Okinawan Vol. 2
Martial Traditions

te, tode, karate, karatedo, kobudo

沖縄手

An Anthology of Articles from the *Journal of Asian Martial Arts*

Compiled by Michael A. DeMarco, M.A.

Disclaimer
Please note that the authors and publisher of this book are not responsible in any manner whatsoever for any injury that may result from practicing the techniques and/or following the instructions given within. Since the physical activities described herein may be too strenuous in nature for some readers to engage in safely, it is essential that a physician be consulted prior to training.

All Rights Reserved
No part of this publication, including illustrations, may be reproduced or utilized in any form or by any means, electronic or mechanical, including photocopying, recording, or by any information storage and retrieval system (beyond that copying permitted by sections 107 and 108 of the US Copyright Law and except by reviewers for the public press), without written permission from Via Media Publishing Company.

Warning: Any unauthorized act in relation to a copyright work may result in both a civil claim for damages and criminal prosecution.

Copyright © 2017 by Via Media Publishing Company
941 Calle Mejia #822, Santa Fe, NM 87501 USA

All articles in this anthology were originally published in the *Journal of Asian Martial Arts*. Listed according to the table of contents for this anthology:

Bolz, M. (1998), Vol. 7 No. 3, pp. 42-55
Silvan, J. (1998), Vol. 7 No. 3, pp. 72-95
Van Horne, W. (1998), Vol. 7 No. 4, pp. 82-99
McKenna, M. (1999), Vol. 8 No. 1, pp. 74-91
Labbate, M. (1999), Vol. 8 No. 2, pp. 80-95
McKenna, M. (1999), Vol. 8 No. 4, pp. 28-47
Labbate, M. (2000), Vol. 9 No. 1, pp. 56-69
McKenna, M. (2000), Vol. 9 No. 3, pp. 32-43
McKenna, M. (2000), Vol. 9 No. 3, pp. 44-57
Paz-y-Meño, a. G. (2000), Vol. 9 No. 4, pp. 22-35
Svinth, J. (2001), Vol. 10 No. 2, pp. 8-17
Florence, R. (2001), Vol. 10 No. 4, pp. 20-43
Bolz, M. (2002), Vol. 11 No. 2, pp. 80-91
Toth, O. & Toth, R. (2003), Vol. 12 No. 4, pp. 66-81

Book and cover design by Via Media Publishing Company
Edited by Michael A. DeMarco, M.A.

Cover illustration
Artistic interpretation of Master Master Itosu Anko (1831-1915), considered by many to be the father of modern karate.
© Illustration by Feodor Tamarsky • www.tamarskygallery.com

ISBN: 978-1893765412

www.viamediapublishing.com

contents

iv **Preface**
by Michael DeMarco, M.A.

CHAPTERS

1 **Kinjo Takashi Kaicho's Advice to Karateka: "Use Both Hands!"**
by Mary Bolz, B.S.

12 **Oral Traditions of Okinawan Karate**
by Jim Silvan, M.A.

36 **The History, Principles, and Precepts of Sakugawa Koshiki Shorinji-ryu Karatedo**
by Wayne W. Van Horne, Ph.D.

55 **Re-Examining Ryukyu Kobudo: An Interview with Minowa Katsuhiko**
by Mario McKenna, M.S.

73 **Elements of Advanced Karate Technique**
by Marvin Labbate

91 **An Interview with Murakami Katsumi: The Heart of Ryukyu's Martial Ways**
by Mario McKenna, M.S.

113 **Developing Advanced Goju-ryu Techniques: Illustrated in the Rising Block**
by Marvin Labbate

130 **Kanzaki Shigekazu: An Interview with To-on-ryu's Leading Representative**
by Mario McKenna, M.S.

144 **To-on-ryu: A Glympse into Karatedo's Roots**
by Mario McKenna, M.S.

158 **Predicting Kumite Strategies: A Quantitative Approach to Karate**
by Guillermo Paz-y-Miño C., Ph.D.

174 **Karate Pioneer Yabu Kentsu, 1866–1937**
by Joseph Svinth, M.A.

187 **Koshin-ryu: The Rebirth of Okinawa's Kojo Family Martial Arts**
by Richard B. Florence, M.A.

214 **Kobudo: Okinawan Weapons are Not All Flash**
by Mary Bolz, B.S.

229 **Basic Foundations in Okinawan Karate: Interview with Canadian Tsuruoka Masami**
by Olga Toth and Robert Toth

248 **Index**

preface

What would you like to obtain from your research and practice of an Okinawan martial art? For an academic, it would be to obtain historical and cultural facts and details. For a practitioner, it would be to gain expertise in the combative skills. If you're interested in both, this second of a three-volume anthology is assembled for your convenience to facilitate your endeavors. These volumes assemble a wealth of material originally published during the two decades when the *Journal of Asian Martial Arts* was in print.

Hundreds of pages and photographs present the richness of Okinawan martial traditions, from the original combatives to those influenced by Chinese and mainland Japanese martial art styles. The variety of topics shown in the table of contents indicate the depth and breath in the chapters, along with the authors who are well-known for their meticulous research and practical skills in specific arts.

These three volumes dive deep into the history and culture of Okinawan martial arts. You'll find coverage of the actual artifacts—the material culture related to weaponry and training methods. Instructions from the masters details both open-hand techniques as well as with weapons. The chapters offer insights into the lives of many masters over the past few centuries, giving the *raison d'être* for these unique fighting arts—their reason for being.

Many streams of arts have contributed to the martial traditions found on the small island: Naha-*te*, Shuri-*te*, Fukien White Crane, Shorin, Goju, Motobu, Shotokan, Isshin, Kyokushin, Pwang Gai Noon, Shito, Uechi, and the list continues. . .

Along with the various styles come the associated training methods, such as conditioning exercises with weights and creatively designed apparatus, such as the punching post (*makiwara*), or stone lever and stone padlock-shaped weights. Some become battle-hardened by active and passive breaking of objects (*tameshiwari*), including wooden boards, baseball bats, rocks, and ice. The extensive use of weaponry is found in many Okinawan styles, often associated with their farming and fishing occupations.

Such a blend of history and culture make the Okinawan fighting traditions a fascinating field of study. Besides being such vital sources of information, these three volumes will prove enjoyable reading and permanent at-hand reference sources in your library.

                                          Michael A. DeMarco, Publisher
                                          Santa Fe, New Mexico
                                          December 2016

chapter 1

Kinjo Takashi Kaicho's Advice to Karateka: "Use Both Hands!"

by Mary Bolz, B.A.

Kinjo wielding sickles (*kama*).
All photographs courtesy of Mary Bolz.

Introduction

"*Ryote o tsukau*" is a phrase often repeated by this great master of Naha, Okinawa. Kinjo Takashi (Kaicho, chairman) is a lone wolf practitioner, so to speak, and teacher of Kobukai Konan-ryu karatedo and kobudo, his own organization which he founded and heads. The *ko* character symbolizes his first name, Takashi. *Bu* is the kanji for martial, literally, stop and spear, implying "stop fighting," and *kai* means organization. The second *ko* means "hard," *nan* means "soft," and, of course, *ryu* means "tradition" or "style."

Kinjo Kaicho's karate training and roots are from the Pangainoon-ryu karatedo of his sensei Itokazu Seiki, who is now 87 years old. Itokazu Seiki was a direct student of Uechi Kanbun of the renowned Uechi-ryu karatedo. In 1978, Uechi-ryu split into four factions, one of which was then called Pangainoon, headed by Itokazu Sensei. Though Itokazu is still living, he is not active due to a cerebrovascular incident approximately eleven years ago and has been in rehabilitation at a local hospital in Naha ever since.

Kinjo Kaicho was very talented in the martial arts from the time he started when he was about eleven years old and proved to be one of Itokazu's top students. He was powerful, agile, and dedicated. So dedicated, in fact, that martial arts is all he wanted to do, and yes, that's all he wants to do today, even in his mid-50's.

Left: Uechi Kanei, one of Kinjo's instructors.
Right: Kinjo with tecchu in grip.

According to Kaicho, there are now fifteen different Uechi-ryu organizations in Okinawa, one of which is called Han Konan-ryu (in Japanese, the pronunciation commonly used; *Pangainoon* in the Fujian dialect, this pronunciation is not used much now in Okinawa) and two Konan-ryu organizations. The other Konan-ryu is the Okinawa Konan-ryu Karatedo Kyokai, headed by Maeshiro Shusei and Itokazu Seisho Sensei and formed in 1992.

Kinjo Kaicho's kobudo sensei was the late famed Matayoshi Shinpo of the Zen Okinawa Kobudo Renmei. Also being one of Matayoshi's very talented and stronger students, he became the vice president, second in command to Matayoshi Sensei himself, of the Zen Okinawa Kobudo Renmei. Unfortunately (or fortunately, depending on the viewpoint), in the early 1990's, he and Matayoshi had a falling out and Kinjo Kaicho formed his own organization for karatedo and kobudo.

From these two main lineages, Kinjo Kaicho represents a continuum of the legacy of Okinawan karatedo and kobudo. There is one theme throughout all his training and teaching emphasized over the two systems from which he comes: *Ryo te o tsukau*, "use both hands." What he is referring to is using both hands efficiently and effectively, never letting one hand just be idle, in both his karate and kobudo techniques.

For example, Kinjo Kaicho always utilizes *hira-te mawashi uke* (open palm slap block) simultaneously while beginning the circle block and then trapping, grabbing, and pulling at the completion of the circle block. This is demonstrated in the photos for the *bunkai* (techniques) of some of his moves.

Technical Section

A1 The attacker comes in with a right punch. Kaicho blocks first with an open right palm circle block followed by a grab with the left hand. The right hand remains ready to move.

A2 The attacker follows immediately with a left-hand punch. Kaicho's left hand still has the attacker's right arm trapped. Kaicho does an inside circle block and grabs with the right hand, immobilizing both of the opponent's arms.

A3 Having trapped the opponent and keeping a firm grip on both of the opponent's arms, Kaicho immediately follows with a fisted-toe front kick (*sokusen maegeri*) to the midsection.

B1 The opponent comes in with a right punch, Kaicho performs *hirate-mawashi uke* (open-palm block with right hand and circle block and grab with left).

B2 The attacker punches to the face with his left hand while Kaicho simultaneously blocks it with his forearm and punches the attacker's face, using, in this case, not both hands, but the one hand very efficiently, doubling as a block and a punch.

B3 This shows the same block/attack technique as B-2 from the inside angle. Notice the preparation of Kaicho's left hand.

B4 Now Kaicho's right hand slides down the opponent's arm; grabs, traps, and pulls the opponent into his left-handed belly punch for the final blow.

C1 Again, Kaicho has just finished *hirate mawashi uke* and is holding a left trap.
C2 The attacker again punches with the left, Kaicho rapidly steps in, cutting off the opponent, using the right arm to block while countering with an elbow strike to the underarm, thereby blocking and cutting off the opponent's attack. Notice he is using his left hand to guard against the opponent's potential punch.
C3 A close-up, outside view of C2.
C4 Kaicho releases and quickly follows with a *koken* (tiger fist) to the abdomen or groin. Here he shows *koken* to the abdomen, but the groin is also one of the main targets. In *koken*, the finger tips are used for jabbing, like nukite.
C5 Kaicho follows with a final *gyaku-zuki* (reverse punch) to the midsection.

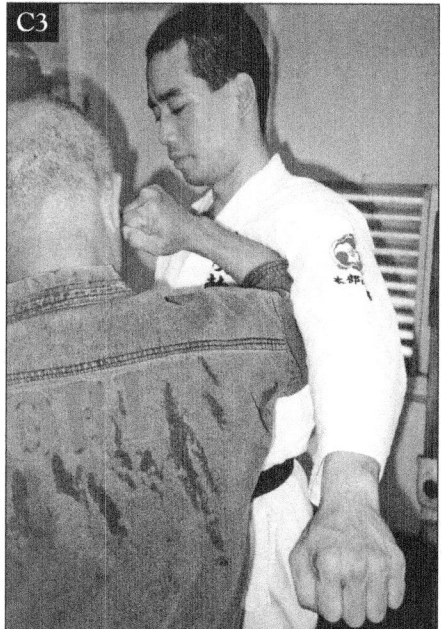

All of these moves are taken from the kata that he created and named *Kobuken*, or "Kinjo's Martial Fist." Kobukai Konan-ryu has nine katas, whereas Uechi-ryu has eight: Sanchin, Kanshiwa, Dai Ni Seisan, Seichin, Seisan, Seiryu, Kanchin, and Sanseiryu, taught in that order from beginner to advanced level. In the Kobukai system, Kobuken is taught after Dai Ni Seisan and before Seichin. Kobuken employs the *zenkutsu dachi* (forward stance) whereas the other katas generally do not, until Seisan kata, and even then it is only used once, on an elbow strike move.

Matayoshi Shinpo, an instructor of Kinjo Kaicho.

In his kobudo, Kinjo Kaicho's trademark of "use both hands" is especially conspicuous in comparison to Matayoshi kobudo. To a knowledgeable kobudo practitioner, it is evident that he learned kobudo from master Matayoshi Shinpo for many years. However, Kaicho's system employs both hands to a greater extent. Kaicho practices the *Matayoshi Nicho Zai* (two-sai kata) and *Sancho Zai* (three-sai kata) with his own modifications by employing the left hand for strikes to the throat. In addition, he has developed his own kata for sai called *Kobuzai*, named after himself. The moves in this kata are very practical fighting moves and the most distinguishing feature is that the sai are almost always held with the *mono-uchi* (striking part, the central, long, sharp-pointed end) pointing at the opponent's throat. The sai is only flipped at the very end of the kata, going back to the attention stance.

Holding the sai in this position not only ensures that one is always ready for fighting, but also makes for a faster, surer block. By not flipping, there is a much longer surface area available for blocking and both hands can be used for blocking, just as in the empty-hand *hirate-mawashi-uke* (open palm block and then circle block with the opposite hand) of karate.

In photo D1, it appears that Kaicho is blocking a neck attack with both sai at once. However, this position is actually held for only a split second. In this position, Kaicho blocks with a deflection by his left sai first (like the open-palm strike in Konan-ryu karate) and then a firmer block with the right sai, which then pushes the bo downward and (photo D2) clears the way for his counter attack to the throat (photo D3).

In photo E1, the downward push-block is shown after the deflecting block has already been performed, simultaneously attacking the throat. The scissors block of the Matayoshi system is shown in photo E2 for comparison with Kinjo Kaicho's version of *jodan-uke* (upper block) in E3.

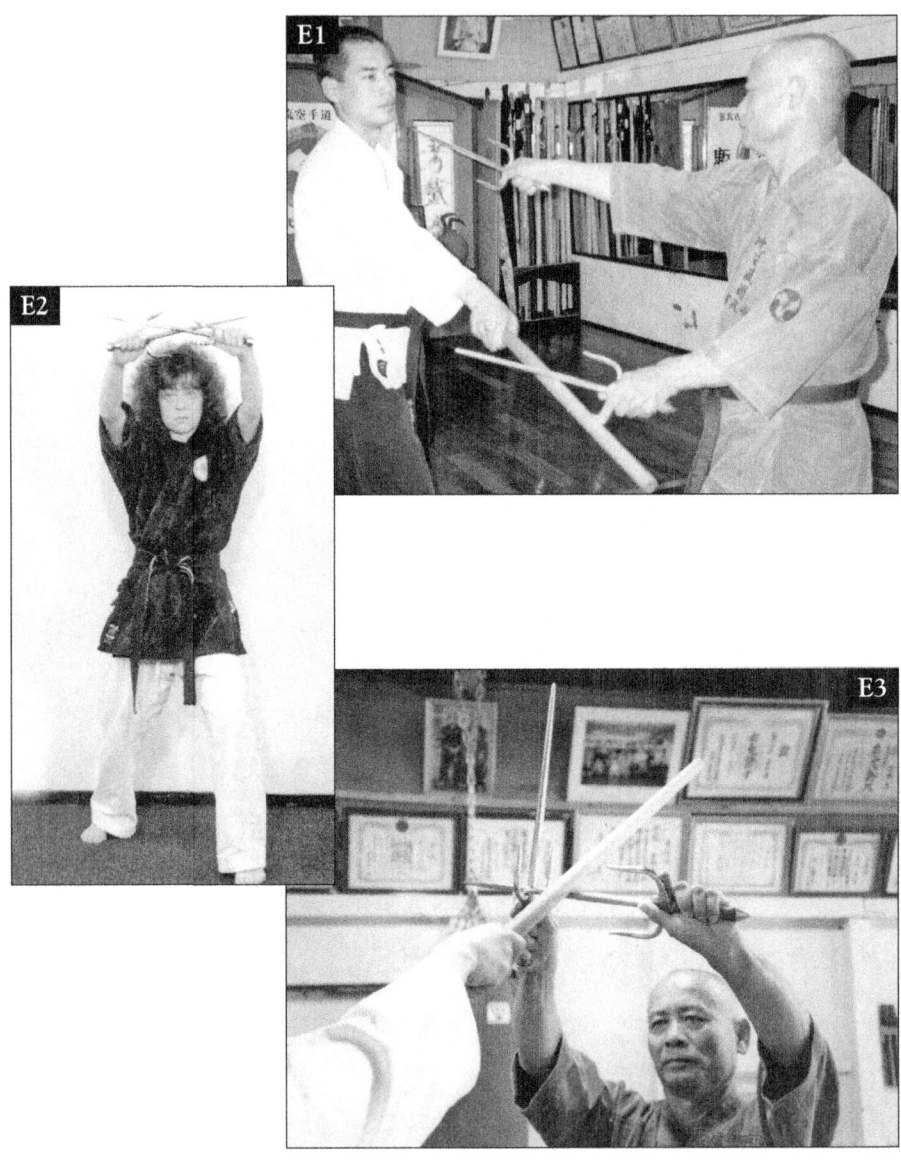

No account of Kinjo Kaicho could ever be given without mentioning his *ieku* (oar) kata. Well-known in Okinawa as second-to-none in his performance of *Tsuken Akachu no Ieku De*, many outside of Okinawa are rapidly coming to know of him through this kata as well.

In photo F1, Kinjo Kaicho executes a block against a temple strike with the bo, followed by an *osae*, a push-down technique and neck attack shown in F2.

In G1, Kaicho pushes the bo over with a lower block simultaneously starting to put in motion his counter attack to the neck (G2). Upon striking the neck, the oar is pulled forward in a slicing motion along it.

Shinden (shrine) at the inside front of Kaicho's dojo in Naha.

Kinjo Kaicho still keeps the names of all the kobudo katas from the Matayoshi system, but has made modifications to each, to replace areas in the katas where he feels the moves were impractical, and where the bunkai was difficult to understand from a fighting standpoint. He has created two other kobudo katas, one for the bo and one for the *tecchu* (palm size stick-like object). The tecchu kata he has named *Kobu no Ti Naka*: "Kobu" after his own name, *ti naka* means "inside of hand." For the bo, in addition to the standard *Choun-no-Kon*, Kaicho has created *Choun-no-Kon Dai Ni*.

In the use of the bo, Kaicho extends his philosophy of *ryo te o tsukau* to mean "use both ends of the bo." Both ends of the bo are utilized without changing his grip, which makes for very fast attacks, such as in the use of escrima sticks, compared to the technique of constantly changing the grip, used in the Matayoshi system.

Kinjo Kaicho seems to live mainly for his martial arts. Besides his own karate and kobudo organization, he has also formed another organization of which he is the president, called Okinawa Kokusai Budo Karatedo Renmei. This organization consists of sensei members and their students from five different karate styles: Konan-ryu, Kinjo Kaicho; Shorin-ryu, Ahagon Naonobu Hanshi; Uechi-ryu, Irei Tadashiki Kancho; Motobu-ryu and Goju-ryu Keishin Kai, Higa Nobuyuki Hanshi. In English, this group uses the acronym OBI (Okinawa Budo International). Kaicho was interested in forming this organization in an effort to keep karatedo united, because all have the same love of budo and the same ultimate goal, even though each has different beliefs concerning technique.

Kaicho and author in front of the *shinden* after a workout.

Kinjo Kaicho's eldest son, Masahiko, is still practicing with him at the honbu dojo. He is Kaicho's attacking partner in the bunkai photos and holds a yondan in karate and kobudo. Kaicho's wife also practices with him and is a sandan in karate and kobudo. Kaicho leads a quite simple life, always studying karate and kobudo. Even when he is not physically practicing, he is thinking about bunkai and studies the moves of many styles. One of the budoka Kaicho seems to admire very much is Soken Hohan, of whom he has a large old photo hanging in his dojo. Soken Hohan was a master who lived to be 94 years-old and was still training up until his death. The photo at Kaicho's dojo shows him at 92, with a bo. One can tell by listening carefully to Kaicho's conversation that that is what he admires about the old masters: their ability to live long and still practice budo. It is what we all in the martial arts hope for, I guess, to practice until we die.

I first practiced under Kinjo Kaicho in the early 1980's, when my sensei, master Nishiuchi Mikio, president of the International Okinawa Kobudo Association, introduced me to him in Okinawa. I lived in Japan for five years when I first started karate, and I return to Japan proper and Okinawa very often. I most recently trained under Kinjo Kaicho this past summer (1997) for one month and literally slept, ate, and trained in his humble dojo once again. I led a very Zen life, living simply and by myself, except when Sensei and his students came to train. During this time, I caught up on the modifications and changes that Kaicho had made in both karatedo and kobudo. I cannot possibly relate my experiences in a short chapter. It was good to be a *deshi* (disciple), again, with no responsibilities as a sensei. My own students and dojo seemed far away, back in the States. I was once again a student in the suffocatingly hot, humid islands of Ryukyu in midsummer with my own sensei.

Acknowledgement

My deepest appreciation to the teacher I have been with the longest, and that is Nishiuchi Mikio Shihan, who introduced me to his sensei, Kinjo Kaicho, back in 1978. My sincere appreciation to Kinjo Kaicho for allowing me to stay in his dojo and train under him again. Greatest thanks to all my students for their support.

chapter 2

Oral Traditions of Okinawan Karate

by Jim Silvan, M.A.

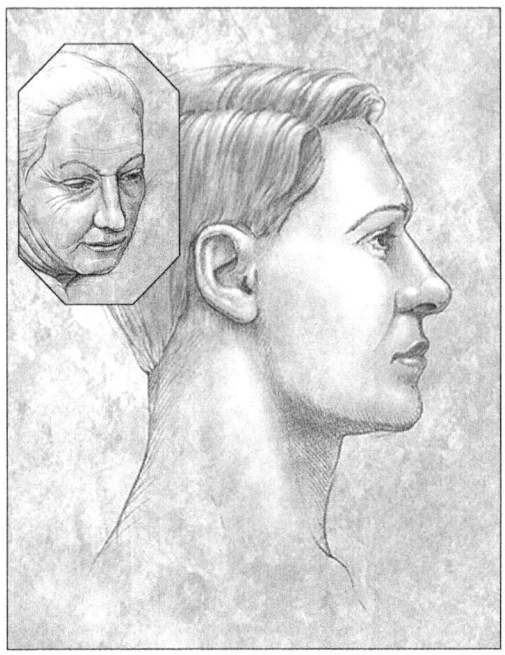

All photographs courtesy of J. Silvan.

Introduction

One area of folklore that has been overlooked is the world of karate. Karate is, and has been for centuries, a subculture with "traditions it calls its own." As such, karate can be studied, analyzed, and interpreted through its folklore. Through analysis, the values, mores, and traditions of the karate world can be delineated. The three most common genres of folklore in karate are legends, folk tales, and proverbs. According to Brunvand, "Folklore may be defined as those materials in culture that circulate traditionally among members of any group in different versions, whether in oral form or by means of customary example" (1968: 5).

Set in days gone by, legends refer to real people and places. Although distorted by oral transmission, legends are also called folk history, or belief tales. A legend focuses on a single episode that is presented as miraculous, bizarre, or embarrassing. Therefore, a legend is an unverifiable story.

Whereas legends are folk history or belief tales, folk tales are the short stories of oral literature. According to Brunvand, "Folk tales are traditional prose narratives that are strictly fictional and told primarily for entertainment, although they may also illustrate a truth or point or moral" (1968: 103).

Seen as a "shorthand" method of communication, a proverb is a "traditional statement passed on in fixed form by oral transmission and assumed to convey some ethical or philosophical truth" (Oring, 1986: 184). Viewed as a mirror to the wisdom of the ages, proverbs are authoritative, they are an appeal to the authority of the ancients and the ancestors.

In the study of karate's oral traditions, proverbs play a very important role. Not only do they justify an instructor's personal perspective of his or her art by transmitting the art's philosophy and tradition, it also justifies the art of karate itself. More often than not, proverbs were written as maxims that were posted on the training hall (*dojo*) walls, thereby allowing the student to study what that particular school viewed as the true essence of karate. Every school has its own maxims and each instructor interprets them differently.

All of the following folklore was collected on a trip I made to Okinawa during the summer of 1995. The interviews took place in settings that were as diverse as the informants themselves. Settings ranged from sushi restaurants, to karate schools, to the informants' homes. Every interview was recorded with the speaker's permission. Professor Shinzato Katsuhiko, the department chairperson for the English Department at Okinawa International University as well as an avid karate practitioner, was present at all but one interview. Shinzato was not present at the interview with Hokama Tetsuhiro Sensei, because of Hokama's command of the English language. Shinzato translated all of the other folk narratives in this paper. Each of the informants were chosen for their unique contributions to the development of karate, and their invaluable insights into its history. They all represent a link to the previous era which has come to be known as karate's Golden Era.

Although the recent history of the martial arts has been well documented, its early history is obscure, full of inconsistencies, and surrounded by controversies. Because the written record is so incomplete, our only link to the past has been what little we can infer from a sparse archaeological record and a rich oral tradition. One of the reasons for this situation can be traced back to the way early karate was taught and practiced. It was always taught within family circles, or among the very closest of friends. Also, it was practiced only in seclusion, sometimes late in the night. People rarely talked about their training with outsiders. In this way, it was kept secret from the outside world. Because of this, little formal documentation exists and whatever evidence we have relies primarily on the oral folk traditions of Okinawan karate.

STORYTELLERS & THEIR STORIES

1) Storyteller: Miyahira Katsuya (1918-)

Now a tenth degree black belt and former president of the Okinawan Prefectural Karate Association, Miyahira began his karate training at the age of thirteen under Chibana Choshin (1885-1969). One of Miyahira's classmates, who was a neighbor of Chibana, introduced Miyahira to Chibana Sensei. Miyahira Sensei studied karate from Chibana for twenty years. However, Chibana was not Miyahira's only instructor. He also studied karate under Tokuda Anbun (1886-1945) and kumite from Motobu Choki (1877-1949).

Left: Chibana Choshin, founder of Kobayashi Shorin-ryu.
Right: Miyahira Katsuya, founder of Shindokan Shorin-ryu.

Following the Second World War, Miyahira returned to his homeland of Okinawa from Manchuria, where he had worked as a schoolteacher, and began his career as a karate instructor. To this day, Miyahira can be found instructing karate students of different levels at his dojo, the Shidokan (Hall of Goodwill), in Tsuboya, Okinawa.

The following interview took place on a very hot, humid day in mid-July 1995. We were welcomed into Miyahira's house, atop his dojo, by his wife, who served us iced tea and fresh fruit. Miyahira felt a little apprehensive about recounting these stories because he found many of them unbelievable. Later in the interview, however, his enthusiasm picked up and he told the stories with much amusement. He always followed each story by explaining their underlying meaning. These narratives had been told to him by his teacher Chibana Choshin and/or by fellow karate students at the age of thirteen to fifteen. However, he could not recall who told him what story or when.

Matsumura Sokon as portrayed by Nakazato Shugoro.

1-A) About Matsumura Sokon (1796?-1893?)

This is a story about Matsumura fighting a bull with a bo [six-foot staff]. Why did this happen? Matsumura was a guard for the king [Sho Ko, r. 1804-1834]. The king had heard how great a martial artist Matsumura was and wanted to test him. The king wanted to make Matsumura fight with a bull to test how strong he was. Matsumura heard this rumor, but the king didn't tell him until several days later. Before the test, Matsumura would go and beat the bull at night wearing certain clothes. He did this often, beating the bull while wearing the same clothes everyday until the event. On the day of the test there was a festival. The bull came out and Matsumura Sokon came out. However, because the bull was in such bad condition from the beatings and recognized the clothing, it just retired, thereby showing how great Matsumura was. [See Kim, 1974: 38-39 for a different version of this story.]

LESSON: This is not a story of how strong Matsumura was, but a lesson that karate men should be smart and intellectual, and not just physical. Wisdom comes after training in karate.

1-B) Matsumura Kokon's Wife

This is a story about a woman karateka, Matsumura Sokon's wife. This woman was from Yonabaru, Okinawa. She was a very strong woman physically, and she wanted to marry a strong man, one who could defeat her. She made an announcement of how strong she was. Once Matsumura Sokon heard this, he challenged her. Then they got married. After they were married, this woman remained very active, but soon Matsumura Sokon got orders to guard a place that belonged to the king. Younger people came to tease Matsumura because he used to be a samurai. One day, the wife came by and shouted strong comments at the youth and they scattered.

LESSON: This story not only tells of how strong Matsumura's wife was but the strength of women in general.

1-C) Itosu Anko (1832-1916)

Itosu Anko [a student of Matsumura Sokon] was very strong, especially his punches. His punch was so powerful that Matsumura would brag to his other students that once Itosu punched an attacker, that was the end of the fight.

LESSON: This story tells how strong Itosu Anko's punch was. The story has been repeated many times so that all of Chibana's students know it [see Bishop, 1989: 103].

• • •

Many stories circulate about great karate men and how they were very cautious after much training. In Okinawa, many people respect caution and being careful.

• • •

Once, a study group of karate students had a discussion about a kata, but they couldn't resolve certain points as to how they should interpret some of the kata moves. Chan Migwa [nickname for Kyan Chotoku, 1870-1945], a member of this group, visited Itosu Anko to help them with their problem. So the group visited Itosu Anko late one night. Itosu opened the door with one hand, holding a club in the other, because when people visit at midnight, something is wrong. After understanding why they had come, Itosu and the students had a long talk about the seven points of kata.

After solving their problem, Itosu asked each of them to demonstrate what they had learned so far. One by one, they demonstrated. Chan Migwa was last. As Itosu Anko told this story to Chibana's Sensei, only one person was impressive—Chan Migwa.

This story tells how hard Chan Migwa was training at that time. Even Itosu admitted how well he was doing.

• • •

Great karate men must have good health all the time because they have to believe they are strong and must be able to react no matter what happens. Because of rumors and expectations among the people, they were obliged to keep in good health.

• • •

Okinawan Proverb: If a karateka is careless enough to catch a cold, people will insult him.

Miyahira: It's no wonder karate men have been cautious not to get sick. That they are so cautious is admirable.

• • •

Karate men in older times took very good care of themselves. In addition to their karate skills, they had knowledge of Chinese medicine. Therefore, whenever they felt something was wrong, they could take care of themselves. Therefore, karate men of the past were better trained. They often thought of themselves as the center of the Earth.

• • •

Chibana told once told me [Miyahira] that ancient karate men were trained in "real" karate and that he, Chibana, had not trained enough, only about 70%. That is why Chibana tried to keep the original kata in their exact form. They had been tested in actual combat. Modern karate men, who had no real experience, too easily change their katas. This was not true karate.

1-D) Students of "Tode" Sakugawa (1733-1815)

Three "Tode" Sakugawa's students once had a fight with a big man from Amami Island. They were Makabe Chan, who represented agility; Okuda, who was powerful; and Matsumoto, who incorporated qualities of both. They challenged the big man one-by-one. Makabe Chan was first and he lost. Next was Okuda, and he too was defeated. However, the third, Matsumoto, easily defeated the big man. Later, this story was interpreted as follows: Makabe who was agile and light represented the Kusanku kata; Okuda, who was very stout, symbolized the Naifanchi kata [see Kim, 1974: 24]; and Matsumoto, who had characteristics of both, represented the Passai kata.

• • •

Matsumura Sokon left certain lessons, maxims, for future generations of karate students. One was, "If we take up karate, we will be rich." Miyahira elaborated on this. Until recently, Miyahira said, he had not understood this point. But now, at his age he does. Miyahira said, "If we are really trained as karate men, physically, spiritually, and emotionally, we can keep balance, thereby giving a good impression to people. This in turn will lead to a good life."

2) Storyteller: Nakazato Joen (1922-)

Nakazato Joen inherited Kyan Chotoku's style of karate now called Shorinji-ryu (Shaolin Temple Style). Born in the small village of Chinen, Okinawa, Nakazato lives there to this day. Nakazato began his instruction under Kyan at age thirteen, and remained with his sensei until Nakazato's induction into the Japanese Army during World War II. Upon his discharge from the military, Nakazato returned home to find that his teacher had died. In remembrance of him, Nakazato thought of calling his karate style

Kyan-ryu, but settled on Shorinji-ryu in honor of the Shaolin Temple in China, the "birthplace" of the martial arts (Silvan, 1993: 55).

A past president of the All-Okinawa Karatedo League, an organization that attempts to maintain karate's traditional heritage, Nakazato is now semiretired from teaching. He spends much of his time as a manager of a retirement center in Chinen. However, he stills oversees the teaching schedule at his Chinen dojo.

When I caught up with Nakazato Sensei, he was busy at the retirement center. Nevertheless, he took time to grant me an interview. Somewhat reluctant to tell many stories, Nakazato suggested other sensei who might have more interesting stories. Nevertheless, the interview lasted two hours. We then retreated to his dojo, where he elaborated on Kyan's karate.

Nakazato Joen, founder of Okinawa Shorinji-ryu

2-A) Matumura's Wife

When "Bushi" (warrior) Matsumura was young, there was a method of holding matches on the street to see how strong they [karate men] were. One night, Bushi Matsumura met a person [in one of these matches] and groin kicked this person many times, but his opponent felt no pain. Later on, Matsumura found out that this person was a woman and they got married. His wife was from a samurai family and had learned karate from someone else.

Matsumura's wife was very strong. She could pick up a sixty-kilogram barrel of rice from the floor with one hand. She was an expert in karate.

Kyan Chotoku (Chan Migwa).

2-B) Kyan Chotoku (Chan Migwa)

Once when Kyan was in a public bathhouse, there was also a man who was very strong and tough. This tough man couldn't find any vessel to scoop the water up with, so he looked around the bath for one. There was a little old man in the bath, and he had a vessel. Because he was an old man, this bully took his vessel. Later, this bully saw Kyan and tried to take Kyan's vessel, but Kyan just held the vessel and didn't move a muscle. People around Kyan spoke to the bully, "Do you know who this man is? He is the great karate man Kyan." The bully ran away.

• • •

Kyan was very fond of cock fighting and he visited the matches often, sometimes taking a chicken to fight. One time, he went to the matches with some of his students and he entered a chicken. Before the chickens fought, his students put sake into the other chicken's water [Bishop, 1989: 80]. When Kyan's chicken fought, it easily won, beating the champion. The owners of the other chickens were angry and attacked Kyan. Kyan easily defeated them while holding onto his chicken.

2-C) Kyan's Teachings

- Karate people should not fight. It makes no sense. People who practice karate are like eggs: if both fight and crack, both will die. However, if only one cracks, he will be seriously injured.

- A karate person should never show the back of his hand [how much training he has].
- You can practice karate everywhere. Even when you are sick and have to stay in bed you can make your hands strong. Even when you are eating, you must be ready. You never know when you will meet the enemy.
- We don't want to injure the enemy. We want to shock their mind so they can reflect. This is the final purpose of karate practice.
- Patience is hard, but if you are patient you will advance.

Shimabukuro Zenpo, second headmaster of Seibukan Shorin-ryu.

3) **Storyteller: Shimabukuro Zenpo (1943-)**

Currently, Shimabukuro Sensei is an eighth-degree black belt in the Seibukan system of Shorin-ryu karate and founder of the International Seibukan Karate Association. Shimabukuro began his martial arts training under the watchful eyes of his father, Zenryu (1904-1969). It was from Zenryu that Zenpo learned the karate method of Kyan Chotoku, his father's instructor. Zenpo also studied karate from his father's good friend, Nakama Chozo, a practitioner of Kobayashi Shorin-ryu karate and student of Chibana Chosin. When not teaching at his dojo in Chatan or visiting one of his branch dojo, Zenpo can usually be found engaged in his real estate business.

Having lived in the United States from 1963 to 1966, Zenpo is well versed in the English language, but he preferred to recite these narratives in Okinawan so that less would be lost in his "broken" English.

This interview took place during one of Shimabukuro's karate classes. He would come over and cite one of the narratives that he had heard from his father and then go back to directing the class.

3-A) Matsumura Sokon's Fight with a Bull

There was a bull that always won its bullfights. The bull was too wild to control and became known as a good fighter around the Shuri area. One day, King Sho Ko, the seventeenth king, heard of the bull's wildness and hit upon a good idea for the main feature for the annual folk dance festival [Bon Odori] in July. King Sho Ko wanted to have his guard, Matsumura Sokon, fight the bull. The plan sounded cruel to the king's retainers, but Matsumura had to accede to the king's request.

Matsumura started going to the cowshed where the bull was kept. Whenever he went there, he punched it between the eyes very hard. He wore a white samurai uniform every time he hit the bull. Because of the constant strikes on its forehead, the bull began to be scared whenever Matsumura showed up.

On the day of the festival, a crowd of people showed up to see a real fight between a man and a bull. When the festival was reaching its climax, the bull came out and was very excited. People were surprised when they saw the bull because it was bigger than they had expected.

Matsumura Sokon showed up and fiercely stared at the bull, moving around the bull, which was irritated. Matsumura tried to shorten the distance slowly and gradually until the bull noticed who he was. People were silently expecting that something serious would happen. But the bull did not move even a step forward. In fact, it began moving backward, and then ran away.

People, including the king and his retainers, were very impressed with the event and realized how great a martial artist Matsumura was.

3-B) Makabe Chan vs. Tannafa Watabu

There was a big fat man called Tannafa Watabu in the Shuri area. He was a boastful and wild man who always teased people to start a fight. One day, he fought with a man called Makabe Chan, who was well known as an agile karate man. Months later, the fat man died from one of Makabe Chan's kicks during the fight.

3-C) Kyan Chotoku

Kyan Chotoku started karate practice when he was a child. Every morning, his grandfather, a retainer of the king, trained him. Training his grandson was sort of his hobby. Some people need a cup of good coffee to wake up every morning. For the grandfather, teaching his grandson was something like a morning coffee.

Kyan Chotoku married an attractive woman from a neighboring village. In those days, such a marriage was unusual, for the young were expected to marry people from their own village. Naturally, the villagers had a grudge against Kyan.

One day, young men from the neighboring village surrounded Kyan on his way home from work. They attacked him, but the young people ended up empty handed. Kyan narrowly escaped from them as soon as he was attacked. Afterward, Kyan often escaped from his pursuers. He knew how to react when a group attacked. Later, the young people learned Kyan was a great karate man. They gave in and started to respect him.

• • •

One day, Kyan was under severe attack from a group. He did not resist them at all. He left himself to whatever they did. The group found themselves beating him thoroughly and then they left. Kyan, who had crouched down, slowly stood up and walked away as if nothing had happened. Although he was beaten up, he defended himself skillfully.

• • •

A mugger once attacked Kyan. He fought back and caught the mugger by the wrist, and took him to the police. On the way to the police station, the mugger tried to break away from Kyan, but Kyan's firm grasp did not allow the mugger to get away.

• • •

Kyan inherited a kata from Kusanku that has been referred to as "Chatan Yara no Kusanku." The term, Chatan Yara, is interpreted as "Master Yara from Chatan Village."

• • •

Talking of kata prefixes and names, there have been no persuasive or historical documents or oral tradition. For example, no karateka knows what is implied in names with numbers, such as: 13, 54 [gojushiho], and so forth. The number could indicate the number of steps or moves in the kata. However, the number of steps or moves are not identical to the numbers in the names. I studied the original meanings of the present-day kata. No karate master has had confidence enough to give a correct interpretation. The questions remain unsolved.

3-C) Maxims
- You cannot be too careful: When we go out of a light room to a dark place at night, we should not go out before our eyes adjust to darkness.
- Wherever we sit, we have to be ready for a quick reaction against some sudden attack.

- When we turn a corner, we had better keep some distance from the corner, just in case.
- When we have to walk home at night, it is advisable to take some blinding missile with us. If a man or a group attacks us, we can throw ashes or sand into his/their eyes to blind him/them.
- Do not tenaciously pursue anyone running away: he may pretend to run away from you until he finds a proper place to attack you. Or he may be leading you to where a gang is to take revenge on you for some reason. Anyway, we have to take old sayings into our heart: A baited cat may grow as fierce as a lion.
- Karate instructors should be an example to the practitioners following them, both physically and spiritually. As karate men, we may be expected to behave in a way to be models from the viewpoint of morality, too.

Hokama Tetsuhiro, curator of Okinawa's only martial arts museum.

4)   Hokama Tetsuhiro (1944-)

Hokama Tetsuhiro is a true twentieth-century renaissance man and martial artist. Born on the island nation of Taiwan, Hokama was raised on a steady diet of karate. Both his grandfather and great-uncle (Shito-ryu founder Mabuni Kenwa [1889-1952]) were practitioners of karate. Hokama's initial martial arts training began while he was a student at Naha Commercial High School. Shortly afterwards, his formal training began under the renown Goju-ryu instructor, Higa Seiko (1898-1966). Following Seiko's death, Hokama continued his Goju-ryu training under Fukuchi Seiko (1919-1975), his senior at the dojo. Hokama is also adept in Okinawan weaponry primarily because of his association with Matayoshi Shimpo (1921-1997).

Hokama divides his time between operating a full-time karate dojo, running Okinawa's first museum devoted exclusively to Okinawa karate (see Silvan and Manyak, 1992), writing books on the history of Okinawa's martial arts, and teaching computer courses at a high school.

When I was finally able to catch up with this extremely busy person, Hokama was more than willing to share his stories with me. Most of the interview took place in my hotel lobby, but we also passed some time at the local *soba* (noodle) shop. Hokama had heard most of these stories in his teenage years from his elders, Higa Seiko and Fukuchi Seiko. He enjoyed telling the stories he believed to be true, but not those he deemed "unbelievable." When he told me stories that seemed unrealistic, he was always quick to point out why.

Higa Seiko.

4-A) Higa Seiko, Hokama's Teacher

For many years, Higa Seiko taught karate to the police, but Higa's body was very frail. One day, a prisoner in the jail confronted him. The prisoner yelled, "Hey, you have any cigarettes?" Higa just laughed and walked away. The prisoner got very angry and attacked Higa, but Higa subdued his attacker by grabbing his neck with his umbrella handle.

Many students of Higa Seiko and Miyagi Chojun (1888-1953) practiced their karate katas during very strong typhoons. During such times, the karate student practices in the doorway, on the roof, or sometimes on the beach. Practicing during times of severe weather is the true test of their mind and body power. If they fail, they only have themselves to blame.

Many stories circulate about famous karate practitioners striking a large animal and pulling its insides out, or driving their fingers through bamboo. Not true! These are only stories to inspire the karate practitioner in his training.

• • •

Many stories tell about strong karate players who fought bulls. One story tells of Seiro Iju, a former mayor of Chinen Village. He would fight the bulls by grabbing their horns and throw them using a judo technique.

• • •

Fukuchi Seiko.

Fukuchi Seiko, a senior student of Higa Seiko, was walking in Naha when he heard cries of, "Help me! Help me!" Fukuchi Sensei walked to where the noise was coming from just in time to see a Japanese serviceman draw a katana and begin to strike a frightened man. Fukuchi jumped in front of the man and caught the sword with his hands. The soldier was astonished and ran away.

• • •

Fukuchi always wore *getas* [type of wooden sandal] when walking. However, sometimes he would slip when walking and he would reach out and touch the grass or a bush and "kip-up" before hitting the ground. This was because of his karate and gymnastics training. If trained in karate, other similar tasks and skills will come naturally.

• • •

One day, a bushi was walking near Shuri Castle when he came across an Okinawan man. As they came closer to one another, it was obvious that neither would step aside for the other. The warrior got very angry and attacked the man. However, the Okinawan was a karate practitioner. As the Okinawan was grabbed, he threw a front kick at his attacker's groin. Just before contact, however, the Okinawan stopped his kick. The bushi realized this man was very dangerous and ran away.

Tomoyose Ryuko watches as Uechi Kanei
demonstrates striking a makiwara.

5) Tomoyose Ryuko (1928-)

One of the leading authorities on Uechi-ryu karate, Tomoyose Ryuko's illustrious martial arts career began when he was seventeen, under the guidance of Shiroma Shinpan (1890-1954), one of Okinawa's most famous karate instructors. Tomoyose trained with Shiroma Sensei for two years before circumstances led him to the legendary Miyagi Chojun. He trained with Miyagi for one and a half years before beginning his study of Uechi-ryu under its founder, Uechi Kanbun (1887-1948). For nearly two years, Tomoyose studied with Kanbun before his untimely death. Tomoyose continued his study of Uechi-ryu under Kanbun's son, Uechi Kanei (1911-1991). Following Kanei's death, Uechi-ryu splintered into several factions, one being the Okinawa Karatedo Kyokai (Okikukai; the largest faction), over which Tomoyose presides.

Of all the sources, Tomoyose spoke the most fluent English and seemed to really enjoy telling his stories. The interview took place at a sushi bar and began almost immediately after the introduction and the first glass of beer. Tomoyose believed these stories to be for entertainment but all had a grain of truth in them.

5-A) Stories Told to Tomoyose by his Older Brother

In the Izumi area on Motobu Peninsula, stood a village that had been cultivated by the samurai class. When the Satsuma clan gained control [in 1609], it was the changing of an era and hard times for the common folk. In these times, the eldest son had to stay with his mother and father to work the family land while the other children had to find land of their own to cultivate.

In this area lived a person who was a master of the bo. He had already cultivated so much land that he had become rich. He hired less fortunate farmers to help their families.

One day, a very strange man, a kind of outlaw, came onto his farm without permission and tried to take all of the crops. Everyone was surprised. Some confronted him by yelling, "What are you doing?" But this outlaw continued stealing, so several of the employees reported to the master. The master came out with his bo and asked, "What are you doing?" But the outlaw had a *kama* [sickle]. When this master tried to strike the outlaw, the outlaw cut the bo. The master was so surprised and became scared. They fought for awhile, but the master's bo was slowly being cut down in size. Finally, from the original six feet, only three were left. In desperation, the master cried for help to his workers. The outlaw was so tired that he left the stolen goods and ran away.

In those days, especially in rural areas, many such masters lived but received no attention because karate was a secret and part of their everyday lives.

• • •

One day, Ko Ryuru [Ryu Ryu Ko a Chinese and one of the ancestors of Goju-ryu] was having lunch at a restaurant. There appeared a young and stout drunk who began making a fuss about trifles at the restaurant. The man disturbed and made fun of Ko Ryuru, who could not help but defend himself from the man's attack and left.

After that incident, the man grew weaker until he needed much care. His parents checked his body. They found their son suffering from some vital blows. The son mentioned that he had fought with a man at a restaurant. They learned that the man was a great martial artist. They took him to the man's house and asked him to cure their son with his Chinese medicine. Since he knew how much he had hurt the son when they fought, he helped the son recover from the effects of his blows. Later, the young man became one of Ko Ryuru's students.

• • •

Motobu Choyu, eleventh headmaster of Motobu-ryu Udun-di.

When Motobu Choyu [1857-1927], Motobu Choki's elder brother, was in Wakayama Prefecture, he let gamblers use his rooms and charged them. One day, one of the gamblers was told to pay up. He was so mad at Choyu that he threw a cup at him. Choyu caught the cup flying directly at him. The way he caught the cup was so impressive and unusual that it indicated he was superior to his brother, Motobu Choki, who was well known on Okinawa.

5-B) A Story from Uechi Kanbun

Ko Ryuru was a student who practiced martial arts. Despite Ko Ryuru's desire to be inconspicuous among the students, his master was convinced that Ko Ryuru was a gifted martial artist.

One day, the master had his well-trained students gather in the dojo. He had to decide on the inheritor for his style. He twisted a rope hard and put it in front of the students. He told them to try to unravel it. They tried one by one, but failed.

The master told Ko Ryuru to try it. He hesitated by asking how could he unravel a rope if all of his seniors had failed at. The master insisted that he should try anyway. He tried, and he unraveled the rope as the master expected. The master announced that Ko Ryuru was the right person to inherit his style.

6) Uehara Seikichi (1904-)

Uehara Seikichi began his formal martial arts training at the age of thirteen under Motobu Choyu. From Motobu, Uehara learned the ancient art of *tuite*, a self-defense system that utilizes wrist and joint locks, throws, sweeps, chokes, punches, and kicks. Originally, this was a family-based art, passed down to the oldest son from generation to generation, until Motobu broke with tradition and taught Uehara. Uehara continued his training with Motobu until his teacher's death in 1927. In remembrance of his teacher, Uehara named this unique fighting system Motobu-ryu Udun-di (Goten-te in Japanese) in 1947. Although hard of hearing, Uehara still personally oversees all of his classes.

Because of his hearing difficulty, Uehara spoke through his student, Kamiunten Fumiko (1954-). Kamiunten has been studying with Uehara for ten years and is a sixth-degree black belt. Kamiunten has earned her teacher's deepest respect and confidence, therefore Uehara felt little would be lost if questions were directed to her. She literally yelled questions in his ears, after which, he would speak out loud to all of us. The interview was conducted at Uehara's house with his wife providing a steady stream of refreshments.

Although one of the more senior karate instructors in Okinawa, Uehara often felt reluctant about repeating these tales and preferred to speak more about his particular art and how it compared to the other styles.

Left: Uehara Seikichi, twelfth headmaster
of Motobu-ryu Udun-di. Right: Motobu Choki.

6-A) About Motobu Choki

When Motobu was working in Kyoto and Osaka in 1922, he taught karate to judo players at the police stations. At that time, Russian boxers, who were traveling around the world for fighting shows, came to Japan. Some judo players challenged them. The boxers easily beat them. No one could control the boxers.

Some of the judo players to whom Motobu was teaching karate suggested that Motobu take part in the show on the spur of the moment, because it was open to all. Motobu came to see the show. He saw judo players beaten and decided to have a match with a leader of the Russian boxers, called George. George was six-foot tall and weighed two hundred pounds. Motobu was small and around fifty years old. During the match, George moved around Motobu, who stayed in the same position. One round was over, then two rounds. In the third round, Motobu started moving and found the timing for his vital punch. George fell to the mat and was carried off to a hospital.

Choki returned to Okinawa in 1923, when he brought some Filipino boxers for a fighting show. He needed some money to publish a book on kumite. However, his elder brother denigrated him for his show business.

6-B) Other Stories from Uehara Seikichi

Uehara took initial instruction in martial arts from Motobu Choyu at the age of twelve, on July 13, 1916.

First of all, he practiced: kick and punch while walking forwards, walking backwards, and turning backwards (which is superior to turning forward exercise seen in judo practice, because the scope of sight is wider when turning backward); both hands punching with a kick; jumping exercise from tiptoe; and push-ups with the fists, fingers, or thumbs, which were done with one hand only in the final stage.

There are two kinds of hand/finger techniques: One is formed by the thumb sitting atop the fist, with the tip extending beyond the fist [*tijukun*]. The other is formed by four fingers thrusting [*jitti*]; this is useful when attacking the ribs or hard muscles toughened by Sanchin exercise.

Summary and Conclusion

The study of Okinawan martial arts folklore is an important interpretive tool for studying not only Okinawan society but the subculture of Okinawan martial arts, an important underpinning of that society.

Several themes were consistent throughout the stories presented. These themes surround karate's values, mores, and culture. On a broader scale, they represent the parameters of Okinawan society.

Important themes or meanings in these stories that reflect Okinawan society and culture are:

- respect for elders
- humility
- self-cultivation is reward enough
- never underestimate an opponent
- moderation is preferred to extremes
- a person's greatest opponent is him/herself
- winning a battle via nonphysical means is the greatest victory
- women are not to be taken lightly but form an important link in society

Besides delineating society's patterns, functions, and meanings, the oral traditions surrounding Okinawan karate serve other functions. Oral tradition can be a methodology for studying history. Not only does folklore address the history and tradition of karate but, more specifically, it is a vehicle for honoring the individuals involved and their distinct contributions. To a karate student, this is of particular importance because one's karate lineage defines and validates the art a person is practicing. An equally important aspect of karate folklore is its ability to entertain. Stories are often repeated "tongue-in-cheek" by the teller, knowing full well that the stories are not entirely true, but nonetheless, are told to perpetuate karate's mystique.

APPENDIX: SOME NOTED HISTORIC FIGURES

Kusanku

Kusanku was a master of Chinese kenpo from Fujian Province. He gave a demonstration of Chinese self-defense on Okinawa in 1761 (Nagamine, 1976: 21). He is also credited with introducing and teaching Chinese kenpo to "*Tode*" (an older term for karate) Sakugawa. *Kusanku* is also pronounced *Kushanku* and *Kuso Kun* in Japanese and *Gong Shangkung* in Chinese-Mandarin.

"Tode" Sakuguwa Kanga (1733-1815)

Tori Hori, a district in Shuri, Okinawa, is famous for its rich martial arts history. It has been the home for many of Okinawa's most famous karate practitioners, among them "Tode" Sakugawa.

Sakugawa Kanga began his tode training under Takahara Peichin (a feudal title) (Silvan, 1993: 33). Sakugawa continued his tode study from Takahara until his death. Takahara gave the young Sakugawa the nickname "Tode" because of his relentless pursuit of martial arts knowledge and training. Following his teacher's death, Sakugawa studied under Chinese *kenpo* (fist way) master Kusanku. Later, he furthered his knowledge of the fighting arts by traveling to China.

Sakugawa contributed much to the development of Okinawan martial arts. His synthesis of tode and Chinese kenpo laid the foundation for Shuri-te (the forerunner of Shorin-ryu), one of the most popular Okinawan karate systems. Many martial art historians refer to him as the "father of Okinawan karate" (Silvan, 1993: 35).

Matsumura Sokon "Bushi" (cir. 1796-1893)*

"Bushi" Matsumura was one of the most influential men in the development of Okinawa-te. Born in Shuri, Okinawa, Matsumura began his martial arts training when he was about fourteen years old. Nearing death and unable to care for his son, Sofuku, Sokon's father, asked his good friend and karate practitioner "Tode" Sakugawa to raise his son (Silvan 1993: 35). Accepting the responsibility, Sakugawa not only raised the boy but taught him the art of te. Sakugawa soon nicknamed the boy "Bushi" for his skill and his spirit. Like his instructor, Sakugawa, Matsumura studied Chinese kenpo and traveled to China to increase his knowledge.

Not only was Matsumura instrumental in the development of Okinawa-te but, in doing so, he transmitted Sakugawa's knowledge as well as developing many of the katas used in karate today. Matsumura is also credited with being the first instructor to organize his system of fighting and giving it a name, Shuri-te (Kim 1974: 43).

> * Note:
> As Bishop points out (1989: 64), there lies a great discrepancy surrounding the exact dates concerning Matsumura. The dates used here and elsewhere in the paper are taken from Hokama Tetsuhiro (see Silvan and Manyak, 1992).

Itosu Anko Yasutsune (1830-1915)

Like his instructor before him, Matsumura Sokon, Itosu was one of the most influential karate teachers in the development of Okinawa karate. Born in Shuri, Okinawa, Itosu studied karate from Matsumura Sokon and Matsumora Kosaku, a Tomari-te expert. However, it was his relationship with Matsumura that had the greatest impact on the development of Okinawan karate. Itosu simplified much of Matsumura's karate and, with Matsumura's encouragement, he spread and popularized the art. In 1901, Itosu introduced karate into the Okinawan public school system as part of the physical education curriculum (Bishop, 1989: 102). In conjunction with this, Itosu developed a new set of katas, the Pinans ("Peaceful Mind"), to be taught because the existing katas were too difficult.

Itosu's contribution to karate far exceeds just the introduction of karate into the school system or his development of new katas. Itosu was a gifted karateka and those who were influenced by him reads like a who's who of karate.

Kyan Chotoku (1870-1945)

Kyan Chotoku was born small and sickly. Hoping to improve his son's health, his father, Kyan Chofu, introduced him to the fundamentals of the martial arts. As his health steadily improved, Kyan sought out Okinawa's more famous instructors to improve his knowledge and technique. Among the instructors he studied from were Shuri-te's Matsumura Sokon and Itosu Anko, and Tomari-te's Oyadomari Kokan (Silvan, 1993: 52).

Despite his small frame and poor eyesight, Kyan was to become one of karate's greatest technicians. Kyan was frequently asked to demonstrate his katas and was often sought out by aspiring karateka. Oftentimes, those visits were by upstart martial artists who wanted to defeat Kyan, thereby making a name for themselves. However, Kyan was never defeated.

Chibana Choshin (1885-1969)

Born in Tori Hori, Okinawa, Chibana began his martial arts training at the age of 15 under the careful guidance of Itosu Anko. Chibana's martial arts career spanned seventy-one years. In 1917, Chibana opened his first dojo in Tori Hori, and began teaching his instructor's karate. However, there were other students of Itosu as well as other stylists. To differentiate his method from the others, Chibana called his system *Kobayashi-ryu* (Young Forest Style). In 1958, he became the karate instructor for the Shuri Police Department. In 1961, he became the first president of the Okinawa Karatedo Federation. In 1968, he received the Kunyonto Order of the Sacred Treasure from Emperor Hirohito. Today, Kobayashi-ryu is the most popular form of Shuri-te karate.

Yabu Kentsu (1863-1937)

An exceptional martial artist, Yabu Kentsu began his formal karate training under Matsumura Sokon. Following his instructor's death, Yabu continued his study of Shuri-te from Itosu Anko. While he was studying from Itosu, Yabu and fellow karate student Hanashiro Chomo became two of the first karate instructors to teach in Okinawa's public school system. His techniques were so good that rumor quickly spread of him defeating the great Okinawan karate fighter, Motobu Choki. However, this story has never been confirmed through written sources or documentation.

Fukuchi Seiko (1919-1975)

Fukuchi Seiko began his study of Goju-ryu karate while a junior high school student under Higa Seiko. While stationed in China during World War II, Fukuchi studied Chinese kenpo. Following his return after the war, Fukuchi resumed his training under Higa.

Matsumora Kosaku (1829-1898)

Matsumora Kosaku, along with Oyadomari Kokan, was one of the early pioneers of Tomari-te ("Tomari Hand"). A highly respected martial artist, Matsumora combined techniques from Chinese kenpo and the indigenous art of te to develop his style of Tomari-te. According to Matsumora, the ultimate aim of karate was the perfection of the individual practitioner in his own mind rather than in physical confrontation (Silvan, 1993: 64).

Higa Seiko (1898-1966)

Born in Naha, Okinawa, Higa Seiko began his martial arts training at the age of thirteen under Naha-te's Higaonna Kanryo (1853-1916). He remained with Higaonna for nearly four years until his death. He continued his training under Miyagi Chojun, his senior at Higaonna's dojo. Higa was a very prominent figure in the martial arts world and gave karate demonstrations throughout Okinawa and Japan. In 1940, he was presented the title of "Skillful Man of Karate" (Silvan, 1993: 24).

Miyagi Chojun (1888-1953)

Okinawa karate owes much to this instructor. He played an instrumental role in getting Okinawa-te accepted by not only his fellow Okinawans, but also by the governing Japanese authorities. Through the efforts of Miyagi and his fellow Okinawan karateka, karate gained official recognition as one of Japan's martial arts. Miyagi gave many demonstrations not only in Okinawa, but on mainland Japan and Hawai'i as well. Miyagi made several trips to China to learn Chinese kenpo and then combined this with what he had learned from his Okinawa-te instructor, Higaonna Kanryo, to develop his own blend of karate, Goju-ryu (a Naha-te style).

Motobu Choki (1877-1949)

Although he never originated a style of his own, Motobu Choki was one of Okinawa's most influential martial artists. Born in Shuri, Okinawa, Choki was denied permission to learn his family style of te, a privilege usually granted only to the first son, in this case, his brother Choyu. Therefore, Choki's initial martial arts instruction came about by secretly watching and mimicking his brother and other martial artists. Because his reputation as a fighter preceded him, he was denied formal instruction by most instructors.

Tomari-te's Matsumora Kosaku and Shuri-te's Itosu Anko finally accepted him as a student. Motobu was widely known for his *kumite* (sparring) techniques and stories—many true and many not.

Motobu Choyu (1865-1927)

The older brother of Motobu Choki, Choyu taught the secret Motobu family Udun-di system that had been passed down from generation to generation by the eldest sons. This "secret" style (later named Motobu-ryu by Uehara Seikichi in honor of Choyu) was a system of *tuite* movements that were unlike the more traditional block-punch karate systems.* Choyu learned this unique system of self-defense from Motobu Anshi and taught the rudiments to Sho Tai, the last Ryukyuan king. Choyu would later break tradition and pass on this system to his top student, Uehara Seikichi, because his son, Chomo, was not interested.

*Editor's note: *Tuite* is the native Okinawan (Hogen) term for "grappling," but a grappling that relies heavily on pressure point activation and joint locks. Literally, it means "grasping hand" and is also written *torite* (Japanese) and *tuidi* (which is closer to the Okinawan pronunciation).

Bibliography

Bauman, R. (1992). *Folklore, cultural performances, and popular entertainment.* New York: Oxford University Press.

Bishop, M. (1989). *Okinawan karate: Teachers, styles and secret techniques.* London: A & C Black Ltd.

Brunvand, J. (1968). *The study of American folklore.* New York: W.W. Norton & Co.

Dundes, A. (1965). *The study of folklore.* Berkeley: Prentice-Hall, Inc.

Geertz, C. (1973). *The interpretation of culture.* New York: Basic Books, Inc.

Kim, R. (1995). *The classical man.* Ontario, Canada: Masters Publications.

Kim, R. (1974). The weaponless warriors. Burbank, CA: Ohara Publications.

Langness, L. (1987). *The study of culture.* Novato, CA: Chandler & Sharp.

Nagamine, S. (1976). *The essence of Okinawan karate-do.* Rutland, VT: Charles E. Tuttle, Co.

Nakaya, T. (1986). *Karate-do: History and philosophy.* Carrollton, TX: J.S.S Publishing.

Oring, E. (1986). *Folk groups and folklore genres.* Logan, UT: Utah State University Press.

Silvan, J. (1993). *Okinawan karate: Its teachers and their styles.* New York: Vantage Press.

Silvan, J., and Manyak, A. (1992) The material culture of the martial arts: Exhibiting Okinawan karate. *Journal of Asian Martial Arts, 1*(4): 100-111.

Urban, P. (1991). *The karate dojo.* Rutland, VT: Charles E. Tuttle, Co.

chapter 3

The History, Principles, and Precepts of Sakugawa Koshiki Shorinji-ryu Karatedo

by Wayne W. Van Horne, Ph.D.

Left: Dr. Thomas Cauley practicing a sai kata. Right: The attacker (Michael Ta) does a front thrust kick. The defender (Thomas Cauley) steps off line and forward and captures the kick while simultaneously striking the attacker's chin with his forearm. By continuing to enter and lift the leg, the attacker will be thrown backward to the ground.

All photographs courtesy of W. Van Horne.

Sakugawa Koshiki Shorinji-ryu Karatedo is a unique system of karate in part because of its comprehensive and encyclopedic nature. It has eighty-five katas and emphasizes classical *bunkai* (interpretation of techniques), theories of movement, generation of power, and the development of ki. It also incorporates systematic training in *taijutsu* (body art, body movement) and other aspects of Japanese unarmed martial systems. Most significantly, it focuses on the classical precepts of budo and the training of an individual's character through karatedo. The current director of the International Division of Sakugawa Koshiki Shorinji-ryu Karatedo is Dr. Thomas Cauley, who studied karate in Japan for seventeen years and was promoted to seventh dan while there. One of the most highly trained karate teachers outside of Japan, Dr. Cauley seeks to transmit to Americans a rich and complex art dedicated to the principles of *budo*, the Martial Way.

History of the System

Sakugawa Koshiki Shorinji-ryu roughly translates as "Sakugawa Orthodox Shaolin Temple System." The name characterizes the system's emphasis on the classical kata and theories of the tradition founded by "Tode" Sakugawa (c. 1733-1815), who is viewed by many karate historians as a founder of the modern karate tradition in Okinawa (McCarthy, 1987: 28). It also emphasizes its legendary derivation from the Chinese Shaolin tradition. The addition of the suffix "-*do*" to karate further explicates its relationship to the Japanese budo and Zen traditions.

According to oral tradition passed on to Dr. Cauley by his teachers in Japan, Ogasawara Jiro (1901-1958), a member of the aristocratic Ogasawara family of Aomori Prefecture in northern Honshu, traveled to Okinawa in 1926 and learned karate from Hanashiro Chomo (1869-1945) (Cauley, 1978: 12-13). Hanashiro is reputed to have been an exceptional karate practitioner and teacher, and was one of the main people responsible for the introduction of karate into the public school system of Okinawa (P. McCarthy, personal communication, January 12, 1997). In turn, Hanashiro learned karate from both Itosu Anko (1832-1915) and "Bushi" Matsumura (1809-1901). Matsumura was a student of "Tode" Sakugawa. Both Matsumura and Sakugawa were legendary figures of early karate, having studied indigenous Okinawan fighting arts, Chinese martial arts, and Japanese weapons systems (McCarthy, 1995: 34, 51). Both Sakugawa and Matsumura synthesized their knowledge of these various arts and were major figures responsible for the origin of the modern karate tradition. Sakugawa Koshiki Shorinji-ryu preserves the katas, techniques, and theory of the Sakugawa-Matsumura-Hanashiro lineage.

Ogasawara Jiro returned to Aomori Prefecture in 1946. He had previously learned a system of empty-hand and weapons fighting passed down within his family.[1] To his knowledge of Okinawan Shorinji-ryu, he added aspects of this family system, most notably *nage waza* (throwing techniques), *kansetsu waza* (joint techniques), *shime waza* (choking techniques), and *osaekomi waza* (holding or immobilization techniques) (Cauley, 1978: 14; T. Cauley, personal communication, October 18, 1996). Ogasawara Jiro's son, Tokushiro (1958-1986), succeeded him as director of the system he founded. In 1986, a Zen priest named Yamazaki Masanao became the current director.

Sakugawa Koshiki Shorinji-ryu also incorporates training in Yuishinkai kobudo, most likely at Ogasawara Jiro's initiative. Thomas Cauley studied this kobudo style under Konishi Yasuhiro (1893-1983), founder and director of Shindo Jinen-ryu karatedo. His direct teacher was Fukuda Shoen, director of Northern Japan Yuishinkai Kobudo. He also studied briefly under the directorship of Inoue Motokatsu and his son, Takekatsu. Both Konishi

Yasuhiro and Inoue Motokatsu learned kobudo from Taira Shinken (1897-1970), founder of Yuishinkai kobudo. Taira had studied kobudo with Okinawan kobudo master Yabiku Moden (1878-1941).

Sakugawa Koshiki Shorinji-ryu has retained its classical Okinawan karate roots, including both the katas and theory of the empty-hand and weapons traditions. In addition, it has augmented this tradition with techniques from classical Japanese martial arts, and integrated them into a highly effective martial art.

Dr. Thomas Cauley.

The International Director

Thomas Cauley is the chief instructor for Sakugawa Koshiki Shorinji-ryu in the United States. He was born on April 1, 1943 in Kinston, North Carolina. He is presently celebrating his forty-first year of practicing and teaching Shorinji-ryu. He lived, and trained, in Japan from 1961 to 1969 and 1974 to 1979. Cauley Kyoshi was appointed chief instructor after seventeen years of resident training in Japan under Okada Jiro, Ogasawara Tokushiro, and Yamazaki Masanao.

Due to his persistence and dedication while in Japan, he also earned rank in other systems through cross-grading, most notably a fifth dan in Shindo Jinen-ryu awarded by the founder of the system, Konishi Yasuhiro. He also received a fifth dan in Shotokan, a fifth dan in Motobu-ryu (by Toma Shian 5 October 1974), a fourth dan in Matsubayashi Shorin-ryu, a third dan in Okinawan Kenpo, a second dan in judo, a second dan in aikido, a first dan in Hakko-ryu jujutsu, and a first dan in kendo. While in Japan, he also attained his doctorate in Asian Studies from Waseda University, the rank of captain in the U.S. Air Force, and the designation of *kyoshi* in Konkoyo Zen. After Cauley Kyoshi returned to the U.S. in 1979, Ochiai Hidy awarded him a fourth dan in Washin-ryu karate.

While in Japan, he married the now deceased sister of then headmaster Ogasawara Tokushiro. According to Cauley, it was after his marriage into the family that his training started in earnest. Seen as a family member by the Ogasawaras, he was expected to devote all of his time to the pursuit of karatedo. He received instruction in the highest levels of Sakugawa Koshiki Shorinji-ryu as well as instruction in the family's traditional arts. Upon returning to the U.S., he was appointed to his current position. Upon the death of Ogasawara Tokushiro in 1986, he was asked to return to Japan to assume the role of head instructor, an honor he refused in order to continue teaching in the U.S.

While training in Japan, he experienced traditional martial arts culture that few in the U.S. have glimpsed first hand. For example, his account of his introduction to his first Shorinji-ryu teacher in 1961 when he was nineteen sounds like a classical Japanese martial arts parable. At the time, he was training in Shotokan (JKA) with Ueki Masayuki at Fuchu Air Force Base:

> I worked with master Ueki Masayuki for three months and then, one night after practice, he introduced me to a kind-looking old man named Okada Jiro. Master Okada taught the Sakugawa Orthodox Shorinji-ryu system. I asked for permission to visit his dojo and study with him. He gave it immediately. The following Monday night, a friend and I traveled to Fuchumura [Fuchu Village], about five miles away. We were promptly thrown out by the senior student. His instructions were that no new students would be allowed into the dojo without prior approval of the master. We were perplexed and stood outside looking at the practice session inside. For three weeks we stood outside the dojo, night after night, wishing we could enter. Finally, Mr. Takahashi told us that master Okada wanted us to go to his home after practice and discuss our desire to learn karatedo.
>
> We ran all of the way to the master's home, were let in the back door, and proceeded to make fools out of ourselves. The master, his wife, my friend, and I were all seated at a low table and Mrs. Okada poured the tea. "Oh boy," I thought, "I am going to drink tea with a karate master!" As soon as I tasted my tea I felt hot tea splashed all over my face and neck.
>
> Master Okada had thrown his cup of tea into my face for rudely drinking ahead of him! He rose, called out to his wife, and retired for the night. My friend and I sat for a moment, and then rose to leave. Mr. Takahashi came in and asked us if we were leaving. "Yes, I think it is time," was my answer.

"But don't you want to learn about karatedo?" he asked. He instructed us to stay in master Okada's home and to sleep on the floor. The next morning Mrs. Okada kicked us awake and fed us. From that day onward Okada Jiro was like my father. The training in the Okada dojo was extreme.

– Cauley, 1978: 39

The martial culture that Dr. Cauley experienced focused not only on rigorous physical training, but also on individualized moral lessons intended to foster the development of ethics and personal character. Another example of the intense training that Dr. Cauley encountered is related in his story of the first time he trained as a student in Konishi Yasuhiro's dojo when he was in his early twenties. Konishi is an important figure in Japanese karate, having studied under Funakoshi Gichin (founder of Shotokan karate), Miyagi Chojun (founder of Goju-ryu karate), Mabuni Kenwa (founder of Shito-ryu karate), Motobu Choki, and Ueshiba Morihei (founder of aikido). Konishi went on to found his own system, Shindo Jinen-ryu karate. The following incident occurred when Okada Jiro took his advanced students to visit Konishi's dojo for black belt training:

As I stepped out onto the practice area I noticed that I was the only *yudansha* [black belt] who had worn his black belt. I knew that I was in for a bad time. I had forgotten that when you visited another dojo you took off your *obi* [belt] and wore a white belt until that particular teacher asked you about your true rank, or told you to wear it in his dojo. I didn't realize that it was a tradition. . . . After practice the sensei [Konishi] directed me to the head of the line with his black belts, all thirteen of them. As I sat at the head of the class, feeling like someone special, all thirteen of those black belts proceeded to choke me unconscious, one by one. After being choked thirteen consecutive times without a break I suddenly developed a certain dislike for my black belt. In fact, it was never again in my mind that it was important to impress my rank upon anyone.

– Cauley, 1978: 39

The traditional training that Dr. Cauley received is reflected in his own rigorous teaching. Strict etiquette is enforced in all his dojos, and training is meticulous, precise, and physically demanding. He seeks to transmit the art he learned in Japan to Americans with its utility and rich knowledge intact.

Techniques (*waza*):
- *tachi waza* (stances)
- *uchi waza* (striking)
- *geri waza* (kicking)
- *shime waza* (choking)
- *ne waza* (grappling)
- *osaekomi waza* (holding & immobilizing)
- *tsuki waza* (punching)
- *uke waza* (blocking)
- *kansetsu waza* (joints)
- *nage waza* (throwing)
- *ukemi waza* (breakfalls)

Weaponry:
- *bo* (staff)
- *kama* (sickles)
- *nunchaku* (flail)
- and other esoteric weapons.
- *sai* (three pronged short swords)
- *tonfa* (wood handles)
- *suruchin* (weighted chain)

Characteristics of the Art

Sakugawa Koshiki Shorinji-ryu is characterized by systematic, integrated, and progressive training that is based on classical methods, techniques, and kata (Van Horne, 1986). There is a structured order for learning basic techniques and katas, with simpler elements learned first and then combined into more complex techniques and combinations only after a significant degree of competency is acquired. Teaching methods are based on the synthesized knowledge, experience, and insight of generations of master teachers, and they have been refined to be extremely efficient and effective.

This systematic method of learning incorporates many principles: coordinated movement, generation of force through body mechanics, distancing and timing (*maai*), movement off the line of an attack (*taisabaki*), various levels of force in offensive and defensive techniques, coordination of breathing with movement, the use of the contraction and expansion of the body, specific meditative states of mind (*mushin*, *zanshin*, etc.), the generation of ki, etc. Ultimately, this training progression teaches a practitioner to synthesize all of these principles and apply them.

The art is also comprehensive, encompassing the practice of a number of specialized categories of techniques that are again ultimately integrated in the art of the practitioners. These include numerous open-hand techniques listed in the column at the left side of this page.

Sakugawa Koshiki Shorinji-ryu also focuses on meridian theory and the flow of ki throughout the body. Applications of many of the categories of techniques noted above focuses on striking, pressing, or otherwise manipulating the many vital points of the body for various effects. The classical interpretations of techniques from kata (*bunkai*) also focus on attacking vital points.

Four primary methods of training are used to practice principles and techniques. First, there is an emphasis on the continual practice and perfection of individual techniques through repetitive group practice of *kihon waza* (basic techniques). Another method is the practice of advanced techniques with a partner including kata applications as well as throws, holds, chokes, joint techniques, etc.

There is an emphasis on katas. There are eighty-five katas: forty empty hand and forty-five with weapons. One aspect of the extensive kata training in Sakugawa Koshiki Shorinji-ryu is that it is encyclopedic: it preserves the classical katas derived from the various traditions of the Okinawan towns of Shuri, Naha, and Tomari, as well as the kobudo katas from various places in Okinawa. However, instead of being a haphazard collection, they have been organized into a very effective progression that cumulatively teaches a student the art's various principles. Learning the katas in sequence takes a student from the basic principles of body movement and mechanics to an understanding of ki and meditative states of awareness. The bunkai also have been rigorously preserved.

Last, *kumite* (sparring) is done full power without the use of protective padding. Participants are not allowed to strike, punch, or kick their partners, but instead are required to have enough control over their techniques to stop them a few centimeters from their partner's body (*sundome*). Kumite also typically involves the application of joint techniques, throws, sweeps, chokeholds, etc., in addition to striking techniques.

Although the physical art of Sakugawa Koshiki Shorinji-ryu karatedo is highly effective, the teachers see the practitioner's moral and spiritual development as its primary purpose. The physical art of combat is simply a venue for the continuing development of a better self through *budo*, the Way of the Warrior. Thomas Cauley views the teaching and dissemination of budo as Shorinji-ryu's primary goal.

The Philosophy of the Art

Cauley Sensei's teaching also emphasizes that situations encountered in training foster insights that promote personal development. He is astute at perceiving aspects of both technique and character that need improvement in individual students. His lessons often focus on correcting these weaknesses through individualized experiences. For example, when I was a beginning student, I once slipped on a puddle of sweat while performing a high kick during kumite. I fell, struck my head, and sustained a concussion. After I recuperated and returned to classes, I was unaware that I had developed an unconscious fear of falling and was inhibiting myself from properly performing high kicks. Cauley Sensei recognized this problem, and one evening he devoted an entire class to kicking practice. Throughout the evening, the kicks we practiced became progressively stronger and higher and eventually included many jumping techniques. As we all became increasingly exhausted, I was forced to perform my kicks without reserve to simply continue the practice. After the class finished, sensei came over to me and stated, "Now you're no longer afraid to do high kicks." I realized then that the session had been in part for my benefit, and learned a lesson about confronting problems to solve them. This insight had been Cauley Sensei's goal. Similar accounts of personal insights generated from Cauley Sensei's lessons are commonly shared among his students.

During the interview for this chapter I asked Cauley Sensei about the distinguishing characteristics of Shorinji-ryu. Expecting a discussion of theory, training methods, or some similar physical aspect of the art I again learned a lesson when his reply focused on the philosophical fabric of the art:

> What makes Shorinji-ryu a fine art and sets it apart from other systems is the budo aspect. It is a whole educational concept rather than just a physical form of karate. It's a full system of life, centering not only on the physical, spiritual, and mental aspects of the art, but also entailing education and morality. One of our responsibilities as much as possible, one of our foremost goals, is to get oneself into the higher educational system. We stress Chinese classics, *anma* [massage], shiatsu, acupuncture, studying the meridians of the body, holistic medicine, Zen. That's why we call our schools Isshinkaikan Institutes of karatedo, not dojos. They're universities of life. Shorinji-ryu is a life pursuit, not a goal. The only goal we have in Shorinji-ryu is to appreciate wisdom.
>
> Most [karate] systems today are sport and tournament oriented. There's a difference between *bugei* and *budo*. Bugei is martial art. Martial means military, and the goal of a martial art is to beat another person in battle. At all costs, do not lose. The main goal is to defeat your opponent.

> *Budo* is the Warrior Way. *Do* means the philosophical search for truth, that's what the word means in our system. In a Martial Way we do not have an opponent, we are our only opponent, and learning of our self is our biggest stepping stone. We learn that winning and losing are not important.
>
> For example, we don't place any emphasis on tournaments. We only have in-style tournaments, we don't have any open tournaments. It's the nature of our art because we really can't compete. In Japan Shorinji-ryu is full contact. There's no protective gear whatsoever—no mouthpiece, no groin protector, no pads. Full power. So it goes both ways; if you and I are going to spar full power, I owe you the respect not to strike you in the face or the groin or any other spot, and I have the utmost respect for my opponent. It's an unwritten thing in our system that you never injure another human being.
>
> That's the basic difference. It is a martial Way, not martial art. We stress harmony, and unity with nature, and cohesiveness with all mankind. Shorinji-ryu teaches us not only how to live, but how to die properly. It is steeped in ancient traditions. It is a Zen way—it's very much a Zen oriented art.

Thus, Shorinji-ryu is a way of life centering on the morality of budo, Zen training, and continuing education in all facets of life. Cauley Sensei also emphasizes the application of personal and moral lessons learned through physical training to personal development and daily living. As with other aspects of his teaching, he often cites personal experiences as examples, such as the following incident that occurred when he was a student in Japan:

> One night, master Okada had accompanied me to the train station and we had stopped at a market and he bought a handful of bananas for his child. We were standing at the train station and talking when a young man, about seventeen years old, came up and grabbed the bananas out of Master Okada's hands and started to run. Master Okada casually reached out and caught the young lad in a tremendous joint technique. He didn't even look at the lad, but asked me if I could accompany him for dinner. I was overwhelmed and baffled. He dragged the young man about three blocks to a Japanese restaurant and threw the boy inside the seating area beside me. Only then, to my surprise, did he look at the young boy. He calmly asked the boy what he wanted to eat. The lad refused, but sensei Okada ordered him the very best on the menu, beef and rice. The boy would not look up at us, and when Master Okada spoke

of things not concerning the incident the lad acknowledged with a red face. Finally, Master Okada asked the lad where he was from. He reported that he had run away from home in Kanagawa City and was going to Tokyo to visit a friend when he ran out of money. After he had finished eating Mr. Okada told the lad to go to his dojo, pry open the back window and take the money and food that was there. "Just don't break anything, and shut the window back so it will not rain on my tatami mats!" said sensei. The lad left with a strict apology. The next day we found him sitting outside the dojo asking permission to learn karate. Sensei found him a job, and the young man is still learning about karatedo today. He has become a fine, young teacher of the Way.

– Cauley, 1978: 39

As an art, Sakugawa Koshiki Shorinji-ryu is rooted in the classical tradition of karate and retains the original theories, applications, and training methods developed by generations of master teachers. As such, it is an extremely effective martial art. However, Sakugawa Koshiki Shorinji-ryu is more importantly a budo, a martial way devoted to moral and intellectual education, to the training of the minds, bodies, and spirits of its practitioners. Today, teachers in both Japan and the United States strive to preserve and impart the training, knowledge, and benefits of this classical art.

TECHNICAL SECTION

Example of Joint Techniques

A1 As the attacker (Randall Brooks) does a middle punch, Wayne Van Horne (the defender) moves forward to the outside of the attacker and off line at a forty-five degree angle. He simultaneously deflects and grabs the attacker's wrist.

A2 Van Horne rotates his hips to turn the attacker's wrist and break his balance.

A3 Van Horne continues to rotate the wrist until the attacker must do a back breakfall.

A4 Van Horne then moves around the attacker's head while rotating the wrist to force the attacker to roll to his stomach.

A5 Van Horne then applies pressure to the wrist and uses his knee to keep the attacker from being able to bend his arm, effectively immobilizing him.

A6 Van Horne lowers the arm and securely immobilizes the attacker with a joint hold.

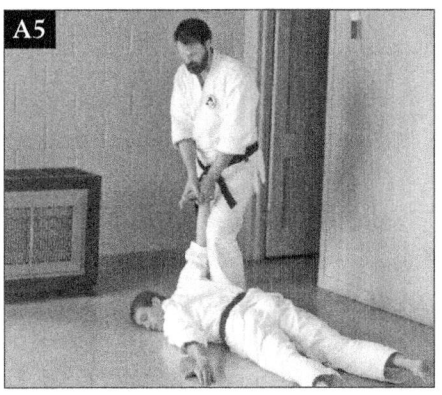
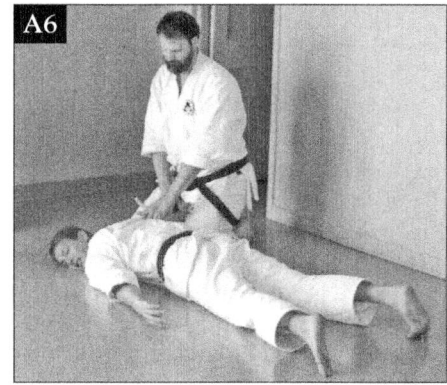

An Example of a Throw

B1 Throws typically rely on moving in harmony with the attacker's force and controlling their motion. As the attacker (Wayne Van Horne) performs an overhead strike, Thomas Cauley (the defender) steps off line and turns away from the attack while grabbing the wrist and elbow of the attacker.

B2 Using the attacker's forward momentum, Cauley controls the arm, causing the attacker to lose balance. The attacker is pulled into a forward breakfall and somersaults in mid-air.

B3   The attacker lands on his back with the defender in control.

C1   The attacker (R. Brooks) punches to the defender's (T. Cauley) head. The defender steps in and under the punch, grabbing the hand and controlling the front foot.

C2   The defender uses the attacker's momentum to pull him forward until he is under his center of gravity.

C3 Still using the attacker's forward momentum, the defender lifts the attacker.

C4-5 The attacker is thrown onto his back.

Joint Technique

Same sequence as the "A" sequence shown earlier, but from a different camera angle.

D1 As the attacker (Barney Foreman) does a middle punch, T. Cauley (the defender) moves forward to the outside of the attacker and off line at a forty-five degree angle. He simultaneously deflects and grabs the attacker's wrist.

D2 Cauley rotates his hips to turn the attacker's wrist and break his balance, throwing him to the ground.

D3-6 He then moves around the attacker's head while rotating the wrist to force the attacker to roll to his stomach.

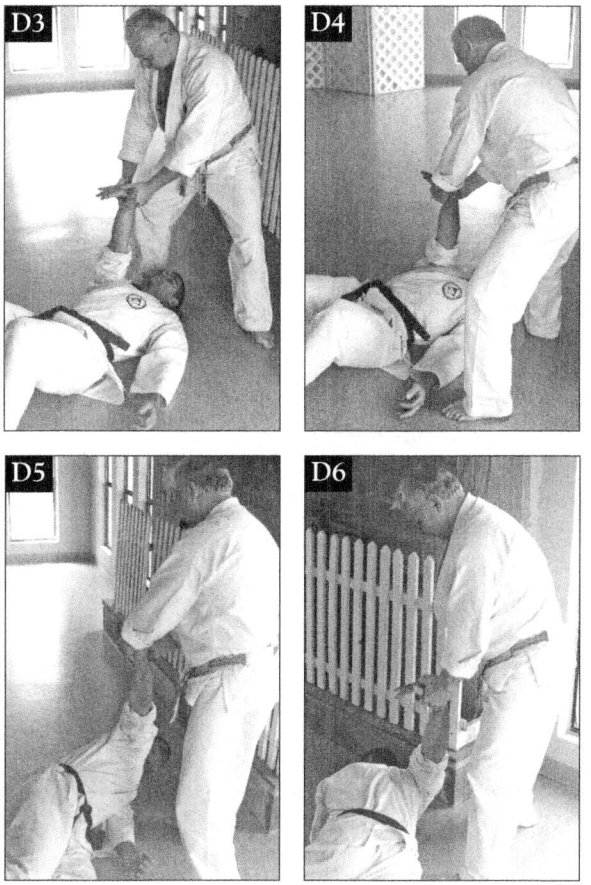

D7-9 He lowers the arm and securely immobilizes the attacker with a joint hold.

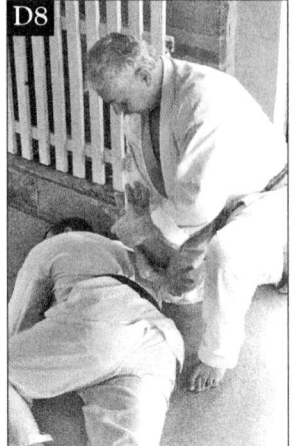
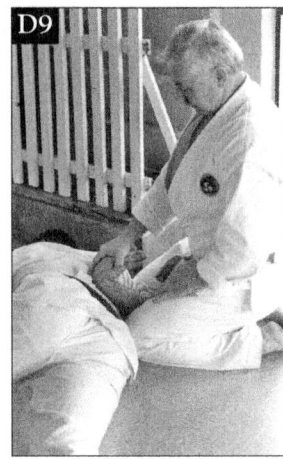

A Choke Hold

E1   The attacker (Michael Ta) throws a middle punch. The defender (Jarret Bailey) parries it and moves forward at a forty- five degree angle to the outside until he is behind the attacker, simultaneously grabbing the attacker's collar.

E2   The defender slips his hand under the attacker's elbow and raises it.

E3   Bailey continues to reach across with his left hand and grabs his own right sleeve. He then tightens his choke hold.

E4   The defender lowers himself backward onto one knee, pulling the attacker backward and off balance, effectively securing his hold. A brief application of this technique quickly causes unconsciousness.

Joint Techniques with Weapons

F1   The attacker (David Rappenhagen) seizes the defender's (Randall Brooks) *bo* (staff).

F2   The defender rotates the bo with a quick wrist motion.

F3   He steps back and down while cutting downward with the bo. This creates a joint technique that can break the wrist, or cause the attacker to release his grip.

G1 The attacker (Timothy Garrett) performs a middle punch while T. Cauley (the defender) steps off line and parries with a tonfa.

G2 Cauley reaches underneath with his other hand and grabs the tonfa, securing the attacker's wrist. Application of pressure to the wrist with the tonfa will cause severe pain and subdue the attacker.

H1-3 Thomas Cauley demonstrates three different joint techniques on Barney Foreman.

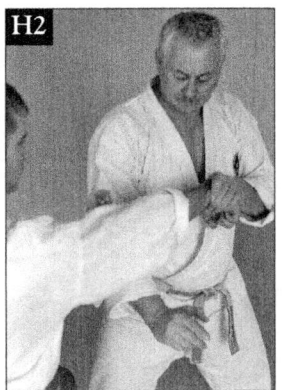

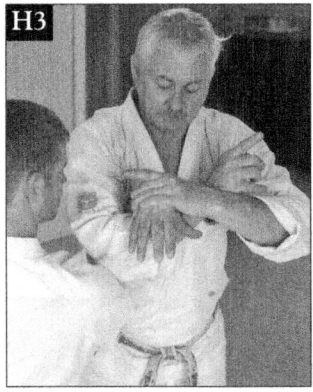

Thomas Cauley performing various katas.

Thomas Cauley and students performing various bo katas.

Note
[1] Due to personal reasons, the style's name has been withheld.

References

Cauley, T. (1978). *The universality of karate and kempo*. Self-published.

McCarthy, P. (1995). *The bible of karate: Bubishi*. Rutland, VT: Charles E. Tuttle, Co.

McCarthy, P. (1987). *Classical kata of Okinawan karate*. Burbank, CA: Ohara Publications.

Van Horne, W. (1986). *Shorinji-ryu karate-do and Zen: A case for the synthesis of cognitive analysis and symbolic interpretation*. Unpublished master's thesis, University of Georgia, Athens.

chapter 4

Re-Examining Ryukyu Kobudo: An Interview with Minowa Katsuhiko

by Mario McKenna, M.S.

Taira Shinken and Minowa Katsuhiko, circa 1970.
All photographs courtesy of M. McKenna.

Introduction

Recently, quite a lot of information has become available on Taira Shinken's life. This has predominantly taken the form of translations of his book and various articles about him from Japanese to English. Although important in the historical and personal information that such translations provide, they do not provide any insight with respect to what kind of person he was and how he influenced the succeeding generation of *kobudo* ("classical martial ways") instructors. Furthermore, there is limited information on the direction and evolution of Ryukyu kobudo after Taira's death. Therefore, to gain a wider personal account of Taira Shinken and the evolution of the Ryukyu Kobudo Hozon Shinko Kai (the organization that Taira founded), the following interview was conducted with Minowa Katsuhiko, one of the few remaining direct students of Taira still teaching in Japan.

The interview was conducted in June and August 1998 at the dojo of one of his students, Yoshimura Hiroshi, on Amami Oshima in Kagoshima Prefecture. In the interview, Minowa relates his experiences and impressions training under Taira. It is hoped that such insights will help us gain a fuller understanding of Taira, both as an instructor and his influence on succeeding generations of kobudo instructors.

Minowa Katsuhiko's Background

Minowa Katsuhiko currently holds the rank of eighth-dan in both Ryukyu kobudo and Uechi-ryu karate. A gentle and quiet man by nature, Minowa Sensei now resides in Naze city on the island of Amami Oshima in Kagoshima Prefecture. Minowa was born on January 10, 1929, on Amami Oshima. After World War II, there were few jobs available on Amami, so, in his 20's, he went to Okinawa in search of work.

Taira's original students at his home (circa 1970). Taira Shiken, seated. Standing (from L. to R.): Nakamoto Masahiro, Minowa Katsuhiko, Kinjo Kazufumi, Nagaishi Fumio (insert), Akamine Eisuke, and Nakasone Koshin.

At the age of 27, he and a group of friends decided to join the local karate dojo, which was run by the late Uechi Kanei. While his friends soon grew tired of karate practice, Minowa tirelessly continued, a passion that has never left him to this day. Two years after receiving his shodan ranking in Uechi-ryu, Minowa entered Taira Shinken's dojo to study kobudo. He devoted most of his energies to studying both Uechi-ryu karate and Ryukyu kobudo. By 1968, he had received his teaching license (*karatedo menjo*) from Uechi Kanei and two years later, received his kobudo teaching license from Taira just before his death in 1970.

After passing on his dojo in Matsukawa, Naha, to one of his students, Minowa returned to Amami Oshima in 1977. He soon established his own association, the Shinshukai (the Association for True Study), where he taught Uechi-ryu and Ryukyu kobudo until he retired from full-time teaching in 1987. After his retirement, he appointed his most senior student, Yoshimura Hiroshi, senior Shinshukai instructor in Amami.

Taira performing Tsukensunakake no Kon Kata.

Taira as a young man in his twenties.

INTERVIEW

▶ When did you first meet Taira Shinken?

That's quite a while ago. I suppose it was about two years after I had entered Uechi Kanei's dojo, around 1960. At that time, Taira Sensei had no dojo of his own. Instead, he traveled from dojo to dojo and would instruct those interested in Ryukyu kobudo. I think at that time he was simply trying to popularize the art. After the war, for one reason or another, people stopped practicing kobudo.

▶ Why do you think people stopped practicing kobudo on Okinawa after the war?

I really couldn't say. Prior to World War II, karate and kobudo were taught together. They weren't considered separate martial art forms. Rather, they were considered complementary. In fact, you were not considered a real Okinawa warrior [*bushi*] unless you had mastered both. It is comparable to two wheels joined on an axle. One cannot run without the other.

▶ When did you begin to study formally under Taira?

Soon after I met him at Uechi Kanei's dojo, I received a letter of introduction from one of Taira's acquaintances that allowed me to study on a regular basis with Taira.

Minowa and the late Uechi Kanei.
Minowa Katsuhiko performing Maezato no Tekko
at his dojo in Matsukawa, Naha, circa 1975.

Minowa giving the author (right) instruction
in the use of double-sickles (*nichogama*).

▶ WHERE DID THE TRAINING TAKE PLACE, SINCE TAIRA SENSEI HAD NO DOJO OF HIS OWN?

Training was conducted out of one of the rooms in his home several times a week.

▶ DO YOU REMEMBER HOW YOU FELT WHEN YOU FIRST WENT TO TAIRA'S HOME?

Extremely nervous! However, I soon realized I had nothing to be nervous about. Taira was an extremely warm and friendly man. He constantly called me Minowasan [Minowa's surname plus the polite suffix "-san," meaning respectful or honorable]. In fact, he called all his students by their surnames.

▶ WHAT DID THE TRAINING CONSIST OF?

Essentially kata practice. Unlike karate, there were no set basics [*kihon*] that students drilled in. All practice was very individual. Taira taught each student according to his ability or interest. If the student was weak in one part of a kata, he was corrected and told to repeat that part until the mistake had been eliminated.

▶ DIDN'T THAT CREATE SOME PROBLEMS IN THE DIFFERENCE BETWEEN THE KATAS AND TECHNIQUES OF TAIRA'S STUDENTS?

Not really. Although the order in which we learned the katas were different, we learned the same katas. Yes, there are differences between Taira's students, but this is to be expected. No two people are alike. As long as the kata is not fundamentally changed, that its ideal and essence are intact, then there's no need to worry. This style of teaching has been used on Okinawa for a long time.

▶ Previously you said that when you learned the kobudo katas from Taira there was no set order?

Not at first, that's right. A curriculum was developed after his death in 1970. Before then, everyone learned the katas in a different order. Unfortunately, Taira failed to teach some of the katas he knew before he passed away.

▶ So these katas are lost forever?

Not necessarily. These katas must have been passed on to someone on Okinawa at some time. So, it's just a matter of finding the right person who knows the katas. For instance, Taira did not teach any of us *Tsuken Bo Sho* and *Dai*, but I managed to learn them from Mie Junshin, a Kobayashi-ryu karate teacher.

▶ You have created several kobudo katas and yakusoku kumite [prearranged attack] sets. For example, Minowa no Tecchu, Minowa no Kon Sho and Dai, and Minowa no Sanbon Nunchaku. Is there any particular reason why you did this?

Actually, I've changed the names of those katas from Minowa to Matsugawa, where my first dojo in Naha was located. Anyway, when I was studying under Taira, there were several weapons in his home such as the *tecchu* and *sanbon nunchaku* that we never practiced. When I asked Taira about this, he simply replied that he had never learned any katas or techniques [*waza*] for those weapons. I never gave it much thought at the time, since I was already working hard enough just trying to learn what Taira was teaching me. However, after I moved back to Naze in 1977, I began to think about those weapons again and started to work out the details for the techniques of each weapon and finally the katas.

▶ Is this your way of giving something back to kobudo?

I suppose it is in a way, but I'm hardly unique. Taira's other students, such as Akamine Eisuke and Nakamoto Masahiro, have also made their own contributions by creating new kobudo katas. Karate and kobudo are not static things. Change is a natural and expected part of life.

"... karate and kobudo are connected, like two wheels to an axle."

▶ THE TECCHU KATA THAT YOU MADE IS QUITE UNIQUE. IN FACT, I AM AWARE OF ONLY ONE OTHER KATA THAT USES THE TECCHU, THAT MADE BY SHORINJI-RYU INSTRUCTOR RICHARD KIM OF AMERICA. WHAT DID YOU BASE THIS KATA AND ITS TECHNIQUES ON?

I didn't know any other kata for the tecchu had been made. I'd like to see it. The techniques contained in Matsugawa no Tecchu are based mostly upon my own ideas about using the weapon. Many of the techniques are very karate-like, but they aren't based on a particular kata. The most unique ways of attacking and defending with the tecchu are found in the last part of the kata. They use large circling motions to parry and unbalance an attacker using a bo. The tecchu also uses quite a lot of strikes to vulnerable parts of the body.

▶ HOW ABOUT THE YAKUSOKU KUMITE [PREARRANGED ATTACK] SETS?

Well, when I was studying under Taira, there really weren't any yakusoku kumite sets per se. There was a bo vs. sai [*bo tai sai*] set and a two-man *bunkai* [analysis of technique] for Sakugawa no Kon Sho that I learned, but those were essentially created by my senior [*sempai*], Akamine Eisuke. It seemed a little strange to me not to have yakusoku kumite sets for the other weapons. Of course, individual techniques did exist for certain weapons like bo v.s. tonfa. These were largely based upon kata techniques, but there were no organized weapon sets. I felt that a lack of weapons yakusoku kumite meant that students could not learn how to use and apply the weapon in a realistic way.

▶ WHEN DID YOU START TO MAKE THE YAKUSOKU KUMITE SETS?

At about the same time that I began thinking about techniques and katas for the tecchu and sanbon nunchaku. From about 1977 on.

▶ THEN THE YAKUSOKU KUMITE SETS BETWEEN TAIRA'S STUDENTS ARE ALL DIFFERENT?

With the exception of bo vs. sai and Sakugawa no Kon bunkai, yes, they're all different.

▶ WHAT ADVICE DO YOU HAVE FOR STUDENTS STUDYING KOBUDO?

Although some people may disagree, I feel you should have a reasonably good foundation in karate before you begin kobudo practice. Ikkyu or shodan would probably be a good time to start learning kobudo.

▸ WHY DO YOU SAY THAT?

Like I said earlier, karate and kobudo are connected, like two wheels to an axle. Fundamentally, kobudo's body mechanics, footwork, stances, etc. are very similar to karate's. For most people learning any new kind of physical skill or activity, it is generally easier to learn without distractions. Adding the extra mental burden of a kobudo weapon can disrupt a student's concentration making it more difficult to learn. By shodan, however, the student already has internalized the fundamental techniques of karate and can better concentrate on learning the correct use of the kobudo weapon.

▸ THANK YOU VERY MUCH FOR TALKING THE TIME FOR THIS INTERVIEW.

It's been my pleasure. Thank you.

SAMPLE OF TECCHU TECHNIQUES

Ryukyu kobudo is the weapon art of Okinawa employing different weapons, some makeshift and some real, for self-protection. Some of the more common weapons include: *rokushaku bo* (six-foot staff), *sai* (metal truncheon), *tonfa/tuifa* (right-angled wooden truncheon), *nunchaku* (wooden flail), and *eku/kai* (oar). It is generally accepted that most of the weapons employed in Ryukyu kobudo were developed from either agricultural or fishing implements (Bolz, 1995: 86; Bishop, 1996: 26). This development is thought to have occurred after the subjugation of Okinawa by the Satsuma *bushi* (warrior) in 1609 and the resultant ban on possessing weapons. Having no other means of defending themselves, the Shuri upper class began to train using simple farming and fishing tools. This, coupled with the introduction of Chinese-based martial arts forms, resulted in the development of modern-day Ryukyu kobudo (Bishop: 26, 1996).

One man who played a significant role in the resurgence of interest in Ryukyu kobudo was the late Taira Shinken (1898-1970). During a time when the study of Ryukyu kobudo was at its lowest, Taira traveled across Okinawa and Japan studying as many weapons and their respective traditions as he could. His years of study culminated in the formation of the Ryukyu Kobudo Hozon Shinko Kai (the Ryukyu Kobudo Preservation and Promotion Association), an organization that survives to this day. The curriculum of Taira's Ryukyu Kobudo Hozon Shinko Kai included instruction in the use of nine weapons and their respective katas that he had learned throughout his years of instruction or that he had created himself.

A couple of the more unusual and little known weapons employed in Taira's Ryukyu Kobudo Hozon Shinko Kai are the *tekko* and *tecchu* (also known as *tikko* and *ticchu* in Okinawa dialect, Hogen, respectively). The tekko can be roughly equated with the "knuckle duster" in the West. While the tecchu is a short tapered wooden or metal rod approximately 20 to 30 cm long.

According to martial arts historians, the use of the tekko appears to have originated when bushi in Okinawa used horseshoes as make-shift weapons to defend themselves against a surprise attack. The weapon was later modified and developed into a simple and effective hand-held weapon (Sells, 1996: 273; McCarthy, 1998, March: 23; Nakamoto, 1983).

The tecchu's origin is similar in many respects to that of the tekko, but less clear. There are two conflicting theories commonly held with respect to its origin. The first theory is that the tecchu was developed from the fisherman's net weaver, suggesting a plebian origin (Minowa, 1998). In contrast, the second theory argues that the long hairpin (*kanzashi*) used by Okinawan bushi was employed as a makeshift weapon when a warrior was attacked by surprise. Hence an upper class origin to the weapon (Nakamoto, 1983).

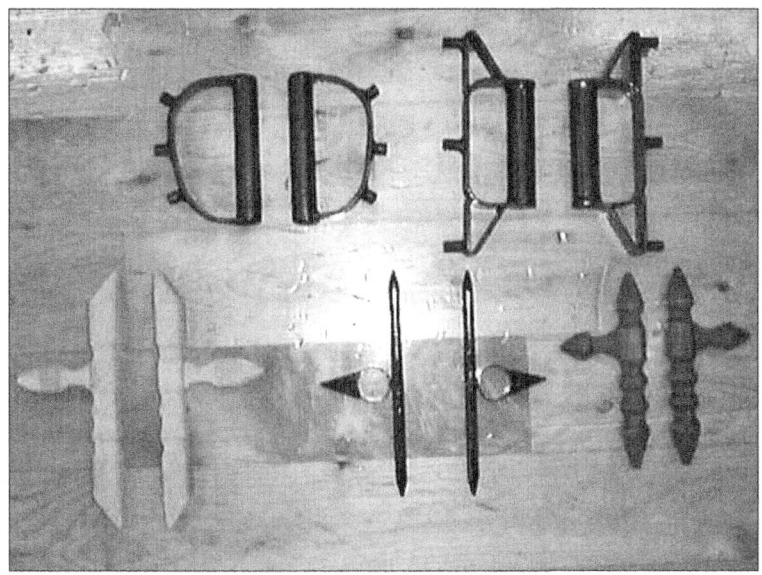

Examples
of tekko.

According to Nakamoto Masahiro, author of *Okinawa Ryukyu Kobudo: Sono Reikishi to Tamashi* (Okinawa Ryukyu Kobudo: Its History and Soul), there is a striking similarity between the tekko and tecchu and the hand-held weapons employed in ancient Greece and Rome. In ancient Greece, boxers wore leather thongs to protect their hands and wrists. As time went on, harder leather was used, turning the thongs into weapons. Later, the Romans added iron or brass studs, creating the cestus, which could be used as a deadly weapon. The Romans continued the development of the cestus creating a spur-like instrument of bronze, called the *myrmex* (literally "limb piercer"), which had a devastating and often fatal impact upon an opponent. The tekko and tecchu became popular weapons for self-defense in old Okinawa, since they are both small, easy to conceal, and like the cestus and myrmex, could produce severe trauma and even death (McCarthy, 1998; Nakamoto, 1983).

In the Ryukyu Kobudo Hozon Shinko Kai, there are presently two katas for these two hand-held weapons. They are Maezato no Tekko and Matsugawa no Tecchu. Taira Shinken developed Maezato no Tekko and named it after his original family name, Maezato (Taira had been put up for adoption as a child) (Nakamoto, 1984; McCarthy, 1998). Maezato no Tekko is based upon techniques he had learned from his grandfather, Kanegawa Gibu, and from the Shorin-ryu karatedo kata Jion (Nakamoto, 1984). However, there appears to be some discrepancy as to which karatedo kata was used as the basis for Maezato no Tekko. Nakamoto has stated that kata Jion was used as the basis for some of the techniques and the *enbusen* (line of performance of the kata), other martial arts historians have argued that Ji'in is more likely the basis for this kata (Sells, 1998).

The second, and to a much greater extent, less known hand-held weapon kata currently practiced in the Ryukyu Kobudo Hozon Shinkok Kai is Matsugawa no Tecchu. Minowa Katsuhiko (eighth dan Ryukyu kobudo, eighth dan Uechi-ryu karatedo), one of Taira Shinken's students, created Matsugawa no Tecchu. Minowa named the kata after the location of his first dojo in Naha, Okinawa. The kata is based upon Minowa's years of study under Taira Shinken, his karatedo background, and his own unique interpretation of the weapon.

Outside of Okinawa and mainland Japan, the hand-held weapon techniques and tradition of the tekko is rare and that of the tecchu is almost completely unknown. With the tekko, overseas kobudo practitioners have gained some exposure to its kata and techniques through the works of one of Taira's students, the late Inoue Motokatsu, such as the *Ancient Martial Arts of the Ryukyu Islands, Vol. 2*, which was published in English. However, to date, there has been virtually no English language information regarding the tecchu. Given the rarity, uniqueness, and lack of English language information on the tecchu and its techniques and tradition, this chapter will focus on the tecchu. In the following sections, the major techniques from kata Matsugawa no Tecchu as well as their applications are illustrated and explained.

Kihon Kame (Basic Posture)

The basic fighting posture when using the tecchu consists of both hands held at mid-level with the left hand and leg positioned forward in a natural posture. This stance is commonly referred to in Japanese as *morote chudan kame hidari mae shizen tecchu*. Due to the tecchu's very limited range in comparison to other kobudo weapons such as the *rokushaku bo* or the *sanbon nunchaku* (three-section flail), speed and mobility are essential when employing the tecchu. Therefore, the body weight is kept slightly forward on the balls of the feet, allowing for greater speed and mobility when defending against an attack.

In addition to shizen tecchu, the tecchu lends itself quite readily to other fighting postures commonly found in Okinawan/Japanese karatedo such as the forward stance (*zenkutsu tecchu*), horse riding stance (*shiko tecchu*), and the cat stance (*neko Ashi tecchu*). However, compared to their karatedo counter-parts, the position of the hips are considerably higher.

Front and side views of morote chudan kame.

Uke Waza (methods of receiving an attack)

Techniques of receiving an attack with the tecchu consist of the standard karatedo closed-fisted variety such as the downward sweeping block (*gedan barai uke*) and the outside middle block (*chudan soto uke*). However, several unique blocks are used to take advantage of the tecchu's deflecting and trapping potential. These include the inside middle block (*chudan uchi uke*), which is used for deflecting and unbalancing an attack; the mid-/upper-level circular block (*chudan/jodan mawashi uke*), which is typically used for hooking or ensnaring and attackers weapon or weapon arm; and the downward sweeping block (*gedan barai uke*) and the upper-level block (*jodan uke*), both of which are also used to deflect and unbalance an attack.

1: mid-level block
2: mid-/upper-level circular block
3: upper- and lower-level blocks
4: downward sweeping block

Atemi Waza (percussion techniques)

The tecchu uses a number of unique techniques that take advantage of its shape and striking potential. Unlike the tekko, the tecchu is not a high-impact weapon that can cause severe damage and trauma. Furthermore, in comparison to other Ryukyu kobudo weapons, such as the *rokushaku bo* or *nicho gama* (double-sickles), the tecchu lacks range or a cutting edge.

Therefore, tecchu strikes instead focus on attacking vulnerable parts of the body, which include the head, neck, torso, and upper leg. The four most common methods of using the tecchu for attacking are: the upper-level strike (*jodan uchi*), which employs the outside point of the tecchu to attack the vulnerable parts of the head and neck; the upper-level reverse strike (*jodan ura uchi*), which uses the inside of the tecchu to attack the head and neck areas; the upper-/mid-/lower-level thrust (*jodan/chudan/gedan tsuki*), which uses the center point of the tecchu to attack primarily the torso and legs; and the upper-/mid-/lower-level stab (*jodan/chudan/gedan nuki*), used primarily to attack the face and torso.

> 5: upper-level strike
> 6: upper-level reverse strike
> 7: mid-level thrust
> 8: mid-level stab

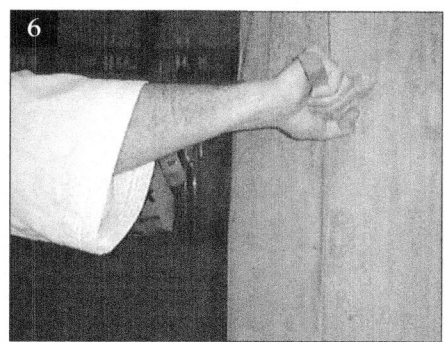
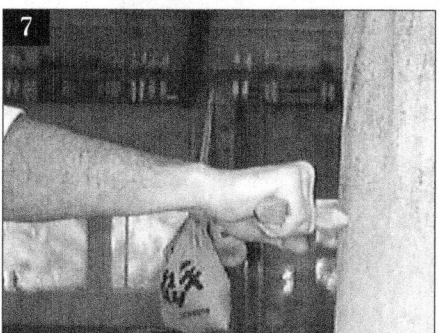

PREARRANGED ATTACKS

Like the other Ryukyu kobudo weapons, the primary means of increasing a person's skill with a weapon after mastery of its fundamental techniques through kata is by *yakusoku kumite* (prearranged sparring). Minowa Katsuhiko has developed a set of ten scenarios for the tecchu defending against an attacker with a rokushaku bo, the most commonly employed weapon in old Okinawa. Below are some simple examples from the yakusoku kumite set for the tecchu vs. the bo, with Minowa Katsuhiko (black gi) as defender and his senior student, Yoshimura Hiroshi (white gi), as the attacker.

1a Yoshimura slides forward and attacks with a right overhead strike. Minowa steps back into a left forward stance and simultaneously receives the attack with a double-handed upper-level block.

1b Remaining in the same stance, Minowa slides forward and, sweeping Yoshimura's bo to the side, targets the torso with a double mid-level stab.

2a Yoshimura slides forward with a right mid-level thrust. Stepping back and to the side, Minowa deflects the attack with a middle left outside circular block.

2b Trapping Yoshimura's bo and forcing it down, Minowa steps forward into a right forward stance and attacks Yoshimura's head with an upper-level reverse strike.

3a Yoshimura slides forward with a right upper-level thrust. Minowa slides back into a natural stance with the right leg forward and deflects the attack with an upper right outside circular block.

3b Hooking the attacker's bo to the outside with his right hand, Minowa steps in and attacks Yoshimura's temple using a left upper-level strike.

4a Yoshimura slides forward into a right forward stance attacking Minowa's leg with a right downward thrust. Minowa steps slightly to the left and parries the thrust with a double sweeping downward block.

4b Minowa quickly steps into a right forward stance before the attacker can retreat and targets Yoshimura's face with a double upper-level stab.

5a Yoshimura steps forward and attacks with a right mid-level thrust. Minowa steps back and to the outside into a horse riding stance with the left leg forward and simultaneously parries the blow with an inside mid-level block.

5b Pushing the attacker's bo to the side, Minowa slides forward into a left forward stance and attacks Yoshimura's thigh with a downward thrust.

6a Yoshimura slides forward and attacks Minowa's leg with a right downward thrust. Minowa steps back into a left leg forward horse riding stance and simultaneously defends using a right upper-level, left downward sweeping block.

6b Minowa then steps forward into a left forward stance and attacks the groin using a right downward whipping strike.

A) Minowa Katsuhiko B) Minowa Katsuhiko, the author, and Yoshimura Hiroshi at Yoshimura's dojo, July 1997.

Conclusion

The tecchu is a unique and obscure hand-held weapon within the curriculum of Ryukyu kobudo. In this chapter I have attempted to give a general overview and introduction of the tecchu's basic techniques, stances, and training methods. It is hoped this chapter will generate some interest in this little known Ryukyu kobudo weapon and encourage others to investigate it and perhaps adopt it.

References

Bishop, M. (1996). *Zen kobudo: Mysteries of Okinawan weaponry and te.* Rutland, VT: Charles E. Tuttle Co.

Bolz, M. (1995). The Okinawan sai: Kobudo weapon for self-defense. *Journal of Asian Martial Arts,* 4(1), 85-99.

McCarthy, P. (1997, March). Taira Shinken: The Funakoshi of kobudo, part 1. *Bugeisha,* 1(2), 18-23.

McCarthy, P. (1997, Summer). Taira Shinken: The Funakoshi of kobudo, part 2. *Bugeisha,* 1(3), 21-26.

Minowa, K. (1998). Personal communication.

Nakamoto, M. (1983). *Okinawa Ryukyu kobudo: Its history and soul.* Naha: Okiinsha.

Sells, J. (1996) *Unante: The secrets of karate.* Hollywood: W. M. Hawley.

Sells, J. (1998). Personal communication.

Acknowledgements

I would sincerely like to thank Minowa Katsuhiko for posing for the photos and for generously providing background information for this chapter and patiently answering any and all questions posed to him by the author. I would also like to thank Yoshimura Hiroshi (fifth dan Uechi-ryu, fifth dan Ryukyu kobudo) for posing for the photos, his encouragement, his patient instruction, and for the use of his dojo. Finally I would like to thank both Michael DeMarco and Richard Florence for their comments and feedback in preparing the manuscript for this chapter.

chapter 5

Elements of Advanced Karate Technique

by Marvin Labbate

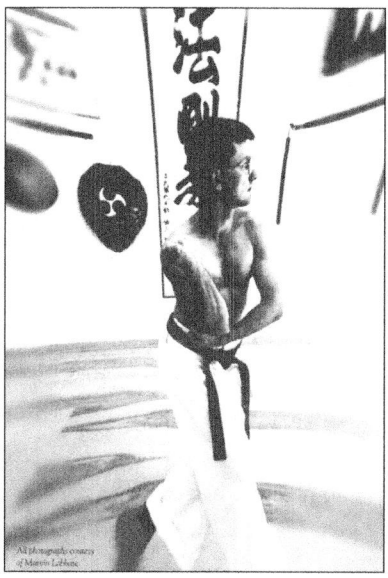

All photographs courtesy of Marvin Labbate.

Every karate student is endowed with a level of strength, speed, flexibility, and endurance that with time and practice naturally develops. Unfortunately, these superficial qualities often mark the primary difference between the beginner and the advanced black belt. This chapter focuses on elements of a deeper subject: the lifelong development of technique. To illustrate the process of development, the chapter probes deeply into the first four steps of Sanchin, the most fundamental kata of Okinawan Goju-ryu.

The version of Sanchin discussed here was developed by the style's founder, Miyagi Chojun, and serves primarily as a catalog of basic principles. It evolved by adding hard (*go*) closed-handed, strength building movements to soft (*ju*), open-handed techniques imported from China. Miyagi taught Sanchin as the first kata and considered it so important that he required students to train exclusively in it for many years. When performed correctly, Sanchin harmonizes both the soft and hard components of structure, movement, and breathing. The goal of this chapter is to systematically reveal these principles by explaining the kata at successively deeper levels of understanding. At the beginner level, the soft principles of Sanchin are introduced and developed. At the intermediate level, hard principles are added. Finally, the advanced student develops the combination of soft and hard to achieve the desired training outcome and improve overall technique. The ideas are so fundamental that they are applicable to any karate style and every student can benefit from the study of Sanchin.

> **Principle #1**
> Practice slowly and carefully, checking and correcting stance with each movement.

Principles of Structure and Movement

The beginning student focuses attention on the principles of structure and movement in Sanchin. This involves memorization of the basic pattern, correct positioning and movement of the body, and harmonizing breathing with motion. The kata should be performed repeatedly each day in front of a mirror, and always with the gi top removed to allow careful inspection of the body's position and form. The beginner uses slow, graceful, tension-free movements and follows each move by checking the body position and adjusting the stance to the correct form.

> **Principle #2**
> Focus the mind on each muscle group in a fixed pattern.

The mind should be focused using the same procedure with each stance: it begins by placing attention at the feet and works steadily up the body until reaching the *tanden*, a spot located just below the navel that forms the center of energy flow in the body. Focus is then moved to the crown point at the top of the head and continues down the body ending again at the tanden. This procedure ensures that each muscle group is considered methodically as part of a consistent procedure of improvement.

Sanchin uses a simple pattern that combines several basic blocks and punches. An overview of the complete kata can be found in Higaonna Morio's highly recommended book.[1] The sequence below shows the movements taken from the ready-stance (*heiko dachi*, A1). The first transition is to a right sanchin stance (*migi sanchin dachi*) and is followed by a double-handed side block (*morote chudan yoko uke*, A2). Following the block, the left hand is chambered (A3), a left two-knuckle punch (*hidari seiken zuki*, A4) is executed, then a left side block (A5). These movements are followed by a step into a left sanchin stance, the right hand is chambered, and a right two-knuckle punch with corresponding side block is executed.

The sequence continues, as shown below starting with A6, with a step into a right sanchin stance executing a corresponding left chamber (A6) and punch (A7). The left hand is then rechambered (A8) and brought across the body while the student looks at an adversary on the left (A9). The right foot then transitions in a crosslegged stance (A10), a 180-degree turn is executed (A11), and the student ends in a left sanchin stance with the right hand chambered. This sequence sets the student up to repeat the basic pattern of three steps and punches in the opposite direction.

Opening steps of Sanchin kata.

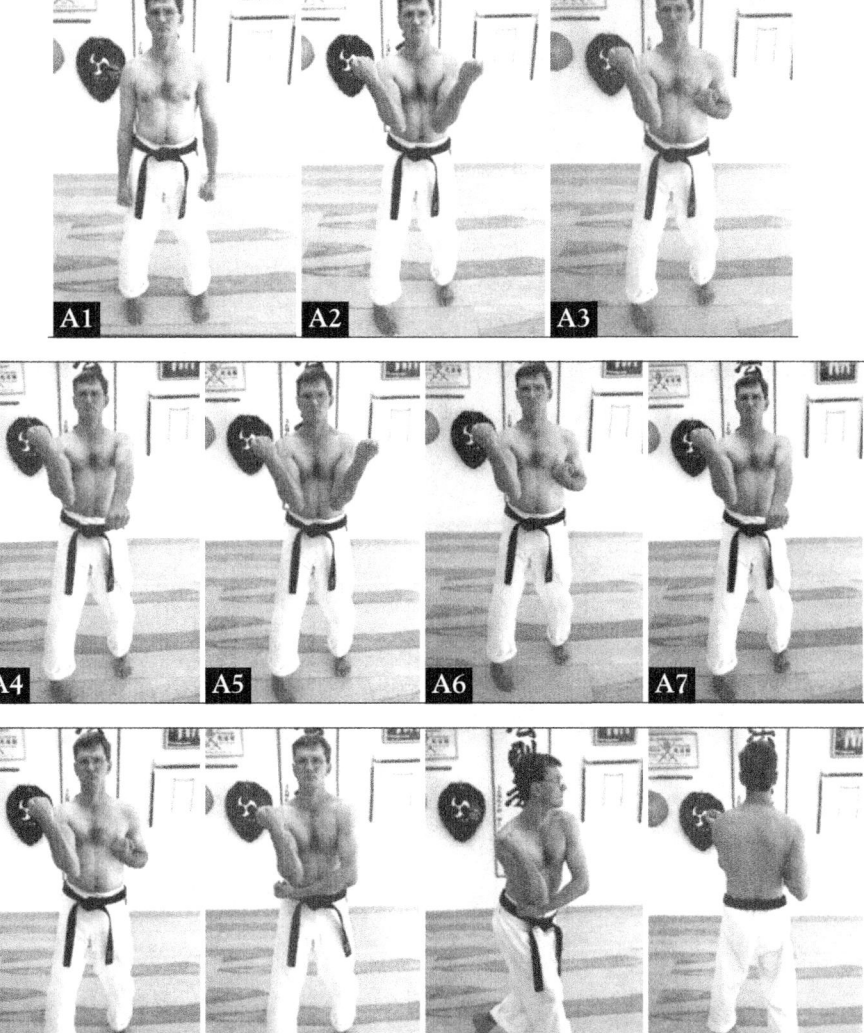

Structure

Applying principle #2, let us now re-examine the central aspects of the opening sequence from the viewpoint of structure. Consider the ready stance shown previously in A1 and begin at the feet: The feet form our link to the universe; our goal is to firmly root the body to the floor and lower the body's center of gravity to provide stability. To achieve this, the position of the feet is critical. Photo B1 shows the correct positioning with the outer edges of the feet parallel, shoulders' width apart.

Ready Stance Feet Positioning

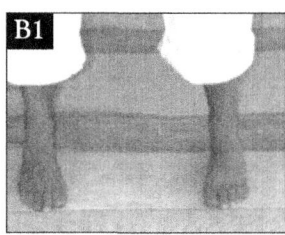 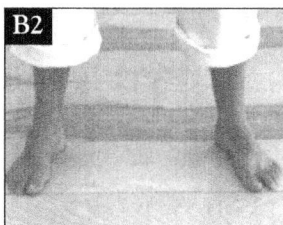

Principle #3
Correctly position the feet so as to grip the floor.

A common error is to position the feet in the more natural stance (B2). Unfortunately, a stable stance cannot be obtained from this position. The same concept applies to the sanchin stance shown throughout the opening sequence. As in the ready stance, careful positioning of the feet is essential to stability. Photo B3 shows the correct positioning for a right sanchin stance. The toe of the left foot and heel of the right foot are aligned, shoulders' width apart. The left foot is aligned with the outer edge forward and the right foot is turned slightly inward. A common error is to position the feet as shown in B4; again, a stable stance cannot be obtained in this position.

Sanchin Stance Feet Positioning

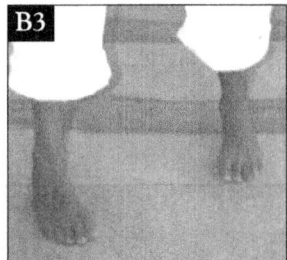 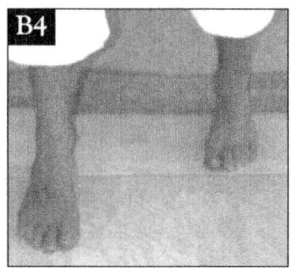

Principle #4
Use peripheral vision to take in the entire scene.

Working up the body, the hips should be carefully aligned facing forward with the back held straight above the base of the spine. Moving to the top of the body, the crown of the head is pushed upward as if to suck energy from the universe while straightening the neck and spine. The eyes look forward and slightly upward, as if looking to the future. When performing in front of a mirror, the gaze should be turned over the right shoulder of the reflection so as to allow the entire body to be perceived at once using peripheral vision. The tongue is placed on the hard palate allowing the free flow of air to and from the body. The chin is tucked slightly inward to improve breathing and prevent strangle holds. The shoulders are always aligned forward and held down.

Notice the position of the arms and shoulders in the double side block in photo A2. The elbow is placed a fist's distance from the body and the arm forms a 90 degree angle at the elbow. The arms form a "V" shape in front of the body with the shoulders firmly down.

Principle #5
Correctly position the arms to ensure an effective blocking technique that will deflect rather than forcibly stop a blow.

Movement

There are four primary transitions in the opening sequence:

- stance-to-stance
- chamber-to-punch
- punch-to-block
- stance-to-turn.

The goal of the beginning student is to remain fluid, stable and upright at all times with the shoulders held down and the hips and shoulders aligned forward. The body does not sway from side to side, nor bob up and down while in motion. To achieve this fluidity the body is held loose with the knees slightly bent.

Principle #6
Move gracefully with circular motions paying special attention to keep the body from bobbing up and down or swaying from side to side.

The stance-to-stance transition occurs between the ready stance and sanchin stance (A1 and A2), or between consecutive sanchin stances. This transition is achieved by moving the body's weight to the forward foot while bending the forward knee slightly to keep the shoulders at the same level. The rear foot is then brought forward in a circular motion that extends to the centerline between the feet. The foot that moves maintains contact with the floor on its outer edge throughout the motion. At the end of the transition the feet are checked to ensure that they are positioned correctly. If an error is found, the foot that moved is the one that made the mistake; corrections are therefore always applied to the foot that moved.

The chamber-to-punch transition shown in photos A3 and A4 is broken down into five segments (in C1 through C5). The transition begins from the chambered position in which the elbow points down and the hand is clenched with the thumb tucked to prevent an inadvertent break (C1). The punch first extends to an uppercut position (C2), then transitions to a vertical punch when the elbow is approximately a fist distance from the body (C3). When the punch is fully extended, it rests in a natural position slightly inward from the vertical position. This position is best determined though a simple arm swinging exercise: swing the arms loosely at the side of the body extending up to shoulder height; after swinging freely four or five times, halt the swing at shoulder height and the hands will naturally hold the correct striking position. The chamber-to-punch transition ends with a cutting motion of the hand when the arm is fully extended. This final movement occurs after the blow is struck and causes the knuckles to grind into an opponent with a twisting motion. The transition ends with the arm locked into its final position (C5).

Chamber-to-Punch Transition.

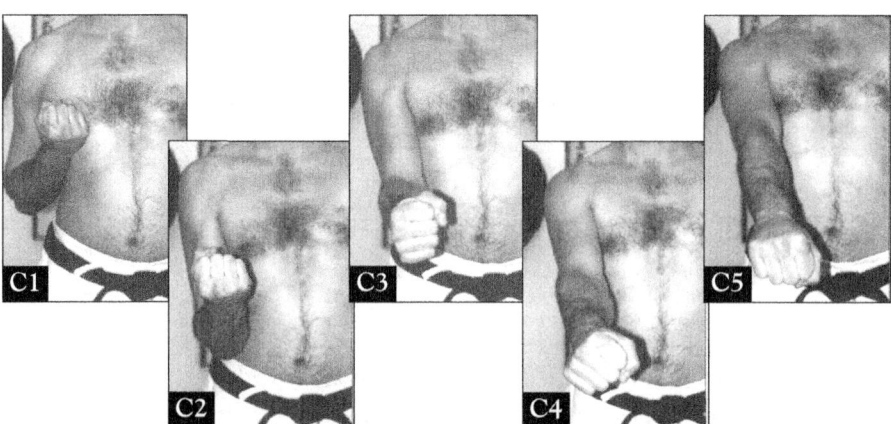

Principle #7
All punches develop from a common transition in which the arm extends forward from the shoulder like a battering ram.

Principle #8
During all movements, the shoulders are held down, the upper arm pinches the pectoral muscles, and the elbows scrape the rib cage.

The punch extends forward from the shoulder, like a battering ram, and does not cross the body. In this manner, the punch is delivered with the full weight of the body behind it. When striking an opponent, the practitioner aligns the body to strengthen the punch rather than weaken it to compensate for poor positioning. Throughout this sequence, the shoulders remain firmly down, the upper arm pinches the pectoral muscles, and the elbow transitions by scraping the rib cage. Two common errors are to raise the shoulders and to allow the elbow to drift outward from the body. Both weaken the technique. It is most important to practice the punch very slowly until it becomes second nature.

The punch-to-block transition follows a circular path much like opening a door: the hand rotates upward while the elbow moves in slightly, causing the upper arm to push against the pectoral muscles. Throughout the transition, the shoulders remain down and the final body position should again be with the forearms in a V-shape with the elbows a fist's distance from the body.

The final transition, stance-to-turn, is shown in photos A10 and A11 and requires that the body remain upright at all times. As the right leg crosses the left, the knees should touch. The turn is performed on the balls of the feet in a manner that ends in sanchin stance. As the body twists out of the turn, the left arm first forms a guard and then moves into the standard side block position, while the right arm is simultaneously chambered in readiness for a punch.

Breathing

The beginning student uses natural abdominal breathing (*zhengfu huxi* in Mandarin) taken from internal energy work (*neidan qigong* in Mandarin, *kiko* in Japanese). Unlike normal breathing that involves movement of the chest, natural breathing uses a slow, deep, abdominal breath centered on the *tanden* (*dantian* in Mandarin). The abdomen is consciously forced to expand as air is inhaled through the nose. The abdomen is allowed to contract as air is exhaled through the mouth. The breath is never held, but instead circulates in a continuous, smooth and natural motion. This form of breathing is used to heal the body and develop physical strength. It has the effect of exercising and developing the abdominal muscles; massaging the internal organs, especially the kidneys; and increasing circulation. This process calms the mind, strengthens the will, and leads to a general improvement in health that allows the student to progress to develop other aspects of technique.

A particularly crucial concept in Sanchin kata is to synchronize breathing with movement. This synchronization manages oxygen to ensure that techniques are always delivered with the full force of mind and body. Consider the initial few movements of the kata from the ready stance shown in the "A" sequence of photos. The first motion, to the double side block, is accompanied by a long breath. The inhalation occurs while the hands rise; the student exhales as the arms fall into position in the double side block. This sets up the breathing pattern for subsequent moves that are generally prepared with inhalation and delivered with exhalation. The subsequent punch is delivered with a long deep breath. While chambering the left hand for the punch, as shown in photo A3, inhalation begins at the point where movement to the chamber is initiated and stops at the precise moment that the hand is in its final resting position in the chamber. Exhalation begins when the punch is initiated; the breath is fully expelled precisely at the point where the punch ends as shown in photo A4. The subsequent side block, photo A5, involves a short breath. As the arm rotates upward, inhalation occurs; breath is exhaled as the arm falls into position in the standard double block.

One further example of this synchronization occurs in the final stance-to-turn transition shown in photos A8 through A11. The breath is inhaled while the left hand is chambered (A8), then exhaled while it traverses the body (A9) and inhaled for the full duration of the turn (A10 and A11). This sequence ensures that oxygen is available for a subsequent punch with the chambered right hand.

Principle #9
Synchronize natural breathing
with motion: inhale while preparing
and exhale while delivering each blow.

Intermediate Go Principles

After learning the basic pattern combining structure with movement and breathing, the intermediate student progresses to strength training. In gongfu parlance this has been termed "iron-shirt training," as it gradually develops a hard surface of solid muscle that provides protection against even the strongest blows. The essence of the idea is to gradually reinforce the basic structures introduced earlier by adding successive levels of muscular tension, thereby building strength and endurance. A central component of this training is to lock down each muscle group into a strong reinforced position with each movement.

At the intermediate level, Sanchin is performed slowly and carefully with all muscle groups in tension and constant attention to form. A common error is for the student to exaggerate the required tension with severe and uncontrollable exertion. Over-exertion can lead to high blood pressure and cause a heart attack or stroke. Further, a muscle under severe exertion tires the student and results in jerky motions. In contrast, a tight solid muscle can provide protection and yet be moved with fluidity. Muscular tension is built gradually over a period of years, through repetition.

Structure

Returning to the right sanchin stance (A2), the mind is focused to induce tension by considering each muscle group in turn as focus moves up the body. With the feet in the position shown in photo B1, the toes grip the floor while the heels turn inward rooting the stance in the floor and gripping it tightly. Focus then moves to the calves and backs of the legs, which should be tightened by a twisting motion at the heels. Then focus turns to the thighs, with the knees bent slightly; the anus is tucked inward; and the tanden is moved upward slightly. This causes the thighs to tighten in an outward twisting motion that protects the groin and places the entire lower body in tension. A common error is for the student to lean backward when performing this technique. The back must be kept straight with the hips aligned forward for stability. A graphic illustration of poor technique can be obtained by attempting this procedure with the feet in the position shown in photo B2: the feet are unable to gain a firm grip in this position and, as a result, little tightening of the body is possible.

Moving now to the top of the body: the crown of the head is pushed upward, the neck becomes tense, and the shoulders, which should be down, also become tense. In the double block position, the top of the arm pinches the pectoral muscles causing the entire muscle group at the shoulder to be locked down into position as shown in photo "D". Next, the hands are clenched firmly, the elbow is moved inward slightly and the small finger on each hand is rotated toward the body. These motions place tension on every muscle group in both the upper and lower arm. Finally, moving further down the body, the muscles in the abdomen at the tanden are tightened.

Upper Arm Pinching the Pectoral Muscles

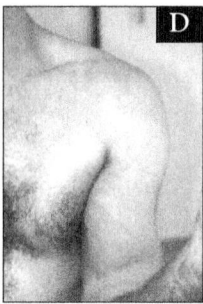

Supplemental Weight Training

To perfect locking of the muscles in the upper body, training is augmented with *chiishi* weights, such as those shown in photos E1 through E5. If these weights are not available, students can obtain a heavy sledgehammer from a local hardware store and simply cut down the handle to obtain a training device with the same characteristics. Chiishi training is initiated by simply placing the device on the floor in front of the student (E1). The student then wraps a hand around the handle and lifts the weight vertically by bending the knees and keeping the arm straight (E2). This first movement places the shoulder muscle group in the correct locked position: it should feel as if the entire shoulder from the neck, across the pectoral muscles, and into the upper arm is one complete and integrated whole. Next, the chiishi is brought upward to position (E3). This position corresponds to a vertical punch. The student should again feel the upper arm pinching against the pectoral muscles and again the entire shoulder group should lock down into an integrated whole. From the vertical punch, the chiishi is then brought to the side block position (E4). This position again locks the shoulder group, but also causes the elbow

Chiishi Training

to be rotated across the body and the small finger of the hand to be rotated inward causing the entire set of arm muscles to become tense and unified. To end the exercise, the chiishi is brought backward, then over the shoulder and back to the vertical punch position (E5). During this motion, the student attempts to maintain the shoulder group in a locked position. This motion is repeated on each side and eventually with two weights simultaneously. A variety of other similar exercises can be used to enhance this form of training.

Chiishi training can be based on repetitions to strengthen the shoulder muscle group in every position used and improve endurance. Alternatively, training can be conducted slowly with each position held so as to develop endurance, flexibility and form. Slow training is used to feel the muscles working: The student holds each position, closes the eyes, and focuses the mind on allowing the weight to take the muscle group to a natural position. The weight works to assemble the muscle group in the correct position and allows the student to develop an instinctive feel for the correct position. When performing the kata, this instinctive feeling will guide the positioning of the body and lead to improved technique without conscious thought.

Progress in chiishi training is immediately noticeable from the manner in which the student picks up the chiishi as shown in photos E1 and E2. Early on, the student picks up the chiishi with the arm muscles and tires the arm quickly. Soon this movement progresses to where the weight is lifted with the entire shoulder group locked into position. Eventually the student lifts the weight with the entire body: the body is rooted in the floor providing a stable position, the center of weight is lowered, the anus is tucked, and all of the other Sanchin principles are applied.

Principle #10
Lock each muscle group into a single integrated whole that is maintained throughout the kata.

Movement

The muscle locking techniques developed using chiishi weights are integrated directly into the performance of Sanchin kata. Throughout each movement, the student pays careful attention to the body's position to ensure that all muscle groups are locking into the appropriate positions. Every movement of the arms, be it punch, block or chamber, should occur with the shoulders down and the entire upper body configured as a single muscle mass.

The student focuses attention on the shoulder group during each punch. As the punch extends, the elbow scrapes the rib cage. The pectoral muscles and upper arm grip tightly together causing a pinching of the muscles just below the armpit. The punch extends like a battering ram with every arm muscle locked into position supporting the arm. The entire weight of the body strikes the punch, not simply the knuckles. To illustrate this point, the student can try extending a punch with the focus of attention at the knuckles. The effect is to loosen the entire arm and shoulder muscle group; this results in a punch that has little force and cohesiveness.

With the body under tension, any movement of the feet inevitably causes a momentary loss of the body's rooting in the floor. As a result, the foot movements between techniques are deliberately quicker and somewhat jerkier than the slow and deliberate movements of the arms. The intent is to minimize the loss of tension during transitions.

Breathing

At the intermediate level, the student begins to learn an alternative abdominal breathing technique called "martial breathing" (*fanfu huxi* in Mandarin). Like natural breathing, this form strengthens and develops the abdominal muscles and provides substantially more oxygen to the body than everyday breathing. Two primary forms of this breathing technique are employed in Sanchin kata. The first is a long deep breath in which air is drawn in slowly and deeply through the nose. The breath is visualized as following a long path around the top of the head, down the neck and back, under the groin, and finally curls itself up at the tanden in the lower abdomen. This long and deep abdominal breath inward is accompanied by the abdomen contracting. When exhaling, air is pushed out as the abdomen expands. The air moves slowly and smoothly, rising up the front of the body to the neck, and is finally expelled through the mouth.

The second form of breathing is a short breath in which air is transferred directly to the tanden while the abdomen contracts. The breath is expended quickly and directly while the abdomen expands. Just as in natural breathing, all breathing is synchronized with the motion of the body when performing the kata. Once again, breath is inhaled when preparing a technique and exhaled when delivering it.

The intermediate student develops the martial breathing pattern to store a reserve of oxygen and to lower the body's center of mass. The chest never moves during this form of breathing since all breath is concentrated in the tanden.

During exhalation, as breath is pushed out of the abdomen, the breath is cut short at about 75 percent with a "ha" sound that originates in the abdomen. This sound is synchronized with a conscious tightening of the abdominal muscles. These muscles tighten first outward and then downward as the student's attention is on the abdomen, lowering the body's center of weight. At the same time, the associated technique is locked into position as described in previous sections. For example, at the precise moment that a punch strikes, the shoulder group should become locked, breath is 75 percent expelled, and the muscles in the abdomen are pushed down, the lower body is tightened, and the body becomes rooted into the floor. The technique thus drives into an opponent's body like a battering ram from a highly stable position with the entire body rigid just at the instant of impact.

> Principle #11
> Combine martial breathing and locking to obtain solid
> and highly stable striking and defensive forms.

During an attack, the body is most vulnerable between breaths since generally there is little oxygen to power movement. This form of martial breathing ensures that the body always carries a reserve of breath with which to respond. Moreover, no visual clue can be taken from the motion of the chest as to the breathing pattern, making it difficult for an opponent to time an attack between breaths. Finally, tightening of the abdominal muscles allows the body to accept a blow to the body with a reserve of oxygen to power a counterattack.

The effect of conscious movement of weight into the tanden can be demonstrated with a simple test. A second person attempts to lift the student, first without weight focused into the tanden and subsequently with the appropriate focus. In the former case, it is relatively easy to lift the student from the ground; in the latter it is nearly impossible. The conscious lowering of the center of weight, coupled with the rooting of the body in the ground by applying tension in the lower body, leads to unparalleled stability. It is generally not possible to dislodge the practitioner from the sanchin stance even with violent thrusts.

Advanced Goju-ryu Techniques

The advanced practitioner builds upon the basic concepts described previously by combining both the hard and soft principles to stress a particular component of technique during a single training session. It is important to develop a number of refinements to the basic concepts.

Building and Controlling Energy

Over the centuries, the Chinese have developed a theory of how the human body interacts with the universe and how energy (*qi*; *ki* in Japanese) is developed, stored, and expended in the human body. The theory is based on the opposing and complementary forces in nature (yin and yang) and attempts to develop an understanding of the human body from this viewpoint. Central to this study is a system of vital energy points and meridians that represent paths of energy flow between major points and organs in the body. For example, one of the primary energy points is the tanden, translated as the "field of elixir," reflecting the vital role that oxygen and breathing play in physical well being. The study of energy flow is a recurrent theme in Daoist philosophy and underlies traditional Chinese medicine and healing practices, such as acupuncture. To master and improve the energy flow in the body, physical disciplines have evolved, such as yoga and qigong, that develop the interaction of movement, breathing, and mental concentration. These healing concepts are the foundation upon which the martial arts are built. Many exercises in karate work and develop specific meridians. Therefore, it should not be surprising that advanced karate attempts to focus the flow and transfer of energy into martial techniques.

The coiled spring.

To illustrate how energy is built and controlled, reconsider the initial sequence of movements in Sanchin. After the initial double block shown in photo A2, the first punch (A4) is performed under increased tension brought about by mental focus. When the next block follows (A5), tension is again increased. This action effectively locks stored energy into the right side of the body. As the left punch and block are subsequently developed, concentration is again focused on increasing tension in the body, this time locking down both shoulder muscle groups. Both sides of the body are now under heightened tension, storing energy. The final punch and block combination, on the right side of the body, further reenforces and increases this tension. Thus, just prior to the turn, the body should feel like a pressure cooker storing energy.

As the feet are positioned for the turn, a subtle modification is made to the hip position as illustrated in photo "F". Instead of holding them in an aligned position, the hips are twisted in the direction opposite to the turn. This maintains the stored energy in the body and should feel as if the body is being coiled up like a spring. When the turn is finally executed, it occurs at very high speed, as if the spring were suddenly released, causing all the stored energy of previous movements to be thrown sharply into the block that follows the turn. Imagine receiving this block on any part of the anatomy; it would be a blow of devastating impact.

Miyagi Chojun believed that a conflict should be ended with the first block. Clearly, a block is not simply a defensive technique. It can be highly effective in immobilizing an opponent when performed with sufficient energy.

> Principle #12
> Carefully build and control
> the expenditure of energy.

Fajing

As a student develops the ability to build and control internal energy, techniques must then be developed to transfer power (*fajing* in Mandarin) into karate techniques. To illustrate this, consider how power can be transferred into the punching technique. In the previous explanations, emphasis was on maintaining the hips aligned forward during the performance of the Sanchin kata. Careful consideration of this position will develop an instinct for the final locked position of each movement. However, the power of a punch comes not from the motion of the arm, but from placing the body weight behind the punch. This motion originates in a subtle movement of the hips that is exaggerated in photos G1 and G2. This sequence breaks down the motion of the punch and highlights the associated hip movement. Throughout the delivery of a punch, the hips lead the body's movement. Just at the point of contact, the entire body reverberates back into the locked position practiced previously, with the hips aligned. In this position, the shoulder muscles are locked down, the arm is aligned with the body in the battering ram position, the body is firmly rooted into the ground, 75 percent of the body's air has been expelled, and the abdominal muscles are tensed.

Efficient hip motion cannot be achieved without careful practice. Three exercises are useful in developing fajing. The first involves the free motion of the hips: The student stands upright in the ready stance, the arms are held loosely by the sides, and the hips are swung freely from left to right by turning the body. The shoulders are held parallel to the floor and the swing is exaggerated as far to the left and right as possible to ensure the free motion of the body.

Hip movement during punching.

In the second exercise, the body is rotated in a similar fashion to the first. However, here the movement is driven from the hips with a shaking movement. The shaking of the body is driven from the hip motion rather than being carried by the twisting of the body. The hip motion should be allowed to die down naturally after two or three shakes from left to right. The initial thrust of the hips eventually reverberates back to an aligned position naturally. Good posture must be maintained throughout these exercises.

In the final exercise, the hip is thrust forward, the body shakes, and eventually comes to a final locked position in which the body is tense and rooted in the ground as described previously at the end of the punch. Over a period of time, the hip motion becomes second nature and is gradually integrated into the overall punching technique. As practice proceeds, the hip motion should become less and less pronounced. It eventually blends into a fluid body motion associated with every punch or block. At this time, fajing becomes an internal component of the motion of the tanden rather than an observable external movement.

Principle #13
Strike not with the hand, but
with the entire body through fajing.

Loading and Reloading

Each technique in the opening sequence has so far been explained somewhat independently. However, the kata can be used to leverage the yin and yang concept of force and counterforce by loading and reloading the body's energy for subsequent movements. This ki control allows every cover and chamber to reload the energy in the body for a subsequent block or strike respectively through a subtle positioning of the body. For example, following a right punch and block the body is locked down into position with the hips aligned. As the left arm is brought to the chamber position, the hips move back slightly, loading the body with energy for the subsequent punch. This principle can also be applied to every block. Generally, each block has an associated cover. Hip movement during the cover has the function of loading energy into the block. The block is executed with fajing, causing the stored energy to be transferred directly into the block and thus increasing the force of the technique.

Principle #14
Load and reload the body's energy to cascade a sequence of techniques.

Concluding Remarks

Sanchin is not a fighting kata, but rather a catalog of principles that develops general technique. These principles permeate all aspects of karate and are the basis for all other katas. For example, every kata involves a variety of stances that include the ready stance, forward stance, etc. In every stance, we can apply the basic principles from Sanchin: The feet are positioned so as to grip the floor. Circular movements are used in each transition to protect vital parts of the body. The feet remain in contact with the floor at all times, preventing sweeps and throws. Each movement is conducted with fluidity; however, at the split second of delivery, each block or punch takes the form of Sanchin. The feet provide stability by being rooted to the ground. Each punch is delivered as a battering ram with the force of the body behind it, and every muscle group locked to reinforce the blow. Each block is itself a blow that sets up the body for a subsequent technique by loading ki into the body for the counterstrike. Breathing is coordinated with movements to conserve energy in the body and extend endurance. Clearly, Sanchin is the source of all these concepts.

The heightened role of discipline in Asian culture allows students to actively pursue Sanchin concepts without the need for reasoning. In stark contrast, students in the United States are conditioned by their heritage to strive for understanding through questioning. The western mind is unable to focus on the "how" of an activity, unless there is first a clear understanding of the "why" that underlies it. This basic cultural difference is often misunderstood and presents a significant barrier to karate students in the United States. As a result, much of the advanced training that occurs only after the attainment of a black belt in Okinawa is lost on US practitioners. This chapter has sought to reveal some of the principles and reasons why students should pursue Sanchin training with diligence: it will surely lead to superior technique and will carryover to every aspect of their martial arts training, irrespective of the style chosen to pursue.

Higaonna, M. (1987). *The Traditional Karate-do-Okinawan Goju Ryu, Vol. 2: Performances of the kata*. Tokyo: Japan Publications.

chapter 6

An Interview with Murakami Katsumi: The Heart of Ryukyu's Martial Ways

by Mario McKenna, M.S.

Murakami Katsumi.
Photos courtesy of Murakami Katsumi, except where noted.

With literally a lifetime of training in Japanese budo, Murakami Katsumi represents an obscure segment of traditional Okinawan karatedo that few people in the West have ever heard of. In an age where the success of a teacher is often judged by the number of students a teacher has or the size of his dojo, Murakami Katsumi has humbly taught a handful of students in his dojo in Tagawa City, Fukuoka Prefecture, for decades. Currently ranked tenth-degree (*judan*) in Kobayashi-ryu by the Kobayashikan Kyokai and ninth-degree (*kyudan*) by Nakazato Shugoro of the Shorin-ryu Shorinkan, the retired junior high school teacher still instructs students in Okinawan Kobayashi-ryu karatedo and Ryukyu kobudo. Murakami's life and teachers reads like a veritable Who's Who of some of Japan's foremost budo experts including: Toyama Kanken (Shudokan), Kyoda Juhatsu (To'on-ryu), Chibana Chosin (Shorin-ryu), Sato Kinbei (taiji, bagua, xingyi, Asayama Ichiden-ryu jujutsu), Inoue Motokatsu (Ryukyu kobudo/Yuishinkai), and Higa Seitoku (Yamane-ryu bojutsu /Motobu-ryu).

Born in Tagawa, Fukuoka, on 1 September 1927, Murakami was greatly influenced by his father, an avid practitioner of judo and kenpo, to study the martial arts. As a schoolboy, he learned many of the modern budo that were common in pre-war Japan such as judo, kendo, sumo, and jukendo. However, it wasn't until he was twenty-six-years-old that he gained his first exposure to Shorin-based Okinawa karatedo from a local teacher named Yara Choui. His appetite had been whetted and two years later he was studying Shorin-based karatedo under Toyama Kanken, eventually receiving his teaching license and opening his first dojo six years later.

Never one to be idle, while studying under Toyama Kanken, Murakami made the acquaintance of Sato Kenbei, a teacher of the Chinese internal arts of taiji, bagua, and xingyi as well as Asayama Ichiden-ryu jujutsu. Impressed by what he saw, he began studying the Chinese internal arts and jujutsu under Sato and ultimately received his teaching license several years later.

Curious about the other traditions of Okinawa karatedo, he began to study To'on-ryu in 1961 in neighboring Oita Prefecture under Kyoda Juhatsu (1887-1968), a student of Higaonna Kanryo (1853-1916) and a senior of Miyagi Chojun (1888-1953). At the same time, he continued to expand his studies in Shorin-ryu karate; in 1963, he began to make frequent trips to Okinawa to study under Chibana Chosin (1889-1969) and his senior student Nakazato Shuguro (b. 1919). While in Okinawa in 1963, Nakazato introduced Murakami Sensei to Higa Seitoku (b. 1921) of Yamane-ryu bojutsu. In 1966, he expanded his knowledge of the bo and the other weapons of Ryukyu kobudo through his studies with Inoue Motokatsu (1918-1993).

Murakami Katsumi's life is truly representative of his generation of budoka: he is a quiet and modest person with a rich and unsurpassed background. In the following interview, he talks about his training and experience in the martial arts and the implications of the martial arts for those who practice them.

INTERVIEW

▶ You studied Ryukyu kobudo under Inoue Motokatsu, isn't that right?

That's correct. However, I originally started my kobudo training under Higa Seitoku, a Motobu-ryu and Yamane-ryu bojutsu teacher. That was during my days as a teacher. I would travel to Okinawa to train, especially during winter and summer vacations. Also during that time, I trained in karate under Chibana Chosin of Kobayashi Shorin-ryu and his senior student Nakazato Shugoro. I was also very fortunate because, in the neighboring Oita prefecture,

I began to study To'on-ryu under Kyoda Juhatsu. However, with respect to my kobudo training, it was primarily under Inoue Motokatsu.

▸ I BELIEVE THAT INOUE LEARNED KOBUDO FROM TAIRA SHINKEN?
That's correct.

▸ WHO INTRODUCED INOUE TO TAIRA SHINKEN?
Inoue was stationed in Burma during WW II and after his return to Tokyo, Fujita Seiko of the Nanbansato-ryu [kenpo] introduced Inoue to Taira Shinken. After Inoue became Taira's student, Inoue would train with Taira when Taira would make his frequent trips to the Japanese mainland. Inoue would also often travel to Okinawa to train with Taira. Inoue had learned most of Taira's repertoire of kobudo katas and received the first grandmaster certification [hanshi] ever issued by Taira Shinken in the same year, I believe. Fujita also introduced Inoue to Konishi Koyu [also Konishi Yasuhiro, founder of Shindo Jinen-ryu] as well as teaching him shurikenjutsu.

Chibana Chosin (standing left) Nakazato Shuguro
(kneeling center) and Murakami Katsumi (kneeling right).

Taira Shinken also named Inoue representative of his Ryukyu Kobudo Hozan Shinkokai [Association for the Preservation and Promotion of Ryukyu Kobudo] for the Tokai area. When Taira was suffering from cancer, Inoue made frequent trips to Okinawa to see him up until the time he passed away in 1970. I think that Inoue also sold several of his and his family's personal belongings to support Taira Shinken while he was sick. He was that devoted to his teacher.

▶ DID YOU EVER MEET FUJITA SEIKO OR TAIRA SHINKEN PERSONALLY?

I never met Fujita Seiko directly, however, we corresponded several times by mail. During that correspondence, he introduced me to the *kyusha* [pressure points] used in Nanbansato-ryu. He also sent me copies of his books detailing the kyusho points, shurikenjutsu, bojutsu and the history of Japanese budo.

With respect to Taira Shinken, I also never had the chance of meeting or training with him directly. However, Taira Shinken approved my Ryukyu kobudo teaching license after he and Inoue Motokatsu discussed my qualifications for promotion to teacher's level in Ryukyu kobudo.

▶ TAIRA SHINKEN SEEMS TO HAVE TAUGHT KOBUDO KATA A LITTLE DIFFERENTLY TO EACH OF HIS DIRECT STUDENTS. FOR EXAMPLE, IN INOUE MOTOKATSU'S BOOK ON RYUKYU KOBUDO [*ANCIENT MARTIAL ARTS OF THE RYUKYU ISLANDS VOLS. 1 & 2*]. INOUE LISTS BO KATA WHICH ARE NOT TAUGHT BY OTHER STUDENTS OF TAIRA SUCH AS AKAMINE EISUKE, MINOWA KATSUHIKO, OR NAKAMOTO MASAHIRO. THIS INCLUDES KONGO NO KON, THE BO KATA CREATED BY TAIRA SHINKEN. DO YOU KNOW ANYTHING ABOUT THE DIFFERENCE BETWEEN WHAT TAIRA'S STUDENTS KNOW AND TEACH? I'M NOT SURE IF TAIRA TAUGHT HIS OTHER STUDENTS HIS KONGO NO KON KATA, OR WHETHER THEY KNOW IT BUT DO NOT TEACH IT.

That's very interesting. I did learn Kongo no Kon, but it was not from Inoue Motokatsu. Kongo no Kon is a very interesting kata. You could say it is part of the Shushi no Kon kata family since in basic technique and performance it resembles Shushi no Kon, but it has its own unique characteristics, such as sliding thrust [*nuki tsuki*] in place of the normal thrust [*tsuki*] in the Shushi no Kon *Sho* [lesser]/*Dai* [greater] series.

Murakami Katsumi (left) and Inoue Motokatsu
in front of the latter's dojo.

▸ INOUE ALSO LISTS A SHUSHI NO KON KO-SHIKI (OLD STYLE) IN HIS RYUKYU KOBUDO BOOK.

Oh, that Shushi no Kon is the original Shushi no Kon from Yamane-ryu bojutsu. However, I did not learn this kata from Inoue but from Higa Seitoku, who had studied Yamane-ryu from Chinen Masami. Higa Seitoku received his master's [shihan] certification in Yamane-ryu from Chinen Masami. I also learned Yamane-ryu bojutsu from my senior, Nakazato Shuguro, who received his teaching license from Chinen Masami.

▸ CONTINUING ON, TAIRA'S OKINAWAN STUDENTS [AKAMINE, NAKAMOTO, MINOWA, ETC.] TEACH THE SAKUGAWA NO KON SHO/DAI BO KATA SERIES. HOWEVER, INOUE MOTOKATSU TEACHES AN INTERMEDIARY VERSION (CHU) BETWEEN SHO AND DAI.

Actually, Sakugawa no Kon Chu resembles the older Yamane-ryu Sakugawa no Kon that I learned from Higa Seitoku. Of course there are differences, but the chu version of Sakugawa no Kon resembles the Koshiki version more than the Sakugawa no Kon Sho/Dai that Inoue learned from Taira Shinken.

▸ INOUE ALSO BREAKS OTHER BO KATAS INTO SHO/DAI VERSIONS WHILE TAIRA'S OKINAWAN STUDENTS DO NOT. FOR EXAMPLE, SOEISHI NO KON AND SHIROTARU NO KON. ARE THESE KATAS SEPARATED BECAUSE ONE IS A MORE MODERN VERSION, WHILE THE OTHER IS BASED ON AN EARLIER VERSION?

Yes, I believe so. The sho/dai versions of these bo kata and their techniques are quite different. For instance, Soeishi no Kon comes from Soeishi-ryu bojutsu, as does Yonegawa no Kon, therefore the techniques used in these katas are quite similar.

▸ WITH RESPECT TO THE NUNCHAKU, TAIRA SHINKEN CREATED TWO NUNCHAKU KATA. HOWEVER, INOUE DOES NOT LIST MAEZATO NO NUNCHAKU SHO/DAI IN HIS BOOK ON RYUKYU KOBUDO. DID YOU LEARN MAEZATO NO NUNCHAKU SHO/DAI FROM INOUE?

I learned two nunchaku katas simply called Nunchaku Sho/Dai. Neither of them used the name Maezato. I believe they are two completely separate katas from Taira's Maezato no Nunchaku Sho/Dai series. I don't know if Inoue learned Maezato no Nunchaku Sho/Dai or if he did know them, whether he didn't teach them for one reason or another. However, for Inoue to create his own katas is not surprising, since nunchaku techniques were common knowledge on Okinawa. For example, Chibana Choshin was quite proficient with the nunchaku, although he never created a formal kata.

Chibana Chosin (sitting) and Murakami Katsumi.

▶ CHANGING THE TOPIC TO KARATEDO, COULD YOU TELL US A LITTLE BIT ABOUT THE KATAS USED IN TO'ON-RYU?

Essentially, the same katas are used as in Goju-ryu with the exception of Gekisai first and second routines *dai-ichi/dai-ni* and Tensho, which were made by Miyagi Chojun. Also, the order in which the katas are taught is different. In To'on-ryu, after learning kata Sanchin, the next kata taught is Rokkishu followed by Seisan.

▶ WHAT IS THE ROKKISHU KATA? I'VE NEVER HEARD OF IT.

It is very similar to Goju-ryu's Tensho kata, but longer, a little more complex, and uses the open hand entirely. Both Kyoda Juhatsu and Miyagi Chojun based their katas on a chapter in the *Bubishi*, Rokkishu ["six hands of chance"].

▶ ARE THE TO'ON-RYU AND GOJU-RYU TRAINING METHODS SIMILAR?

Yes, they're basically the same. There are small differences in the execution of technique such as the fist being chambered just above the hip as in Shorin-ryu, compared to it being chambered at chest level as in Goju-ryu. However, with respect to katas, most of the To'on-ryu katas use the open hand instead of the closed fist found in Goju-ryu. I asked Kyoda Juhatsu about this and he replied that Higaonna Kanryo had told him to do what was comfortable for him, whether it be a closed fist or open hand. Also, in some respects, the To'on-ryu katas are plainer than their Goju-ryu counterparts. For example, in the kata Sanseiryu, the To'on-ryu version does not use any front kicks, while the Goju-ryu version does.

▶ THE TO'ON-RYU HEADQUARTERS IS LOCATED IN OITA PREFECTURE, ISN'T IT?

Yes, that's right. Kyoda Juhatsu's son, Kyoda Juko, tookover after his father retired from active teaching; sadly though, Juko passed away at the age of 62. With respect to Kyoda Juhatsu's dojo, he taught out of the garden in his home. He didn't have a formal dojo as such. Outside in his garden, he had makiwara, nigirigame, and other training equipment. I remember that sometimes Miyagi Chojun's students would come to the dojo to visit or to ask for instruction. Apparently Miyagi had said in his later years that if you had any questions about katas, to ask his senior Kyoda Juhatsu.

▶ ARE THERE ANY OTHER TO'ON-RYU SCHOOLS IN OITA PREFECTURE?

Yes, there is one run by Mr. Kanzaki Shigeru [in Beppu]. However, I am not sure if he is still actively teaching or not. He's a little bit younger than me, 71-years-old, I believe.

Murakami Katsumi (left) and Kyodo Juhatsu at the latter's home in Beppu, Oita Prefecture.

▶ WHAT KIND OF PERSON WAS KYODA JUHATSU?

He was an educator in the true sense of the word. His occupation was being a principal of an elementary school for most of his life. He was a man of great integrity, I felt. Prior to moving to Oita, Kyoda had taught a number of students not only academically, but also physically and mentally, through karate practice.

▶ HOW WAS HE WHEN YOU LEARNED KARATEDO FROM HIM?

He was extremely patient and kind when he taught karate to his students. It made quite an impact on me.

▶ How did you find learning To'on-ryu, since you already had a strong background in Shorin-ryu?

Not terribly difficult.

▶ Why then did you seek out Kyoda Juhatsu to learn karatedo, since you had already studied Shorin-ryu and Ryukyu bojutsu?

That's right, I had studied Shuri-te and wanted to investigate the Naha-te tradition. I simply wanted to gain a deeper understanding of what Ryukyu budo was. Not just simply technique, I wanted to understand the heart of Ryukyu budo. Maybe I was a little strange wanting to study both traditions since many teachers at that time said you couldn't study both Shuri-te and Naha-te at the same time. Maybe they were right, but at the same time I thought maybe they're wrong. So, I went and studied Naha-te anyway. It really isn't all that odd. Take Mabuni Kenwa for instance. He had studied Shuri-te from Itosu and then later Naha-te from Higaonna. He also went on to study Chinese kenpo [*quanfa*], Ryukyu kobudo, and other martial arts. Anyway, I just felt that I wanted to know more, so I sought out Kyoda Juhatsu.

▶ You studied Shuri-te from both Toyama Kanken and Chibana Chosin. Were there any differences between the two in what you learned?

Although they both taught Shuri-te, not surprisingly, there were differences. This is not surprising since they are two different people with two different personalities. Chibana learned his karate from Itosu Anko, while Toyama learned from Itosu and also Yabu Kentsu, who was his chief instructor [*shihan dai*]. So, their Shuri-te were quite different. For example, the kata Gojushiho, Passai, and Chinto were essentially performed the same, but you can see differences in the kind of techniques being executed.

▶ You later studied Ryukyu kobudo under Inoue Motokatsu.

Yes, but before that I had studied Yamane-ryu bojutsu from Higa Seitoku and learned Shushi no Kon, Sakugawa no Kon, and the like. Again, I wanted to expand my knowledge of Ryukyu budo and to study more deeply, so I began to study under Inoue Motokatsu. At about the same time I began to study the internal Chinese martial arts from Sato Kinbei.

▶ Who was Sato Kinbei?

Sato Kinbei was from Miyagi Prefecture in northern Japan. He also had a background in several jujutsu schools, such as Daito-ryu aikijujutsu and Asayama Ichiden-ryu. I believe Mr. Sato first started his training in the Chinese internal arts in 1959 after Wang Shujin, a taiji, baqua and xingyi teacher, visited Japan from Taiwan to demonstrate the internal martial arts. Not only Mr. Sato came to watch Mr. Wang's demonstration, but many other notable teachers in Japan came to watch, such as Fujita Seiko [Koga-ryu ninjutsu and Nanbansato-ryu], Ohtsuka Hironori [Wado-ryu], and Konishi Yasuhiro [Shindo Jinen-ryu].

This was the first time that taijiquan was demonstrated in Japan. After seeing Mr. Wang's demonstration, Sato Kinbei was completely amazed and asked to be accepted as one of his students. Interestingly enough, at that time, Mao Zedong's regime was modernizing the Chinese martial arts into martial sports for fitness and competition. Mr. Sato was truly lucky to have learned the old style internal martial arts of China before these changes took place. Nowadays many people throughout the world practice taijiquan for health purposes and not as a form of martial arts training.

Top: Receiving instruction in kata from Chibana Chosin.
Bottom: Chibana Chosin's students performing kata Naihanchi Shodan.

▸ Could you explain a little bit more about Wang Shujin?

Wang Shujin was the first person to teach the Chinese internal martial arts in Japan. Wang learned xingyi from Zhang Zhankui and xingyi and bagua from his teacher's friends, Li Cunyi and Xiao Ha. When Zhang Zhankui died, Wang moved to Taiwan with the Nationalist Party [Kuomintang] and learned taiji from Chen Panling. Chen Panling had been vice president of the Central National Arts Center in Nanjing, and was a leading figure in the Nationalist Party. He is said to have known a great deal about different kinds of martial arts, and published numerous books.

Sato Kinbei studied under Wang for eight years after Wang came to Japan in 1959. During this time, Wang lived in a single room in a wooden apartment building in Sakuragaoka near Shibuya, Tokyo, cooking his own vegetarian meals. At that time, he had no place to practice or teach, so each morning he practiced for about two hours in the woods around Meiji Shrine. After this, Wang would return to his home, eat breakfast, then go to work at the Sumihigashi City Hospital. Sato Kinbei did not pay to learn from Wang, but did pay for Wang's living expenses and his twice-a-year trips to return to Taiwan.

▸ Sato Kinbei also taught you Asayama Ichiden-ryu jujutsu. Could you explain a little bit about it?

Asayama Ichiden-ryu as an *atemi* [striking] and *gyakute* [reversal] art. Sato Kinbei learned Asayama Ichiden-ryu from Ueno Takashi [16th generation grandmaster]. In December 1955, Sato Kinbei was named Ueno's successor. The Asayama Ichiden-ryu is first learned using only empty hands, but later, techniques incorporating a short wooden stick [37 or 25cm long] or a steel fan are introduced. Sato Kinbei was introduced to Ueno by the expert on traditional martial arts Takamatsu Sumisuke [also Takamatsu Toshitsugu], who lived in Nara. Interestingly, it was through Sato Kinbei's introduction that Hatsumi Yoshiaki [also Hatsumi Masaaki; Togakure-ryu ninjutsu founder] first studied under Ueno and later under Takamatsu Sumisuke.

▸ You have studied many different forms of martial arts. Is there anyone in particular that you are fond of?

No, there isn't anyone in particular that I like. They are all unique. It's not like I feel, "Oh it's Monday, so I should practice taijiquan," or "It's Thursday, so I have to practice Shorin-ryu." Personally, no matter how hard I practice or how well I perform a technique, I never think, "Oh, I'm never going to perfect this technique." That is not the focus of my training. What is important is that in each moment I am focused on that technique, I lose myself in it and enter into a state of *mushin* ["no mind"]. This type of training is a form of Zen training, more specifically Soto Zen.

Zen Buddhism teaches that the truth of your existence can only come from yourself, and can only be achieved through forgetting your own self or ego. In order to forget your own self, you must have a singular concentration on the moment which requires you to remove all other distractions or obstacles. When you achieve "no mind," you have removed all distractions and have perfect concentration and are able to see the truth for what it is. You have forgotten yourself.

In karate, kobudo, or Chinese kenpo, when you practice your goal should be the same: to achieve that singular concentration and forgetting yourself. The katas and movements found in budo are Zen. Their common denominator is the elimination of the self. When you can achieve this state of forgetting yourself, it is an absolutely wonderful feeling.

Left: Nakazto Shuguro (right) and Murakami Katsumi free sparring.
Right: Nakazto Shuguro (left) and Murakami Katsumi (right)
during their days training at Chibana Chosin's dojo.

▶ TRADITIONALLY, THEN, THE GOAL OF THE MARTIAL ARTS AND ZEN ARE THE SAME.

For me they are. The state of mind found in budo is one of looking at and reflecting on one's self. It is the same state of mind that is found in *zazen* [seated meditation]. The practice of budo is not about technique or violence, it is not anti-social. However, it is about getting along with your fellow man. When you practice any martial art with another human being, you must harmonize with him or her. This kind of encounter between two people and the resultant harmony between the two of them is the central theme inherent in all budo. For example, technically speaking, when you suddenly have an encounter, at that moment a struggle arises. And in that encounter at that very moment, you must harmonize with that person. There is no struggle. There is no opposition. This cannot happen by using only technique or power, which actually work in opposition to harmonizing with your opponent.

At the moment of the encounter, you harmonize with the other person's power and join with it. It is a natural response and does not oppose anything. So, in the realm of budo you cannot only think of technique, you must also think of how to harmonize with the other person. The harmony we strive for in our day to day encounters with others is simply a reflection of the law of the universe.

▶ SO, THE MOST IMPORTANT THING FOR SOMEONE PRACTICING BUDO IS NOT TECHNIQUE, BUT THEIR DAILY ACTIONS AND BEHAVIOR?

That's right! All the students that my teachers [Toyama, Kyoda, Chibana, Inoue, and Sato] instructed gave something back to society. They refused to instruct anyone of low character or moral standing because these people would give nothing back to society. Their instruction was to help you become a valuable and productive member of society. It must be that way. This is how all my teachers taught and instructed me how to teach.

When I studied under Kyoda Juhatsu, he always said that our training was to build both a strong body and a strong mind. A person learning budo only for the sake of learning to fight gives nothing back to society and is beaten by the smallest things he may encounter in life. This kind of person is useless. However, if your mind is strong, no matter what trials you may encounter in life, your will power and your determination will see you through them. As a prerequisite, the first and most important thing to develop is a strong and healthy body. I honestly feel that this is the proper way to train.

▶ SO EVEN WHEN YOU ARE NOT PRACTICING KARATEDO OR KOBUDO YOU SHOULD BE TRAINING YOURSELF?

That's right! Everything is training! Your karate training should not be something separate from your life, it should be a part of your daily life, your daily activities. In each and every facet of your life and your daily encounters you should carry the same [state of] mind you have as you practice in the dojo.

▶ IN CLOSING, OUT OF ALL THE TEACHERS YOU HAVE STUDIED FROM, WAS THERE ONE IN PARTICULAR WHO HAD A STRONG INFLUENCE ON YOUR LIFE?

I would have to say that all my teachers had a strong and common influence on me. Chibana Chosin not only taught me the physical aspects of karatedo, such as its techniques and katas, but from time to time he would recite Buddhist scripture. This really did create a strong moral and spiritual basis for my karate practice. Kyoda Juhatsu would also recite Buddhist scripture during my days training under him, as did Inoue Motokatsu. Personally, the Buddhist scriptures contain the secrets or the basis of budo's underlying philosophy.

Recent photo of Murakami Katsumi (left) and Nakazato Shuguro.

General Background of Ryukyu Weaponry

Ryukyu kobujutsu is the civil weapons art of the ancient Ryukyu kingdom. Some of the more common weapons include: *rokushaku bo* (6' staff), *sai* (metal truncheon), *tonfa* (right-angled wooden truncheon; *tonfua, tuifa*), *nunchaku* (wooden flail), and *eku* (oar; *ieku, kai*). It has been argued that, with the exception of the sai, most of the weapons employed in Ryukyu kobujutsu were developed from either agricultural or fishing implements (Bolz, 1995: 86; Bishop, 1996: 16).

The beginnings of Ryukyu kobujutsu are thought to have occurred after King Sho Shin-O and his administration issued the "Age of Eleven Distinctions" document in 1507, which reportedly outlawed the private ownership and stockpiling of weapons (Kerr, 1958/1980: 86; McCarthy, 1999). However, there is some confusion regarding this matter. Sakihara Mitsugu claims that the statement in question was actually found on a monument erected in 1479 and called the "11 Great Achievements of the Age." Sakihara translates the relevant section of achievement four as "Brocade and embroidered silk are used for garments and gold and silver are used for utensils. Swords and bows and arrows exclusively are accumulated as weapons in the protection of the country" (Sakihara, 1987: 165). Sakihara explains that "In 1926 Iha Fuyu misread the passage therein to mean 'this country used the armor for utensils,' and assumed that the king had confiscated all arms which were then made into practical tools such as farm implements. Thus originated the fallacy of a disarmed, peace-loving Ryukyu..." (Sakihara, 1987: 199).

Whether or not the first weapons ban is a myth, the Satsuma bushi's subjugation of Okinawa in 1609 and subsequent tightening of restrictions on the possession of weapons is a verified fact. Whatever the origins of Ryukyu kobujutsu, the Satsuma ban resulted in its further refinement. Having no other means of defending themselves, the Shuri upper class began to train using simple farming and fishing tools (Bishop, 1996: 100). This, coupled with the tradition of Chinese-based martial arts forms, resulted in the development of modern day Ryukyu kobujutsu (Bishop, 1996: 101; McCarthy, 1999).

Although there is scant literature to confirm the exact beginnings of Ryukyu kobujutsu, there is enough evidence to suggest that the use of the bo has a relatively long and reasonably well-documented history on Okinawa (Taira, 1964: 37; Nakamoto, 1983: 22, 62, 64). The earliest reliable account of the use of *bojutsu* (staff techniques) appears in the book, *Okinawa's 1,000 Year History*. In it, there is a passage that describes the nobles (*anji* or *aji*) using staff techniques around 1314 (Taira, 1964: 37). Almost one century later, we find China solidifying cultural and trade ties with the Ryukyus by establishing the first Chinese settlement in Kume Village in 1393. This settlement consisted of thirty-six families whose purpose was to introduce Chinese culture (politics, business, commerce, music, literature, and martial arts) to the Ryukyus (McCarthy, 1999; Nakamoto, 1983: 64). It has been suggested that techniques for the staff were imported via these original thirty-six families (Taira, 1964: 37; Nakamoto, 1983: 64). Further evidence corroborating the use of the staff on Okinawa can be found in *The Biography of Jiryo*, where *yaribo* (festival dances using a 6' or 3' staff) are described being performed during the Keicho Period (1596-1614) (Taira, 1964: 37).

Of all the weapons in Ryukyu kobujutsu, the staff was by far the most common means of self-defense in the old Ryukyu kingdom. This can be readily seen in the number of staff katas handed down from centuries ago in comparison to other weapons and their respective katas (see chart on next page). Conservative estimates place the number of extant staff katas from twenty-seven to around thirty (Murakami, 1995: 5; Nakamoto, 1983: 69, 70). The following bojutsu techniques have been translated and excerpted from Murakami Katsumi's, *Ryukyu Bojutsu no Higi* (The Secret Techniques of Ryukyu Bojutsu), published in Japanese in 1995. They include techniques for yielding to an attack as well as methods of joint manipulation found in many Ryukyu staff kata. It is hoped that the reader will gain a better understanding and appreciation of the depth of the techniques used in Ryukyu bojutsu through this brief introduction.

RYUKYU KOBUJUTSU
WEAPONS KATA

#	BO – KATA NAME	#	SAI – KATA NAME
1	Shushi no Kon sho/dai	1	Tsukenshitahaku no Sai
2	Sakugawa no Kon sho/dai	2	Tawata no Sai
3	Shirotaru no Kon	3	Chatan Yara no Sai
4	Yonegawa no Kon	4	Hantagawa Kuragawa no Sai
5	Choun no Kon	5	Hamahiga no Sai
6	Hantagawa no Kon	6	Yaka no Sai
7	Tsuken Bo	7	Kojo no Sai
8	Tsukensunakaki no Kon (Eku)	8	Jigen no Sai
9	Chinen Shichiyanaka no Kon	..	....
10	Urasoe no Kon	#	TONFUA – KATA NAME
11	Sesoko no Kon	1	Hamahiga no Tonfua
12	Soeishi no Kon sho	2	Yaragawa no Tonfua
13	Sueyoshi no Kon sho/dai	..	....
14	Chatanyara no Kon	#	KAMA – KATA NAME
15	Tenryu no Kon	1	Kanegawa no Nicho Gama
16	Tokumine no Kon	..	....
17	Kachin Bo	#	TEKKO – KATA NAME
18	Sukun no Kon	1	Maezato no Tekko
19	Shihokiri no Kon	..	....
20	Koho no Kon	#	TINBE – KATA NAME
21	Manme no Kon	1	Kanegawa no Tinbe
22	Shokyu no Kon	..	....
23	Kongo no Kon	#	SURUCHIN – KATA NAME
24	Daiton Bo	1	Maezato no Suruchin
25	Soshi no Kon	..	....
26	Oshiro no Kon sho/dai	#	NUNCHAKU – KATA NAME
27	Tsuki Bo	1	Maezato no Nunchaku sho/dai

TECHNICAL SECTION

In the martial arts, a person must be able to automatically gauge the distance of an attack and know whether to move away from it or into it. Consequently, the ability to meet an attack by yielding, moving into it, and fighting at close quarters is of great importance. Jujutsu, karate, and Chinese internal arts (taiji, xingyi, bagua) are all renowned for their emphasis on yielding to an attack and fighting at close quarters. The technique of fighting at close quarters uses very little motion, but is extraordinarily powerful. These close quarter tactics and strikes are not limited to empty-hand techniques, but can be also be found in the Okinawa bo kata of Chinen Shichiyanaka no Kon and Sakugawa no Kon. In the following section, we will examine some of these close quarter techniques and how they are executed.

PART I
Yielding to an Attack:
Striking and Bending the Attacker Backwards

SEQUENCE I

1a An attack can be either a strike or thrust with a *bo* (staff) or a sword. Meeting the attack you should step back at a 45-degree angle with your left leg and, at the same time, hook and deflect the bo downwards, pulling the attacker forward. Alternately, you can strike the attacker's arm or wrist.

1b Take advantage of this reaction and in one quick motion strike the attacker's face. The distance between the bo and the attacker's face is such that you are able to make a strong attack in comparison to targets on other parts of the body.

SEQUENCE 2 - Variation

2a Alternatively, you can step forward and turn using your right foot, placing you at 90-degrees to the attacker while simultaneously deflecting and hooking his bo. This will open up his right side.

2b You can then quickly strike the attacker's face.

The important thing in the execution of these techniques is to move in and meet the attack. If this is done, the attacker's weapon and face are exposed, making them easy to strike. Also, deflecting and hooking the attacker's weapon must be done in one motion.

SEQUENCE 3 - From Taijiquan

The important thing about striking is not the strike itself, but the timing of one's block, the position of the body, and the movement of the feet. The flowing and yielding blocks used in taijiquan are a perfect example of how to meet an attack and fight at close quarters. Using these blocks, one is completely protected and an attacker's force is used against himself. This technique of moving away and yielding to an attack can also be seen in karate and Chinese boxing.

3a   In taijiquan, an attacker's punch can also be met by stepping to the side while simultaneously deflecting and hooking it downward.

3b   Similarly, the attacker's balance can be broken by reversing direction and striking the attacker's face with a palm heel strike.

3c   Furthermore, the neck of the attacker can be grabbed or struck using a ridge hand strike, bending him backwards. Alternatively, the attacker's clavicle can be struck with a knife hand strike.

PART II
The Use of Joint Techniques: Kansetsu Waza

SEQUENCE 4

Techniques for manipulating an attacker's joints (elbow, wrist, shoulder) are easily applied to using a bo. Jujutsu is well noted for its extensive use of joint manipulation techniques. However, in jujutsu as well as bojutsu, this does not simply mean grabbing an attacker's wrist, arm, or elbow, but consists of creating the perfect conditions for seizing an attacker's joints. We will illustrate some of the joint techniques used in bojutsu.

4a The attacker steps forward using a right thrusting attack with a bo (alternately the attack can be a side strike). Meeting the attack, you should step back at a 45-degree angle with your left leg and, at the same time, hook and deflect the bo downwards, pulling the attacker forward.

4b Immediately strike the attacker's chest with a right thrusting attack. At this moment, you have created an opening.

4c Slide the bo between the attacker's bo and his arm, simultaneously hooking it and stepping to the left.

4d Continue stepping to the left and turn your bo to the right, entwining the attacker's arm until you are at a 45-degree angle.

4e By continuing to step to the left, the attacker can easily be thrown to the ground.

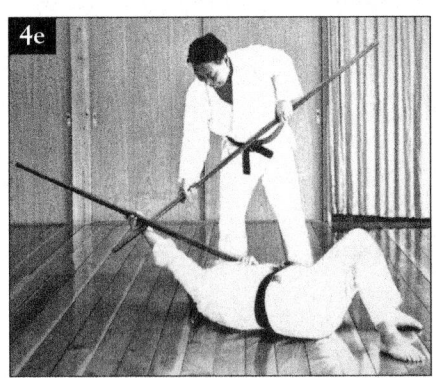

MURAKAMI KATSUMI TRAINING TIMELINE

- 1927 Born in Ichiba. Tagawa City, Fukuoka Prefecture. As a child, studies judo, kendo, sumo, and jukendo.
- 1953 Introduction to Okinawan karatedo through Yara Choui.
- 1955 Begins to study karatedo under Toyama Kanken.
- 1959 Begins to study taiji, baqua, xingyi, Asa Yama Ichiden-ryu jujutsu from Satou Kinbei.
- 1961 Received his teaching license (*shihan menjo*) from Toyama Kanken and opened his first dojo.
- 1961 Began studying To'on-ryu from Kyoda Juhatsu.
- 1963 Began studying Kobayashi Shorin-ryu from Chibana and Yamane-ryu bojutsu from Higa Seitoku.
- 1966 Received his teaching license from Kyoda Juhatsu.
- 1966 Received his teaching license from Chibana Chosin.
- 1966 Began studying Ryukyu kobudo from Inoue Motokatsu.
- 1970 Received his teaching license in Ryukyu kobudo from Taira Shinken.
- 1973 Taught karate and kobudo at the Australia Goju-kai headquarters from July 21 to August 11.
- 1974 Became the chief representative for the Ryukyu Kobudo Shinko-kai for the Kyushu area.
- 1977 Received his kyoushi certification from Inoue Motokatsu in Ryukyu kobudo.
- 1977 Received his kyoushi certification from Miyahira Katsuya in Kobayashi Shorin-ryu.
- 1980 Received his teaching certification from Sato Kinbei in taiji and xingyi boxing.
- 1981 Received his teaching certification from Sato Kinbei in baqua.
- 1988 Received his menkyou kaiden in Asa Yama Ichiden-ryu Jujutsu from Sato Kinbei.
- 1990 Received his Certificate of Service and Dedication to the Ryukyu Kobudo Shinkokai from Inoue Motokatsu.
- 1997 Named a consultant to Inoue Motokatsu's Ryukyu Kobudo Hozon Shinkokai.
- 1998 Promoted to tenth-dan in Kobayashi-ryu Kobayashikan Kyokai and ninth-dan in Shorinkan Shorin-ryu by Nakazato Shugoro.

Illustration by Oscar Ratti and courtesy of Futuro Designs & Publications.

References

Bishop, M. (1996). *Zen kobujutsu: Mysteries of Okinawan weaponry and te*. Rutland, VT: Charles E. Tuttle Co..

Bolz, M. (1995). The Okinawan sai: Kobujutsu weapons for self-defense. *Journal of Asian Marital Arts, 4*(1), 85-99.

Florence, R. (1996). An interview with Uehara Seikichi on the Motobu-ryu Udundi bujutsu. *Journal of Asian Martial Arts, 5*(3), 66-89.

Kerr, G. (1958/1980). *Okinawa: The history of an island people*. Tokyo: Charles E. Tuttle Co.

McCarthy, P. (1999). *Ancient Okinawan martial arts, vols. 1 and 2*. Tokyo: Tuttle Publishing.

Murakami, K. (1995). *Ryukyu bojutsu no higi* (The secret techniques of Ryukyu bojutsu). Tokyo: Aiyudo.

Nakamoto, M. (1983). *Okinawa dento Ryukyu kobujutsu: Sono rekishi to tamashi* (Okinawan traditional kobujutsu: Its history and soul). Naha: Okiinsha.

Taira, S. (1964). *Ryuku Kobudo Taiken*. Ginowan: Joujushorin.

Acknowledgments

I would like to thank Murakami Katsumi for allowing me to interview him and for providing me with the photos from his personal collection that accompanied this interview. In addition, I would also like to extend my appreciation to him for granting me permission to excerpt his work *Ryukyu Bojutsu no Higi*. Finally I would like to thank Charles "Joe" Swift who made this interview possible by kindly introducing me to Murakami Katsumi.

chapter 7

Developing Advanced Goju-ryu Techniques: Illustrated in the Rising Block

by Marvin Labbate

All photographs courtesy of M. Labbate.

Introduction

The difference in skills between a beginning and an advanced karate student should be marked by more than levels of strength, speed, flexibility and endurance. These qualities can be improved with time and practice. This chapter considers something deeper concerning the lifelong development of technique. The focus here is on the principles of advanced blocking techniques in Okinawan Goju-ryu and their associated applications. This chapter builds upon the core principles of structure, movement, and breathing developed in a previous article on Sanchin kata (Labbate, 1999). The standard rising block is used as a vehicle to explain blocking principles, however, the ideas apply to all of the standard blocks.

In common with other blocks used in traditional karate, the rising block has often been criticized as an ineffective fighting technique. Although this criticism is justified at the beginner's level, the advanced practitioner develops a qualitatively different technique. The advanced level block transfers internal energy into the block from the center of the body, uses inner sensitivity to intercept, adhere, and redirect an opponent's energy, and body-shifting to gain a position of advantage. Correct distancing, timing, and hand-eye coordination are developed through partner training. The final block is a combination of hard and soft principles that allows it to serve a broad variety of defensive and offensive applications.

The Beginner's Level

Beginning students are generally taught a mechanical rising block that allows them to develop the gross movement and coordinate their arms (Oyama, 1981). This basic block is shown in Sequence 1. From the ready position (1a), the student transitions to a simple covering position (1b), then forms a cross with the covering arm and the blocking arm (1c), and finishes with a lifting motion in which the blocking arm rotates into its final position, a fist distance from the forehead (1d). The covering position provides a first line of defense while the lifting motion is supposed to force an opponent's punch upward and away from the face. Unfortunately, this lifting motion is useless against a powerful opponent who will simply punch right through the intended block with a direct strike to the face.

Building on this basic block, intermediate level skills are then taught in which the student begins to develop the ability to deflect while blocking. In this block, rather than crossing the covering arm with the blocking arm, the blocking arm takes a direct 45-degree path from the chamber to its final position. Although slightly more difficult to grasp, this alternative block deflects an opponent's punch rather than opposes its force. The intermediate block is practiced in both stationary and moving two-person blocking (*tanshiki*) drills where the defending student steps backward to block an attackers blow. These two-person drills provide reflexive training and begin to develop hand-eye coordination, timing, speed, and distancing.

Building further upon the intermediate level of blocking skill, a more advanced level can be developed through body conditioning. Stationary and moving two-person forearm conditioning drills are used to develop resilience and strength in the arms. At this point, the "block" is often considered as a deflecting strike. The strike occurs with full power using a strengthened arm capable of withstanding the speed and strength of an opponent. This block represents the classical *go*-form: a hard technique issued with strength and speed to confront the aggressor. Unfortunately, this hard technique is of little value if the opponent is simply stronger or faster: clearly more is needed.

Transferring Internal Energy

The next stage of development involves the transfer of internal energy into the block from the center of the body. This concept has already been discussed from the viewpoint of transferring internal energy into punching movements in a previous article on Sanchin kata (Labbate, 1999). The idea can also be employed to transfer power directly into the rising block using a shaking motion. To teach this movement, a progressive sequence of drills is used that exaggerate and train the motion of the body. As a student becomes more proficient, these exaggerations gradually decrease until the motion becomes an internal element of the blocking technique.

The preliminary drills focus on the development of the "karate drum" shown in Sequence 2. Standing in a loose ready stance (2a), the student quickly swings the arms and shoulders clockwise and counterclockwise as far as possible to the right (2b) and left (2c). This swinging motion serves to exaggerate and develop the necessary motion of the hips. A second exercise is then used in which the student drives the swinging action from the hips while holding the arms and body loosely. This latter exercise transitions the student to focus on movement of the hips rather than the shoulders. A third exercise completes the development of the basic turning motion: the hips are driven backward and forward while the shoulders are held in position aligned forward.

Sanchin style locking is next added to the progression of drills and is shown in Sequence 3: from the ready position (3a), the body is forced through focused tension directly into the locked position (3b). The body becomes firmly rooted to the ground, the body weight is lowered, and each muscle group is brought under tension in a single motion.

Principle #1
The karate drum drills teach the fundamental principles of loading, shaking, locking, and rebounding.

Putting these exercises together, the student can finally develop a complete "karate drum" technique: the hips are driven forward, then allowed naturally to reverberate or rebound back into their final position aligned forward, and finally Sanchin style locking occurs at the close of the technique.

After mastering the basic karate drum drills, the student may move forward to drills that cause power to be directed into a particular technique as shown in Sequence 4. In the case of the rising block, this is called an "upshake." Swinging the arms in the style of the karate drum, the rising block positioning is integrated. For a block with the right arm, the body is rotated as far as possible to the right, the right hand is chambered, and the left arm covers (4a). The shoulders are then rotated, as far to the left (4b) as possible, the left hand remains in the cover position, and the right hand transitions upward in an intercepting motion (4c). The body reverberates back into a final position with the hips aligned forward, the left hand chambers, while the right elbow rotates upward into the block in a redirecting motion until reaching its final position (4d). This cover, intercept, and redirect motion is coordinated and driven from the hips. Sequence 4 exaggerates the body motion to develop the required form, as the student progresses the movements become incrementally smaller until they are an internal aspect of technique.

Principle #2
Develop power in the rising block
by directing internal energy.

At the end of this technique, the student applies the locking motion taught as part of the karate drum drills. The student must focus on aligning the hips forward at the end of the block, with the body tightened as in Sanchin kata. Putting these pieces together, the deflecting strike is enhanced to become a powerful strike driven from the hips by internal energy. After the block is complete, the body is locked down as in Sanchin for a split second at the moment of contact when the block completes.

The up-shake is just one of four basic shaking motions that can be applied to all of the basic karate techniques. It can be used to transfer power into any upward movement toward an opponent, for example, rising block, uppercut punch, and elbow strikes. A similar down-shake is used in techniques that move downward into an opponent, for example, down-block, downward strikes and punches. For techniques that involve forward motion of the same hand and leg, such as a lunge punch, palm-heel strike, shuto, etc., an open-shake is used. In contrast, a closed-shake is used for techniques that involve opposite hand and leg movements, for example, a reverse punch, palm-heel strike, etc. Collectively these shaking motions form the principles by which internal energy is transferred into every aspect of structure and movement. These gross movements are practiced only to train the body. Eventually the hips are coordinated with every technique and the associated movement will happen naturally.

To develop hand-eye coordination, speed, timing, and distancing, the blocks are practiced with a partner. Each level of partner training progressively adds new principles from those listed above, first in stationary, and then in moving drills. In these exercises the timing of the attack is organized by the attacker to be at uneven intervals so that the defender is forced to track and intercept the incoming blow with precision.

> **Principle #3**
> Up-, down-, open- and closed-shakes allow power
> to be applied to every karate technique.

Two-Person Sensing Techniques

To make further progress, the advanced student must make a substantive transition to combine the hard techniques of Sanchin with new, soft techniques. The basis of this transition is two-person sensing techniques, a concept that has always been at the center of developing advanced Goju-ryu karate (Higaonna, 1996). The essence of this concept is to make contact with the opponent and retain this contact until the opponent is defeated. In combat, the first point of contact is typically through a block. Having made contact, the opponent's every move can be sensed through feeling so as to maintain control without having to watch his or her movements. This control also makes it possible to confront additional opponents while engaged in combat.

> **Principle #4**
> Two-person partner drills, conducted at uneven intervals,
> are used to develop hand-eye coordination, speed, timing, and distancing.

A number of two-person drills are available to develop this skill. A variety of these drills, that illustrate the basic progression, are explained here to give a feel for the training methods. The drills are cumulative, each building upon the previous to develop and enhance the training process. It is important to practice the drills softly in a relaxed stance. They are intended to develop sensitive, fluid motion rather than force and strength.

> **Principle #5**
> Practice two-person sensing techniques slowly and softly to develop the ability
> to sense and anticipate an opponent's movements without watching.

The first drill is illustrated in Sequence 5 and is concerned with learning to maintain contact by grabbing and sticking. Two students begin in the open-hand middle block position with hands positioned so that a hook is formed at the wrist. The students touch by locking these hooks together (5a). From this grabbing position, both students rotate the hand from outside to inside forming a hook on the opposite side of the wrist (5b). This process is repeated backward and forward. The object of the drill is to develop the sense of sticking to an opponent, grabbing with the hook of the hand, and controlling the contact at all times.

Sequence 6 shows a second drill in which the range of contact is extended to include a palm-heel strike. One partner strikes slowly and carefully (6a) while the other carefully follows the strike inward maintaining light contact at all times. The defender guides the strike to a cupped hand positioned just off the body. The defender then becomes the attacker (6b) and returns the palm-heel while the partner practices the same technique. This drill begins to develop the feeling of following a blow. The attacker determines the speed, power, and direction of the blow while the defender simply focuses on maintaining contact. Through drills of this type, students learn to adhere in the presence of motion and to follow a partner's movement rather than block and lose contact.

Sequence 7 shows a drill that is intended to develop the skill of redirecting the energy of an opponent. Like the previous drill, one student uses a palm-heel strike to attack while the other follows the inbound motion to defend and maintain contact. However, at the last moment, prior to the strike making contact, the defender redirects the blow by rotating the hips away causing the blow to miss the body entirely (7a), following which the roles of defender and attacker are reversed (7b). This is more difficult than the previous drills in that it requires the attacker not to overcommit and the defender to sense when the attack has terminated in order to begin a return attack. Through gentle soft motions it is possible to develop a sense for redirecting the opponent's energy away from the body and loading the internal energy into the body. Notice that the basic hook developed in the first drill is used to control the direction when redirecting the incoming blow.

Sequence 8 illustrates a final drill bringing together the skills of sticking, sensing, loading, redirecting, and rebounding. As before, the drill begins with a palm-heel strike by the attacker (8a) in which the defender sticks and follows (8b). The strike is then blocked, loading energy for a counter while redirecting the opponents energy (8c). Finally, the defender counters with a palm-heel strike (8d).

The principles of sensing, sticking, and redirecting are now used in all of the standard partner training drills. However, these drills are utilized to focus on maintaining contact rather than delivering the appropriate sequence of blocks and blows. Sequence 9 shows a blocking drill conducted in this manner. First the students practice these drills with their eyes open, then with their eyes closed. The object is to maintain contact at all times, anticipating the opponent's movements by sensing the position of their body. The drill begins from the ready stance (9a). In this case, the initial attacker is on the left side of the photo. The attacker strikes to the face and the defender makes initial contact through a rising block (9b). The defender then counters to the body and the attacker senses this movement. The attacker maintains contact, feeling the motion of the defender to intercept the incoming blow. At the point of interception the attacker is touching in two places (9c), allowing the point of contact to move to the new block and allowing the right hand to be chambered while maintaining contact (9d). After this attack to the body, the attacker strikes to the groin (9e), and is in turn blocked by the defender who maintains contact (9f). Roles then reverse with the defender striking to the face.

Principle #6
Practice two-person sensing techniques in blocking drills with a partner with the eyes closed to develop the senses.

In combat, we seek to maintain contact at all times so as to read the opponent with our senses. When contact is lost it is generally a cue to attack since the opponent is repositioning to attempt some alternative technique.

Principle #7
Use body-shifting to allow a blow to pass and reposition the body to advantage.

Body-Shifting

Body-shifting (*taisabaki*) is a technique in which the goal is to move in relation to the attacker both to avoid a blow and gain a position of advantage (Okazaki and Stricevic, 1984). The simplest form of this concept is termed "opening the door." If the defender is standing in a ready stance, and the attacker attempts to strike with the left hand, the defender moves the right foot backward, rotating the body by 90-degrees to avoid the blow. This technique places the defender on the inside and in position to counter. A similar technique with the right foot can be used to avoid a left forward punch. Although this technique is simple, it is preferable to position the body to the outside of the attacker where there is less likelihood that the attacker will be able to use a second technique.

Body-shifting movements can be achieved on any angle, not simply backward. For example, Sequence 10 shows how to combine the technique with the rising block. The attacker attempts a right-punch, the defender intercepts and adheres to the blow, moving to the left on a 45-degree line with the left foot, while maintaining contact and following the opponent (10a). The right foot is then positioned so that the defender is in an advantageous position, on the outside of the attacker, with the groin protected from kicks (10b). During this movement, the rising block is used to expose the ribs by grabbing with the muscular part of the forearm. Body-shifting ensures the correct distancing to effect the counter (10c). Irrespective of the stance in use, when moving to the left, the left foot moves first followed by the right; when moving to the right, the right foot moves first followed by the left.

Principle #8
When moving to the left. the left foot moves first followed by the right;
when moving to the right, the right foot moves first followed by the left.

It is important to overcome the student's natural tendency to step back during the delivery of a blocking technique. Stepping backward is useful as a teaching tool when students are learning the basic gross patterns of blocking as it prevents their inadvertently being hurt. At more advanced levels it produces a defensive mind-set and represents an error in conditioning that places the student at a distinct disadvantage by causing loss of contact. This in turn prevents the ability to sense and control the opponent's movements. Movement to the side, as shown above, is a common alternative and is a distinct improvement as it allows sensitivity techniques to be used.

The Advanced Level Block

Combining the transfer of internal energy with sensitivity techniques and body-shifting, students can at last progress to more advanced level blocking techniques. The advanced level block is shown exaggerated in Sequence 11 to highlight the main ideas. Although these photos show stationary poses, it is important to recognize that the entire photo sequence is performed as one fluid motion.

Instead of blocking from the chamber at 45-degrees in a deflecting motion, the block is positioned first to intercept the incoming blow as shown in photo 11a. This occurs at the earliest point the chambered hand can reach the incoming blow and takes the shortest path to interception. The position of the interception is almost vertical and occurs with the muscular part of the forearm. It provides the first point of contact and the defender immediately adheres to the opponent. The motion of the arm continues upward in a circular motion redirecting the opponent's energy (11b). The defender's arm then rotates into its final position pulling the opponent's arm out of danger by adhering and redirecting at the point of contact (11c). No force is required

to achieve this block irrespective of the power and speed of the incoming blow. It occurs as a light, effortless, and fluid motion maintaining contact at all times.

As the block begins to redirect the blow, notice that the defender's hips are back, loaded, as shown in photo 11c. As the defender redirects the opponent's energy with the block, he steps straight in and strikes with a counter punch using the additional power generated from turning the waist (11d). This strike occurs with the full force of the loaded energy. The defender remains in contact at all times even though striking a blow. The counter strike occurs before the opponent has time to form a subsequent attack. Following the counter-strike the defender is reloaded in the opposite direction with both hands in contact. A wide variety of follow-through attacks can now be achieved while remaining in contact with either hand.

Principle #9
Intercept, stick, redirect, lock, counter, and reload in single fluid motion.

TECHNICAL SECTION

We have so far considered the rising block as a deflecting technique, as a powerful strike, and as a method for redirecting an opponent's energy. However, the technique can be used in wide variety of applications. A few of these are demonstrated here to give a flavor for the more general utility of the technique.

Grappling Techniques

At close quarters the block is useful in obtaining space. For example, in Sequence 12 the attacker is grappling close in and in order to use any techniques the defender must create some space (12a). The defender first grabs the attacker (12b) and strikes to the forearm to loosen the opponent's hold. Then the opponent's pushed away using the "block" (12c). While remaining in contact to read the opponent's movements, multiple strikes can then be made.

Typical grabs, such as that shown in Sequence 13, can also be confronted using the block. In these applications, the chambered hand is always used to trap and control the opponent. For example, in Sequence 13 the attacker grabs the defender (13a) who immediately clasps the grabbing hand (13b). Holding the grab in place a block is used downward to soften the opponent's arm and pull him forward (13c). At the same time, the wrist is turned downward causing the opponent to be sucked into a subsequent strike to the neck (13d). Notice that after initial contact is made (13b), the defender never looses contact until the attacker is defeated.

The technique can be used in other grappling positions, such as that shown in photo 14a. Here the defender steps backward and holds the attacker's head downward (14b). This provides direct access for a downward strike to the nape of the neck (14c). Again, after initial contact, the defender remains in contact until satisfied that the attacker is defeated.

Penetration Punch

Sequence 15 shows the use of the "block" as a penetration punch. Initial contact occurs during the block where the attacker expects a standard block (15a), instead, the blocking arm rotates upward fully, striking the attacker in the temple (15b, 15c). Notice that contact is maintained throughout the technique. The defender keeps the attacker's arm under control while delivering the punch. The attacker's own energy is used to drive the defender's strike in at the temple.

Choke

Sequence 16 shows how to use the "block" to enter a choke. The application begins with the attacker pushing (16a). The defender then traps downward to obtain contact (16b). While maintaining contact, a rising block is then performed directly to the neck (16c). The opposite hand is then moved under the blocking arm to grab the opposite collar (16d). The knuckles on the blocking hand are then forced upward into the opponent's neck by pulling the opposite hand downward at the same time as forcing the blocking hand upward (16e). Tight contact is maintained through the blocking arm at all times leading to strangulation (16f).

Principle #10

A "block" is multi-role technique that can be used in a wide variety of applications that include grappling, striking, choking, take-downs, as well as blocking.

Take Down

The block can also be used as part of a take-down. For example, in photo 17a, the attacker ducks to avoid a blow and grabs at the ankle while striking to the hip joint. The take-down is affected by striking with the "block" (17b) while pulling at the ankle until the opponent falls (17c).

The applications presented here are by no means exhaustive. They simply represent a cross-section of representative uses for the rising block alone.

Concluding Remarks

The Goju-ryu principles presented at the beginner level provide simple basic forms that were never intended to guide the practitioner in applications. They are primarily learning tools to progress along the path to advanced technique. Most of these basic ideas can be used in a multitude of applications in combat. However, to be useful they must be based on the principles of structure, movement, and breathing developed through Sanchin kata. Subsequently, advanced principles must be added: transferring internal energy into every technique, sensing skills to intercept, adhere, and redirect an opponent's energy, and body-shifting to position the body. Correct distancing, timing, and hand-eye coordination must be developed progressively through stationary and moving partner training. As overall technique improves, the quality and subtlety of kata training grows to incorporate more advanced movements. Thus each incremental improvement is fed back into every aspect of progressive training. Finally, applications evolve not as a staged set of movements, but rather as an artistic combination of the practitioner's ideas and training. Karate is then no longer concerned with mastering a technique. In the end it is concerned with mastering oneself.

References

Labbate, M. (1999). Elements of advanced karate techniques. *Journal of Asian Martial Arts*, 8(2), 80-95.

Oyama, M. (1981). *Mastering karate*. New York: Grosset & Dunlap.

Higaonna, M. (1996). *The history of karate*. Norwich, UK: Dragon Books.

Okazaki, T., and Stricevic, M. (1984). *The textbook of modem karate*. Tokyo: Kodansha International.

chapter 8

Kanzaki Shigekazu: An Interview with To-on-ryu's Leading Representative

by Mario McKenna, M.S.

The inset photo is from his early years: Kanzaki (front center); his bearded teacher Kyoda Juhatsu; classmate Murakami Katsumi (front right).
All photos courtesy of Kanzaki Shigekazu.

Few karate students in the West would recognize the term *To'on-ryu* and still fewer would recognize the name Kanzaki Shigekazu. Yet this man is a link to the karate of a bygone era—a karate in which an intimate bond existed between teacher and student, where training was a matter of survival and not of sport, and where humility and compassion represented the ultimate goals of training.

Kanzaki Shigekazu was born Kanzaki Kazuya to Japanese parents in Japanese-occupied Korea in 1928. Upon his family's return to Beppu, Oita Prefecture, a teenaged Kanzaki Kazuya entered the Japanese Self-Defense Force. Young and full of energy, he found himself caught-up in several scuffles, including some with American servicemen. Deciding he should do something about it, he eventually came under the tutelage of Kyoda Juhatsu, classmate of Goju-ryu founder Miyagi Chojun and direct student of Higashionna

Kanryo, Naha-te karate's most famous proponent. From that time onward, Kanzaki was a student of Kyoda Juhatsu until the latter's death in 1968. So close was the relationship between Kyoda and Kanzaki, that Kyoda presented Kanzaki with the name "Shigekazu" upon Kanzaki's recognition of mastery of To'on-ryu. The name was derived from the first Chinese ideogram of Kyoda's first name, "Ju" (which can alternately be read as "Shige"), which was combined with the "Kazu" of his first name, giving him his new name "Shigekazu." All of Kyoda's sons also use this "Ju" character in their first names: Juki, Juchoku, and Juko.

Kanzaki Shigekazu, in a White Crane stance found in the Nepai kata.

Kanzaki Shigekazu is the most senior practitioner of To'on-ryu in Japan today. Now into his seventies, the retired Japanese Self-Defense Force officer relates his training under Kyoda Juhatsu and his own unique insights into karate. The following interview took place at a local community center near Kanzaki Sensei's home in Beppu city, Oita Prefecture, on April 9, 2000.

TECHNICAL SECTION

▶ COULD YOU PLEASE TELL ME YOUR DATE OF BIRTH, AND THEN SOMETHING OF YOUR KARATE BACKGROUND?

I was born on March 20, 1928. I first started training in karate in 1950, about five years after the war ended. Japan was still a fairly volatile place and there were plenty of bars and the like. I had gotten into a few scuffles with some American soldiers, so I thought I should do something about that.

Eventually, I heard of an Okinawan by the name of Teruya Rinko, who was well known for taking on the local Yakuza armed with a boat oar [ekudi]. Teruya is a very Okinawan name and if you looked it up, I'm sure you could find it. So, I went looking for him in the hope that he would teach me, but he refused. He told me that he had been taught by a very famous Okinawan sensei when he was a junior high school student in Okinawa and that this same teacher was living in Beppu. So, Teruya Rinko took me to Kyoda Sensei.

▸ SO YOU MET KYODA SENSEI THROUGH ONE OF YOUR FRIENDS?

Yes, through Teruya Rinko. The first thing I learned was how to stand and walk in the style of the Sanchin kata. I practiced this as hard as I could for about three months, just walking up and down. During those three months, Kyoda Sensei constantly watched me, deciding what kind of a person I was. Then New Year's came and Kyoda was there at the New Year's celebration. At that moment I decided that I didn't want to quit karate training. After those three months had passed, Kyoda started to formally teach me karate. We practiced on top of tatami and they soon became worn and tattered.

▸ THIS WAS AT KYODA SENSEI'S HOUSE?

Yes, at his house. Kyoda Sensei's third son, Juko, who also practiced karate, worked for NTT [Nippon Telephone & Telegraph] and lived at the company dormitory. Kyoda Sensei's tatami in his home often became ragged and ruined from our practice, so we started practicing in Juko's dormitory room. However, someone was living below him, so we had to make sure we didn't make any noise when we practiced. Absolutely no noise at all. [*Note: Kanzaki Sensei stands up and demonstrates the very quick, circular sliding footwork of Sanchin on top of the community center's tatami, making no noise at all*]. Even when we practiced stepping in to attack with strikes or kicks, we had to be very quiet.

▸ WAS KYODA SENSEI STRICT WHEN HE TAUGHT KARATE?

Kyoda Sensei did not teach a student another kata until he thought he could do the previous ones. Of course, you practiced basics and Sanchin first. We always practiced Sanchin at the beginning and at the end of practice. Then slowly you were introduced to Seisan, Sanseru, and other katas.

▸ SO, AT FIRST YOU ONLY PRACTICED SANCHIN FOOTWORK FOR THREE MONTHS AND AFTER THAT THE BREATHING, HAND POSITIONS, BLOCKS, AND PUNCHES. HOW LONG DID IT TAKE TO LEARN THE ENTIRE SANCHIN KATA?

Everything was very slow. At first you practiced the kata without any focus or power and slowly you built up your strength. Later, Kyoda Sensei would check your focus.

▸ SO, ALL TOGETHER IT TOOK ABOUT SIX MONTHS TO ONE YEAR.

That's right. Watching someone do Sanchin kata, you can tell what level he is capable of practicing at.

▸ WHAT ABOUT OTHER PRACTICES, LIKE BLOCKING, PUNCHING, ETC.?

You did that by yourself, but Kyoda Sensei was always watching and checking. Changing the topic a little, the blocks used nowadays ... how should I put this? Looking at karate katas today, the blocks just simply throw the arm out and stop. The block should be a sweeping action. It should sweep out and snap back. The blocks nowadays are just thrown out there. They're just for show, just to make the katas look good. Look at the Seipai kata standardized for competition, the blocks just stop dead. Snapping the block out doesn't look good. This is just one point of the basic difference between the karate of today and that of yesterday.

With respect to katas when I was learning, it was up to the student to study and find what techniques were in the katas and how to use them. Kyoda Sensei never explained directly what the meaning of a technique in a kata was.

▸ KYODA SENSEI NEVER TAUGHT THE MEANING OF A TECHNIQUE?

Almost never. It was up to the student to figure out. We would practice by ourselves and then show Kyoda Sensei what we thought the technique could mean. If he wasn't satisfied, he would tell us to go and practice and investigate the technique more. But, by studying and researching karate techniques this way, your body soon learns and remembers it. Nowadays, if you just learn a kata and then stop practicing it for a few years, you forget everything. You have to repeat a technique over and over and constantly think about its meaning. There was one part of Sanseru kata that I could not figure out for the life of me. Kyoda Sensei taught me what it meant. That was the only part of a kata he directly explained.

▸ IF KYODA SENSEI WAS SATISFIED THAT YOU UNDERSTOOD THE TECHNIQUE HE WOULD SAY "GOOD," "ALRIGHT" OR SOMETHING?

Yes, just a one word answer. Kyoda Sensei's son, Juko, eventually moved into a house owned by his wife's family and practice was conducted outside when the weather was good.

▸ WHAT DID YOU DO WHEN IT RAINED?

Kyoda Sensei would conduct spiritual training inside. It usually consisted of lectures or stories. I remember being extremely cold sometimes when we were practicing outside during the winter. We'd be barefooted and practicing on top of the snow (laughing).

▶ SEEMS LIKE IT WAS QUITE AUSTERE TRAINING. IT MUST HAVE BEEN QUITE HARD. THE BASIC TECHNIQUES, SUCH AS CHUDAN UKE, KAKE UKE, TUSKI, WERE BASICALLY THE SAME AS WHAT IS FOUND IN MOST OKINAWAN KARATE STYLES?

Basically, they're the same.

▶ YOU MENTIONED THAT WITHIN TO'ON-RYU THERE ARE FIVE KATAS: SANCHIN, SEISAN, SANSERU, SUPAREMPEI/PECHURIN, JION, AND NEPAI?

Jion is not one of Higashionna Sensei's katas. It comes from Yabu Kentsu.

▶ IN TO'ON-RYU THERE ARE THREE VERSIONS OF THE SEISAN KATA ?

No, there are two. One from Higashionna Kanryo and one from Higashionna Kanyu.[1] Kyoda Sensei learned the Kanyu Seisan first and then the Kanryo version when he entered the latter's dojo. But Kyoda did not teach the Higashionna Kanryo version of Seisan as that was included in the Goju-ryu kata.

▶ ARE THERE MANY DIFFERENCES BETWEEN THE KANYU AND KANRYO VERSIONS OF SEISAN?

They're not that different. [*Note: Kanazaki Sensei demonstrates the Kanyu version of Seisan. It is easily recognizable as Seisan and is quite similar to the Kanryo version in Goju-ryu with respect to technique and enbusen* (pattern)]. However, much of the footwork and stances are considerably different. Furthermore, the Kanyu Seisan contains several techniques that its Goju-ryu counterpart does not have, such as a cross-step kick similar to that in Isshin-ryu's Sunsu kata.

▶ WITH RESPECT TO SANSERU, KYODA SENSEI LEARNED THIS KATA FROM HIGASHIONNA KANRYO. HOWEVER, IT IS RUMORED THAT MIYAGI CHOJUN DID NOT LEARN THIS KATA FROM HIGASHIONNA SENSEI. IS MIYAGI CHOJUN SENSEI'S SANSERU A DIFFERENT KATA?

It's completely different. Miyagi Sensei's son, Miyagi Kei, received instruction from Kyoda Sensei. He looked intently at Kyoda's Sanseru, noting that it was completely different. Kyoda Sensei's Sanseru uses twice the amount of movement than Miyagi Sensei's. Kyoda Sensei's uses many long jumping and lunging movements that the Goju-ryu Sanseru doesn't have.

▶ Then from who did Miyagi Sensei learn Sanseru?
I couldn't say.

▶ Does To'on-ryu's Sanseru have a double front kick?
No! But the To'on-ryu version covers a greater distance, the width of about five tatami.[2]
[Note: *Kanzaki Sensei again stands up and demonstrates Sanseru kata. It indeed covers at least twice the distance of the Goju-ryu version and strikes this interviewer as very much "Chinese" in its use of* maai *(combative engagement distance) and strong lunging attacks. There is also a complete absence of the use of front kick* (mae-geri) *in the kata*].

▶ The next kata practiced in To'on-ryu is Suparempei?
No, Pechurin. Pechurin is Pechurin; Suparempei is Suparempei. Kyoda Sensei said that Higashionna Tanmei only taught Pechurin.[3] Suparempei is most likely another kata. Remember, after Higashionna Tanmei passed away, Miyagi Chojun traveled to China.[4] I cannot say for sure because it was such a long time ago, but that may have been where the Goju-ryu Suparempei kata came from. But as far as I know, Kyoda Sensei only taught Pechurin.

▶ In Murakami Katsumi's book, Karatedo to Ryukyu Kobudo, there are photos of Murakami performing Pechurin. Have you seen this book?
Yes, but the photographs are a little off. There are Suparempei techniques mixed in with it.

▶ So, it is not purely Pechurin kata?
Yes, techniques of Suparempei are included in it. There mixed in with it.

▶ But many of the techniques in Pechurin and Suparempei are very close?
Yes. Some of the techniques do resemble each other.

▶ Therefore, Pechurin and Suparempei are essentially the same in technique and as kata.
They are basically the same. Perhaps it was Miyagi Sensei's trip to China that affected the name change in the kata. But I am certain that Higashionna Sensei referred to that particular kata as Pechurin.

▶ I'm not sure which book I read it in, but it said that Pechurin was Kyoda Sensei's favorite kata.

Hmm, no that's not true. I don't recall Kyoda Sensei having any particular kata as his favorite. I do recall at an Okinawan Cultural Festival in Kumamoto Prefecture that Kyoda Sensei performed Sanseru kata and injured his foot quite badly when he was doing one of the sword foot [*sokuto-geri*] techniques in the kata. He came down so hard on the stage floor that he injured his foot. He put so much power into each technique. When I watch Goju-ryu Sanseru, I don't see those kinds of techniques and that kind of power displayed. Kyoda Sensei could perform these kinds of powerful techniques with or without sound of his feet.

▶ THERE IS ALMOST NO INFORMATION AVAILABLE ON TO'ON-RYU IN EITHER ENGLISH OR JAPANESE.

That's correct. Recently, my students have asked me to take some photographs or something to leave behind. Maybe using a digital camera or something like that. But I don't know. I don't really know those kinds of things.

▶ OVERSEAS, THE NAME OF MIYAGI CHOJUN IS WELL KNOWN, BUT IN THE CASE OF KYODA JUHATSU, PLEASE EXCUSE ME AS THIS IS A LITTLE IMPOLITE, HIS NAME AND TO'ON-RYU ARE VIRTUALLY UNKNOWN.

That's true. But in the old days, Kyoda Sensei's name was well known, for example, in the Zen Ku Ren [*Zen Nihon Karatedo Renmei*; All-Japan Karatedo Federation]. He often appeared at many of their functions, so I suspect that To'on-ryu was well known back then. But he wasn't well known throughout Japan.

▶ PRESENTLY, WHO IS TEACHING TO'ON-RYU IN JAPAN?
No one!

▶ WHAT ABOUT YOUR STUDENTS?
They are not teaching. Most of them have risen to quite high positions at work and are too busy. They've become department heads of some company and don't have any free time to teach. But, there may be one of my students teaching in Moji in Kita Kyushu. He might be teaching, but I'm not sure. He loves budo as he also practices iaido as well.

▶ DON'T YOU FEEL YOU SHOULD LEAVE SOMETHING BEHIND OF TO'ON-RYU?
I feel I should leave something behind of To'on-ryu. Pictures or something.

▶ NEIPAI CAME VIA GOKENKI.[5] WHY DID KYODA SENSEI LEARN THIS KATA FROM

GO KENKI?

What can I say? Kyoda Sensei was part of the Karatedo Kenkyu Kai along with Go Kenki, Miyagi, Yabu, and others, a time when there weren't any *ryuha* [lit. "traditions and sects"; styles] as we know them today. They got together to learn and study about karate. Nowadays, different ryuha will not get together and exchange information, which strikes me as rather strange. It was never like that in the past.

▶ THEREFORE, IN YOUR OPINION, THE MODERN IDEA OF RYUHA IS MEANINGLESS?

Meaningless. At that time, Go Kenki was part of that group and taught that kata to those interested and Kyoda Sensei was interested.

Kanzaki Shigekazu sitting among members
of the Self-Defense Force Club.

▶ HIGASHIONNA SENSEI'S KATAS ARE THOUGHT TO BE BASED IN CRANE BOXING. DO THE TECHNIQUES FOUND IN NEIPAI RESEMBLE THOSE FOUND IN OTHER NAHATE KATAS SUCH AS SEISAN, ETC.?

Yes.

▶ IS THE TO'ON-RYU NEIPAI THE SAME AS THE NEIPAI ILLUSTRATED IN THE BUBISHI?

No, it's different. I believe it's similar to the one Tokashiki Iken learned from Sha (Mandarin: Xie) Sensei, a Whooping Crane boxer from Fuzhou, China.

▸ IN TO'ON-RYU, NEIPAI IS THE LAST KATA? IT'S CONSIDERED THE HIGHEST FORM? IS THE ORDER FIXED IN WHICH THE KATAS ARE TAUGHT IN TO'ON-RYU?

Basically the kata order is Sanchin, Seisan, Sanseru, Jion, Pechurin, then Neipai. Now basically the order is fixed, but it wasn't like that in the past. Nowadays people teach too many katas and teach them far too quickly without properly researching them by themselves to understand their meaning. The way kata is taught has changed, I think. It was up to the student to research the technique as much as he could and only after he could not figure out the technique for himself did he ask the sensei.

▸ HOW LONG DID IT TAKE YOU TO LEARN THE TO'ON-RYU KATA IN THIS MANNER?

About ten years or so, practicing three or four times a week.

▸ WITH RESPECT TO JION, KYODA SENSEI LEARNED THIS KATA FROM YABU KENTSU, HOWEVER THIS IS A SHURI-TE KATA.

Sorry to bring up the past again, but there is the Jion kata practiced by the Japan Karate Association and there is the Jion that was taught by Yabu Sensei. But I believe that Jion as taught by Yabu Sensei is not originally a Shuri-te based kata. Funakoshi Gichin says this in his early books on karate.[6]

A rare photo of Kyoda Juhatsu (right) and Miyagi Chojun performing prearranged sparring techniques (*yakusoku*).

▸ Did Kyoda Sensei learn any other Shuri-te kata?
Not that I know of.

▸ Does To'on-ryu practice push-hands (*kakie*) like Goju-ryu?
Well, look here [Note: *Kanzaki Sensei points to an old picture of Kyoda Juhatsu and Miyagi Chojun in their teens; see photo at right*]. From this stance all techniques of attacking and defending were practiced.

▸ Did you use the makiwara when you practiced?
Yes we did, but we used a slightly different way of punching. We used a vertical fist until we made contact with the makiwara and then we turned counter-clockwise until the fist was 3/4 twisted. Strike vertically and then twist the punch into the opponent. Keeping the fist vertical until contact and then twisting through is the strongest way to punch.

▸ Did Kyoda Sensei teach any weapons kata such as the bo or sai?
He did teach bo kata, but I don't remember him ever saying what the name of the kata was.

▸ Was this bo kata passed down from Higashionna sensei?
No. It came from Kyoda Sensei's own training. Kyoda Sensei also taught the use of the nunchaku and sai. He had all these weapons and other training equipment in his home.

▸ I have heard a rumor that when Higashionna was in China, he studied the use of the staff and the broadsword. However, I have never heard of any of Higashionna's students teaching use of these weapons.
I never heard of Kyoda ever learning these weapons from Higashionna.

▸ Both Kyoda Juhatsu and Miyagi Chojun learned karate from Higashionna Kanryo. Excluding the katas that Miyagi Chojun reportedly made himself—such as Geki-sai Dai Ichi/Dai Ni and Tensho—there are four common katas between Goju-ryu and To'on-ryu. Although there are obvious differences in technique, Goju-ryu has several other katas, such as Seinchin, Shisochin, etc. Are these other katas from Miyagi Chojun's own research and practice?
I have no idea. Kyoda Sensei was transferred from time to time because he was a schoolteacher. Miyagi Sensei could have learned those katas when Kyoda Sensei was not around. I really don't know.

Kanzaki Shigekazu parries right with the sai.

▸ You mentioned previously that it was up to the student to practice and learn the meaning of each technique in a kata and later the student would show Kyoda Sensei what he thought the technique meant. Then Kyoda Sensei would correct the student. Were there any pre-arranged sparring sets?

Yes! Kyoda made sets of techniques for basic techniques like middle-punch [*chudan tsuki*], front kick [*mae geri*], etc.

▸ How about arm and leg conditioning (*koteikitai*)?

Yes, but we also used a training tool for practicing hooking (*kake*) and striking. It was made from a small telephone pole that Juko had brought home from work. You could practice deflecting, punching, striking, and kicking on it. Naturally, this practice toughened your arms and legs.[7]

▸ Did you also use other equipment such as old style dumbbells (*chiishi*) and gripping pots (*nigirigame*)?

Yes, we did. Kyoda Sensei had the nigirigame ordered all the way from Okinawa.

▸ How many people have received teaching licenses from you?

Two. But, like I said, they have become too busy with work to teach. Since one of them is a policeman, he may be teaching, but I'm not sure.

▶ WHAT WAS KYODA SENSEI LIKE WHEN HE TAUGHT KARATE?

God, he made us practice Sanchin kata constantly and I thought, "Why do I have to practice this kata all the time?" Then I'd have to train with the different equipment. He was really tough on us when he was teaching, but when you were just having a conversation, he was so kind. He would often talk about the spiritual aspects of karate or about how to carry ourselves in public. For example, he would tell us to always walk on the right side and never right down the center of the street: one, to give ladies a path to pass by; and, two, to protect yourself in case you were kicked or attacked by someone. Or to always keep alert when riding the train or what not. To always be watching.

▶ DO YOU HAVE ANY PARTICULAR MEMORIES OF KYODA SENSEI?

He was such a good man. He taught us karate well into his 80's, up until the time he died.

▶ DID YOU EVER HEAR ANY STORIES ABOUT HIGASHIONNA SENSEI FROM KYODA SENSEI?

I often asked myself why people want to know about Naha-te's roots. You know: "What did Higashionna Sensei teach?" "How did he practice?"... I thought about researching our karate roots many times while Kyoda Sensei was still alive, but I never did. When I think about it now, it seems strange. For some reason or other, I couldn't bring myself to ask Kyoda Sensei my questions. I think Kyoda Sensei was the same way with respect to Higashionna Sensei. You tend to hold back with respect to your teacher. You feel you can't ask your teacher too many questions. It was extremely difficult for me to ask him questions. I just couldn't. I was his student. Because he was my teacher, I just held back. It's strange, isn't it?

▶ IT'S A WAY OF SHOWING RESPECT, RIGHT? DID KYODA SENSEI BECOME ANGRY IF YOU ASKED HIM QUESTIONS?

No, not at all. But as his students, we felt we couldn't ask him those kinds of things, especially with respect to techniques. He really wanted the student to first and foremost learn for himself.

Technique from Samseru Kata

In photo 1a, Kanzaki moves to the outside to evade an attack, then grasps the opponent around the neck from behind with his left hand, supporting the grip with his right hand at the opponent's armpit area. With this secure hold, he easily takes the opponent down to his left side (1b).

Technique from Samseru Kata

Moving to the inside, Kanzaki deflects an attack with his right open palm (2a). He counters by pushing the opponent off-balance with his left arm and rolling him over his left leg. Simultaneously, Kanzaki moves into a solid stance allowing a follow-up punch to the opponent's mid-section (2b).

Technique from Samseru Kata

Kanzaki evades an attack by moving to the outside and immediately places his left forearm against the opponent's neck while grasping the opponent's uniform at the armpit with his other hand (3a). He rotates his body to the right, pulling with his right hand while his left forearm bears against the side of the opponent's neck, taking him face-down to the ground (3b).

Notes

1. Higashionna Kanyu (1848-1922) was a cousin of Higashionna Kanryo. Like his younger cousin, Kanyu also trained in Chinese martial arts with Aragaki Seisho (1840-1918/20). However, unlike Kanryo, he was better known as a gifted musician rather than excelling in Chinese martial arts.
2. Tatami are straw mats used as floor covering in Japanese homes and are approximately 90 cm x 180 cm.
3. Literally "old man." *Tanmei* was often used as a term of respect to one's elders.
4. Kanzaki is referring to the fact that after the death of Higashionna, Miyagi Chojun, with Aisho Nakamoto (1881-1945), traveled to Fuzhou in 1915 for training and research.
5. Wu Xianhui (1886-1940) (Jap. Go Kenki), a Fuzhou tea-merchant and instructor of White Crane Chinese boxing, was the co-founder of the Karate Research Society (*Karatedo Kenkyu Kai*).
6. Kanzaki is referring to two early books on karate by Funakoshi Gichin, *Ryukyu Kenpo Toudi* (1922) and *Rentan Goshin Toudi Jutsu* (1925), which classifies the Jion kata as Shorei-ryu (i.e. Naha-te based kata) in contrast to Shorin-ryu (i.e. Shuri-te based kata). However, it should be noted that in *Kobou Kenpo Karate-do Nyumon* (1938), Mabuni Kenwa took issue with the Shorin-ryu versus Shorei-ryu distinction and argued that it was an inaccurate and inappropriate means of classification.
7. Kanzaki is referring to an old karate training device that resembles a "wooden man" (Jap. *moku-jin*) and is illustrated in some of the older pre-war texts on karatedo, such as *Karatedo no hanashi* (page 44), by Nakasone Genwa; and *Karate-do Taiken* (page 96), edited by Nakasone Genwa. Kanzaki referred to it as a *kakete*, which would translate roughly as "suspended hand."

chapter 9

To-on-ryu:
A Glimpse into Karatedo's Roots
by Mario McKenna, M.S.

Kyoda Juhatsu (1887-1968), the founder of To'on-ryu.
All photos courtesy of Kanzaki Shigekazu.

Introduction

One style of Okinawa karate that is virtually unknown both overseas and even in Japan proper is To'on-ryu. Except for the occasional passing reference to To'on-ryu in English language karate history books (Alexander 1991; Bishop 1989; Hokama 1998), information regarding this style and its founder, Kyoda Juhatsu (1887-1968), is virtually non-existent.

To'on-ryu has been most often described and dismissed as being "similar to Goju-ryu." This is not surprising since the To'on-ryu founder, Kyoda Juhatsu, received instruction from Higashionna Kanryo (1853-1915), the same Higashonna Kanryo who instructed Goju-ryu founder Miyagi Chojun (1888-1953). Regrettably, such explanations fail to adequately describe just who Kyoda Juhatsu was and what his system encompassed. In this chapter, a little light will be shone on the life of Kyoda Juhatsu and To'on-ryu's development.

Kyoda Juhatsu

Kyoda Juhatsu was born on December 5, 1887, during the latter stages of the Meiji restoration. It was a turbulent and chaotic time in Japan's history, where social and political change was the norm. He was the fourth son of Kyoda Jukyo and his wife. He was nicknamed "Sutagwa" in his childhood and "Sutachi" in his adulthood. The young Kyoda's life was uneventful and, by all accounts, he was a quiet and modest person. Although it is not known at exactly what age he gained his first exposure to the fighting arts, we do know that his mother brought it about. Kyoda's mother was a relative of Higashionna (Okinawa Hogen: Hijianna) Kanyu, who took the young Kyoda to receive instruction in Chinese martial arts (Man. *quanfa*; Jap. *kenpo*) (McKenna, 1999; Murakami, 1991).

Very little is known about Higashionna Kanyu (1848-1922). It is believed that he, like his younger cousin of five years, Higashionna Kanryo, had trained in Chinese martial arts with Aragaki Seisho (1840-1918/20). However, unlike Kanryo, the older Kanyu was better known as a gifted musician rather than excelling in Chinese martial arts (McCarthy, 1999). Nevertheless, the *Ryukyu Shinpo* related an interesting tale about Higashionna Kanyu in a January 24, 1914 article titled, "Okinawan Martial Artist." Kanyu's intensity and courage can be glimpsed in the following:

> On Okinawa, there is a tale of the martial valor of one Higashionna Kanyu, related to the short spear [*tinbe*]. During the Kume Village Great Tug-of-War, there were two teams: *Daimon* [Great Gate] and *Seimon* [West Gate]. The towns participating in the Daimon were Higashi and Kumoji, whereas the towns participating on the side of Seimon were Nishi and Izumisaki. However, one year after the Tug-of-War, trouble broke out over a trivial matter. At that time, Higashionna [Kanyu] stood in front of Daimon with a short spear in his hand, and stared down several opponents, not giving in even a single step. – Miyagi, 1987: 126; Tokashiki, 1991: 83

Sometime between 1901 and 1903, Kyoda Juhatsu began to study a Fujian-based martial art from his father's acquaintance, Higashionna Kanryo (Murakami, 1991; Tokashiki, 1991; Kinjo, 1999). In his youth, Higashionna had studied extensively under Aragaki Seisho and Kojo Taite (1837-1917) of Kume Village. He later studied Whooping/Singing Crane Fist (*Minghequan*) from Xie Zhongxiang (1852-1930) in Fuzhou, Fujian Province (Tokashiki 1991; 1997). Along with Itosu Anko (1813-1915), many considered Higashionna one of the foremost innovators of karate on Okinawa at the turn of the twentieth century. A few months later, Miyagi Chojun began studying from Higashionna.

Kyoda Juhatsu surrounded by students.

Like most karate training in the early twentieth century, instruction was tailored to the needs of the individual with a strong emphasis on the application of technique (*oyo* or *bunkai*). Kyoda Juhatsu spent several long months learning the basic footwork and breathing of Sanchin, the fundamental kata Higashionna used. In fact, as did all of Higashionna's students, Kyoda Juhatsu spent the first few years mastering Sanchin; basic applications, e.g. push-hands (*kakie*) and prearranged sparring (*yakusoku kumite*); and the use of supplementary strengthening exercise equipment (*nigirigame, ishisashi,* and *chiishi*) before Higashionna taught him other kata.

Once these fundamentals had been adequately mastered, Higashionna would teach one or more additional katas and their respective applications. These included: Seisan, Sanseru, and Pechurin/Suparempei.[1] Kyoda was the only student to learn all four of the katas directly from Higashionna Kanryo. Furthermore, unlike Miyagi, Higashionna is believed to have taught Kyoda the use of Chinese weaponry, including the spear and broadsword (Hokama, 1998; McCarthy, 1999).

Higashionna was not Kyoda's only teacher. While attending the Okinawa Prefectural Teachers' College, Kyoda studied karate under "the sergeant," Yabu Kentsu (1863-1937), one of the greatest Shuri-te (the style originating in Shuri) exponents (Kinjo, 1999). From Yabu, Kyoda learned the Jion kata, which he later included in his To'on-ryu. Kyoda also briefly studied under Yabu's teacher, Itosu Anko (Watatani and Yamada, 1978).

Following the deaths of Higashionna Kanryo and Itosu Anko in 1915, Kyoda, along with several other prominent young karate teachers, such as Miyagi Chojun and Mabuni Kenwa, continued their teachers' campaign to popularize the art of karate throughout Okinawa and mainland Japan. The pre-World War II era was a tumultuous time in Japanese history. "National essence" (*kokutai*) was aimed at reshaping all of Japan, including Okinawa, into one unified people and relied heavily on what Van Wolferen has described as "a rapid 'samuraization' of the country: a dissemination, among the lower layers of the population, of the disciplinary ideals and extremist 'loyalty' code that had exemplified the education of the samurai" (Van Wolferen, 1989: 62).

Hence Japan's ancient martial arts of kenjutsu and jujutsu were more often than not seen as an idealized means of developing the "national essence." In his role as an educator, Kyoda set about popularizing karate in accordance to kokutai by establishing several karate clubs at the elementary and junior high schools at which he worked prior to World War II.

Kyoda also lent his talents to the establishment of several karate associations and research societies. The first of these was the Okinawa Karatejutsu Kenkyu Kai (Okinawa Karatejutsu Research Club/Association), which opened in 1925 and established the first permanent training center for karate (Kinjo, 1999). Besides Kyoda, there were many famous karate teachers who instructed at the Kenkyu Kai, including: Choju Oshiro, Choshin Chibana, Mabuni Kenwa, Miyagi Chojun, Hanashiro Chomo, Motobu Choyu, and Wu Xianhui (Jap. Go Kenki; 1886-1940).

Of all the instructors who participated in the Karatejutsu Kenkyu Kai, perhaps Wu Xianhui had the most lasting and profound influence on all the others. Wu Xianhui is somewhat of an enigmatic figure in Okinawan karate history and there is little factual evidence surrounding his life. It is known that he was Chinese and immigrated from Fuzhou in 1912. He was a tea merchant by trade and resided in Naha's Higashi-machi (Tokashiki, 1991). Wu was also an instructor of White Crane boxing (Man. *Baihequan*; Jap. *Hakutsuru-ken*). Wu taught Kyoda the Nepai kata (Kinjo, 1999).

By 1930, Kyoda, along with his colleagues from the Karate Kenkyu Kai, was again vigorously involved with promoting karate, this time by establishing the Karate Kenkyu Kai as the official branch of the Okinawa Prefectural

Athletic Association (*Okinawa Kenritsu Taiku Kyokai*) (Kinjo, 1999). In December 1933, the Greater Japan Martial Virtues Association (*Dai Nippon Butoku Kai*) officially recognized this organization. This was a significant event in that Okinawa karate was officially recognized as a Japanese budo.

After the Butoku Kai officially recognized karate, Kyoda was one of the first Okinawan karate teachers to receive his "expert certification" (*kyoshi*) from the Okinawa governor, at the Butoku Kai's request, in 1934 (Murakami, 1991). Kyoda was a strong proponent of the "instructor, expert, master" (*renshi, kyoshi, hanshi*) licensing system that the Butoku Kai used and was instrumental in promoting it on Okinawa and later on mainland Japan. In addition, Kyoda was named the chief director and head instructor of the Butoku Kai's Naha branch.

The final organization Kyoda was directly involved with was the Okinawa Prefectural Karatedo Promotion Society (*Okinawa-ken Karatedo Shinko Kai*), established in January 1937. Along with Yabu Kentsu, Hanashiro Chomo, Kyan Chotoku, Chibana Chosin, Miyagi Chojun, Gushukuma Shimpan, and Nakasone Genwa, Kyoda participated in a March 1937 meeting and helped created the "twelve basic forms of karate." These kata were the origin of today's Shorin-ryu Kihon-gata I and II (Sells, 1999).

The To'on-ryu Style

After World War II, Okinawa lay in ruins. Few if any of the pre-war karate organizations had survived the Battle of Okinawa. For most karateka who survived, hardship and poverty marked the first few years following the end of World War II. Not surprisingly, karate practice took a back seat to simple survival. It was during this chaotic era that Kyoda Juhatsu retired as a school principal and moved to the southern Japanese island of Kyushu, settling in the hot springs resort town of Beppu, Oita Prefecture. He began to teach his brand of karate, calling it To'on-ryu. Kyoda did not have a formal dojo as such, teaching out of his home garden instead. In the garden, he had striking posts (*makiwara*), clay gripping jars (*nigirigame*), single-ended stone weights (*chiishi*), and other training equipment.

Of Kyoda Juhatsu's teachers (Higashionna, Yabu, Itosu, and Wu), by far Higashionna had the most profound impact on him. Indeed, Kyoda devoted well over a decade of his life to learning Higashionna's karate. So loyal was Kyoda to his teacher, that he named his karate style after him: To'on-ryu (literally "Higashion[na] style"). To'on-ryu takes its name from the Chinese reading (*on* or *ondoku*) of two of the characters in Higashionna's name.

Although both Kyoda and Miyagi studied under Higashionna Kanryo, Kyoda's To'on-ryu is in many ways completely opposite to Miyagi's Goju-ryu in the execution of technique. To'on-ryu is characterized by swift springing movements and places little emphasis on rooted stances, a Goju-ryu characteristic. Generally speaking, To'on-ryu techniques are executed in a much more circular, smooth, and flowing pattern than their Goju-ryu counterparts. There is definitely a more distinctive and obvious Chinese flavor to To'on-ryu. This can be especially seen in To'on-ryu's use of low kicks as well as the open hand in contrast to the closed fist of Goju-ryu.[2] It is interesting to note that many people believe that it was Miyagi Chojun who initiated the change from empty hand to closed fist. However, this appears not to be the case. Kanzaki Shigekazu, a direct student of Kyoda Juhatsu, stated that Higashionna Kanryo had told Kyoda to do what was comfortable for him, whether it be a closed fist or open hand.

TO'ON-RYU KATA

Sanchin

Like his teacher Higashionna, Kyoda was a staunch believer in Sanchin kata practice and was often quoted as saying: "Karate begins and ends with Sanchin" (Kinjo, 1999: 313). Kyoda's method of instruction was virtually identical to the way he had learned under Higashionna: "Sanchin for the first three years!" In the first year, Kyoda taught the basic foot movements, hand positions, and strikes, as well as the correct method of breathing for the kata. Importance was placed on basic footwork that, in contrast to modern Goju-ryu, emphasized using the toes to grip the floor instead of the ball of the foot. Kyoda likened Sanchin's foot movements as being similar to moving the feet over hot coals, that is moving quickly and smoothly in a light, sliding action (Kinjo, 1999). Generally speaking, the feet are held straighter and wider apart in comparison to the Goju-ryu Sanchin stances. For Kyoda's students, basic footwork alone took several months of training and was later taught in conjunction with striking, kicking, and blocking techniques.

To'on-ryu Sanchin breathing is also considerably different to that in modern Goju-ryu. Goju-ryu employs deep and slow inhalations through the nose followed by a powerful, almost bellowing exhalation of air from the contraction of the abdomen through the mouth, coupled with a tightening of the glottis (roughly sounding like a prolonged "hah"). This *ibuki* method of breathing is reported to have originated after Miyagi Chojun returned from his research trip to Fuzhou in 1915 (Tokashiki, 1991). In contrast, Kyoda taught the method of breathing he had learned from Higashionna. While performing Sanchin, students breath out normally and continuously, but after the hand is returned to the Sanchin guard posture, a very brief, sharp exhalation is performed, akin to blowing dust from one's hand (roughly sounding like "su").[3] Therefore, To'on-ryu does not use two stages in its breathing like Goju-ryu. Goju-ryu inhales as the arm is retracted and exhales as the punching arm is extended. As the arm is brought back into the Sanchin guard posture, another inhalation is performed with a final exhalation as the arm stops in the guard posture. In contrast, the To'on-ryu practitioner inhales as the arm is retracted, but then continually exhales as the punching arm is extended and returned to Sanchin guard posture.

By the second year, Kyoda's students were expected to conduct their own personal research and investigate what techniques the kata contained. Finally, by the third year, students were expected to begin to apply the various techniques contained within the kata in simple and complex patterns (Kinjo, 1999). Modern karateka could scarcely imagine learning in such a manner. Indeed, Kyoda's methods embraced what has been described as, "[sic] a set of standards no longer fashionable to a generation so dominated by materialism" (McCarthy 1999: 5).

Rokkishu

After learning the Sanchin kata, Kyoda next introduced his students to the techniques of Rokkishu. Rokkishu is very similar to the techniques contained in Goju-ryu's Tensho kata, but these techniques were never systemized into a formal kata. It is believed that both Kyoda Juhatsu and Miyagi Chojun based their techniques on a chapter in the *Bubishi* entitled "Rokkishu," or the "Six Hands of Chance/Energy."[4] It is of interest to note that martial arts historian Kinjo Akio has argued that, although Tensho and Rokkishu contain the hand formations illustrated in the *Bubishi*, it is more likely that Kyoda and Miyagi took their inspiration from an alternate source, perhaps forms of a Fujian origin (Kinjo, 1999). However, what this alternate source may be is still a point of speculation.

Seisan

Seisan then follows Rokkishu. There is some confusion as to exactly how many versions of Seisan Kyoda was proficient in, but it is believed that he was familiar with at least three. According to Kanzaki Shigekazu, Kyoda had learned both Higashionna Kanyu's and Kanryo's Seisan (Kinjo, 1999). In contrast, Murakami Katsumi has stated that Kyoda had also learned a version of Seisan from a man named Miyagi, who learned the form in China.[5] Murakami also states that according to Kyoda, this Miyagi was the elder brother of a man who rented a room in the Kyoda family house when he was a youngster. This Miyagi had two elder brothers, one who was quite a bit older and proficient in karate. The second eldest traveled to China and studied martial arts. It was the younger man Kyoda learned from. This man did not use any other kata. According to this man, he taught the kata exactly as he learned it in China.

Kanzaki Shigekazu practicing
Seisan kata as he learned from Kyoda.

It is believed that Kyoda received strict instruction in Seisan kata from Higashionna Kanryo. Kanzaki noted that Kyoda was especially strict with him when teaching one of Seisan's important kicks, the *sokuto-geri* (sword-foot kick). Kyoda often recounted an interesting story about the sokuto-geri to his students. Kyoda said that when Higashionna demonstrated this technique, there was a loud cracking sound. The next day when Miyagi Chojun visited Higashionna's house, Higashionna was separating the floorboards. Higashionna said to Miyagi, "there seems to be something wrong with the floor. Go take a look." When Miyagi Chojun went under the house to have a look, one of the large supporting beams under the floor was broken cleanly in two and the house was sinking down as a result (Murakami, 1991)!

According to Murakami, "The kick [sokuto-geri] in Seisan is used as a finishing technique in a kill-or-be-killed situation, and is very frightening" (Murakami, 1991: 94). Accordingly, the sokuto-geri must be performed with great power when practicing, sometimes resulting in broken floorboards. Not surprisingly, Kyoda used to check the floor before practicing this kick. He said that once he didn't check the floor well enough, and that he injured his foot quite badly (Murakami, 1991).

A young Kanzaki demonstrates the "kake-uke" and an elbow strike of the Sanseru kata. Note the resemblance of the hand with an eagle claw techniques found in some Chinese systems. Right, Kanzaki demonstrating movements from the Pechurin kata.

Sanseru

Sanseru is the next kata in To'on-ryu and was reputedly Higashionna's specialty (Kinjo, 1999). Interestingly, Higashionna's most famous and prolific student, Miyagi Chojun, reportedly did not learn Sanseru (Kinjo, 1999).[6] Despite his family's wealth, Miyagi Chojun was called up for a compulsory two-year tour in the military in 1910, and posted in Miyazaki Prefecture on the island of Kyushu. On the other hand, Kyoda, who had graduated from the Okinawa Teachers' College in 1909, was free from such obligatory military service because he did not meet the minimum height requirements as well as being an elementary and junior high school teacher (Kinjo, 1999; Shinbunsha, 1937). Therefore, it was during Miyagi's absence that Kyoda is believed to have learned Sanseru and because of that, Miyagi was reportedly very envious of Kyoda (Kinjo, 1999).

Pechurin

Pechurin (also known as Suparempei) is generally regarded as the highest kata in Naha-te (the style originating around Naha). After thoroughly teaching Sanchin, Higashionna Kanryo taught Seisan, Sanseiryu, and finally Pechurin (Murakami, 1991). According to Murakami Katsumi (1991; 1999) Pechurin is the longest Naha-te kata and contains all of the techniques of the Naha-te tradition. Many karate practitioners believe that there are many

At a Beppu Self-Defense Force dinner
gathering, Kyoda Juhatsu sits at far right.

secret techniques hidden within this kata and much practice and personal investigation is necessary to unlock its secrets. Interestingly, Kyoda Juhatsu taught this kata to only a handful of students: his son Kyoda Juko; Beppu Self-Defense Force karate instructor, Kanzaki Shigekazu; and his senior student and former Okinawan Government representative, Irah Choko.

A young Kanzaki in a posture found in the Jion kata.

Jion

As previously mentioned, it was during Kyoda's college days that he studied under Shuri-te expert Yabu Kentsu, a man who reputedly had amazing punching power (Kinjo, 1999). From Yabu, Kyoda learned the Jion kata. It is also rumored that during Kyoda's studies of Shuri-te, he also learned the Pinan kata as well as the Sochin kata, but this has not been substantiated.

Kyuda Juko (left), youngest son of Kyoda Juhatsu, performing Nepai kata in his garden. Kanzaki in a simular pose.

Kyuda Juhatsu in his early 80's relaxing at home in Beppu.

Nepai

During the several years Kyoda Juhatsu was involved with the Karate-jutsu Kenkyu Kai he learned White Crane boxing from Wu Xianhui, including the Nepai kata. Kinjo Akio (1999) has speculated that Kyoda included Nepai in his To'on-ryu because Higashionna's training was believed to be a form of Crane boxing as was Wu's.

Nepai is clearly illustrated in the *Bubishi* and means "twenty-eight," referring to the number of strikes and/or fighting postures contained within the kata.[7] Wu also taught his version of Nepai to Shito-ryu founder Mabuni Kenwa, who called the kata Nipaipo or "twenty-eight steps." However, the Shito-ryu version is considerably different from the To'on-ryu version, which still contains its "Chinese flavor" and obvious combative origins.

Conclusion

Kyoda died on August 31, 1968, at the age of 81. Among his student, Kyoda is remembered for the respect and humility he demonstrated after class. After class Kyoda would often speak at length and with respect about Higashionna Kanryo and would also recite Buddhist scripture. Murakami Katsumi remembers Kyoda in the following words:

> He was in the true sense of the word an educator. His occupation was being a principal of an elementary school for most of his life. He was a man of great integrity, I felt. Prior to moving to Oita, Kyoda had taught a number of students not only academically, but also physically and mentally through karate practice. – Murakami, 1999

For Kyoda Juhatsu, as with many Okinawans of his generation that studied karate, he refused to instruct anyone of low character or moral standing because he felt these people would give nothing back to society or karate. Ever the educator, Kyoda felt that karate training was to build both a strong body and a strong mind and that it was through this training that a person would become a valuable and productive member of society (McKenna, 1999). After his death, Kyoda's teachings were carried on by four of his students: Iraha Choko (1901-1986), Kyoda Juko (his third son, 1926-1983), Kanzaki Shigekazu (b. 1928), and Murakami Katsumi (b. 1927). Regrettably, out of these four students, only Kanzaki Shigekazu and his students are still teaching To'on-ryu, in Beppu, Oita Prefecture.

Notes

1. Although it is generally accepted that the advanced open hand kata of modern Goju-ryu were all brought to Okinawa from southern China by Higashionna (Yagi, 1984; Nagamine, 1986; Sakuda, 1987; Higaonna, 1998; Kinjo, 1999), more recent evidence suggests that Higashionna's teaching consisted of only four katas: Sanchin, Seisan, Sanseru and Suparempei/Pechurin (see Tokashiki, 1991, 1995, 1997).
2. It should be noted that To'on-ryu also uses the closed fist which is chambered just above the hip as in Shorin-ryu, compared to it being chambered at chest level as in Goju-ryu (McKenna, 1999).
3. For an overview of Sanchin kata, see Labatte (1999), and Toguchi (1976).
4. Ibid. 2
5. This was not Goju-ryu founder Miyagi Chojun, but a different man with the same surname.
6. The late Matayoshi Shinpo has also related that Miyagi Chojun did not learn the Sanseru kata from Higashionna. Miyagi may have learned Sanseru on his trip to Fuzhou in 1915 (Lohse, 1999).
7. The *Bubishi* and its contents have been translated into modern Japanese and English. Detailed translations and commentary can be found in Otsuka (1986), McCarthy (1995), and Tokashiki (1995).

References

Bishop, M. (1989). *Okinawan karate: Teachers, systems, and secret techniques.* London: A&C Black.

Fujiwara, R. (1990). *Kakutou waza no reikishi* [The history of combat]. Tokyo: Baseball Magazine.

Higaonna, M. (1998). *The history of karate: Okinawan Goju-ryu.* Thousand Oaks, CA: Dragon Assc. Inc.

Hokama, T. (1998). *History and traditions of Okinawan karate.* Hamilton, Ontario: Masters Publication.

Kanzaki, S. (2000). Personal communication.

Kinjo, A. (1999). *Karate denshin roku* [A true record of the transmission of karate]. Okinawa: Tosho Center.

Labatte, M. (1999). Elements of advanced karate techniques. *Journal of Asian Martial Arts,* 8(2): 80-95.

Lohse, F. (1999). Personal communication.

McCarthy, P. (1995). *Bubishi: The bible of karate.* Rutland, VT: Charles E. Tuttle.

McCarthy, P. (1999). *Ancient Okinawan martial arts: Koryu uchinadi.* Rutland, VT: Charles E. Tuttle.

McCarthy, P. (1999). Personal communication.

McKenna, M. (2000). Interview with Murakami Katsumi: The heart of Ryukyu's martial ways. *Journal of Asian Martial Arts*, 8(4): 28-47.

Miyagi, T. (1987). *Karate no reikishi* [Karate's history]. Naha: Hirugusha.

Murakami, K. (1975). *Karatedo to Ryukyu kobudo* [Karatedo and Ryukyu kobudo]. Tokyo: Seibidou Hakko.

Murakami, K. (1991). *Karate no kokoro to waza* [The spirit and technique of karate]. Tokyo: Shinjin Butsu Orai Sha Hakko.

Murakami, K. (1999). Personal interview.

Nagamine, S. (1986). *Okinawa karate: Sumo riki meijin den* [Okinawa karate: Legends of sumo and karate masters]. Naha: Shin.

Nakamoto, M. (1983). *Okinawa dento kobudo: Sono reikishi to tamashi* [Traditional Okinawa kobudo: It's history and soul]. Naha: Okiinsha.

Okinawa Asahi Shinbu. (1937). *Okinawa-ken jinji roku*. Naha: Okinawa Asahi Shinbu.

Otsuka, T. (1986). *Okinawa den Bubishi* [The transmission of the Okinawa Bubishi]. Tokyo: Baseball Magazine.

Sakuda, M. (1987). *Karate meijin retsuten* [Biographies of karate's masters]. Naha: Gakkan Okinawasha.

Sells, J. (1999). *Shito-ryu history*. http://www.west.net/~msource/shito history.htm

Toguchi, S. (1976). *Okinawan Goju-ryu: Fundamentals of Shorei-kan karate*. Santa Clarita, CA: Ohara.

Tokashiki, I. (1991). *Gohaku-kai nenkanshi* (yearbook). Naha: Published privately.

Tokashiki, I. (1995). *Okinawa karate hiden Bubishi shinshaku* [Okinawa karate secrets: A new interpretation of the Bubishi]. Naha: Published privately.

Tokashiki, I. (1997). *Karatedo kobudo: Kihon chousa houkokushou* [A basic investigative report on karatedo and kobudo]. Okinawa Prefectural Board of Education. Naha: Nansei.

Van Wolferen, K. (1989). *The enigma of Japanese power: People and politics in a stateless nation*. London: MacMillan.

Watatani, K., and Yamada, C. (1978). *Bugei ryuha dai jiten* [An encyclopedia of martial arts]. Tokyo: Tokyo Copy Co.

Yagi, M. (1984). *Karate seikai wo wakeru* [Karate takes flight to the world]. Okinawa: Kobundo.

Acknowledgement

Special thanks to Charles "Joe" Swift for his translation of the *Ryukyu Shinpo* newspaper article, "Okinawa no Bujutsu-ka" and with the "Seisan" section of Murakami Katsumi's book, *Spirit and Technique of Karate*.

chapter 10

Predicting Kumite Strategies: A Quantitative Approach to Karate

by Guillermo Paz-y-Miño C., Ph.D.

All photographs courtesy of G. Paz-y-Miño C.

One of the skills that needs careful development while practicing *kumite* (freestyle fighting) is the understanding of the attacker's body language. This, I believe, requires both individual learning to "predict" the attacker's intentions as well as teamwork to observe and analyze kumite performed by others. The main goal in this case should be to dissect the subtle movements that precede a kick or a punch. We all know that no matter how unique an attacker may be, his kumite becomes predictable after sparring with him for a few times. Likewise, there are general behavioral patterns applied to humans which can help us anticipate when an individual is about to attack without having to necessarily experience a previous fight with the individual in question. This idea is by no means new. Boxers, martial arts competitors, full-contact fighters, and even the "ultimate" fighters (who brake each other's bones at the Octagon) spend hours studying videos and trying to predict how future opponents will fight. This is as crucial in sparring as it is in understanding the fighting characteristics of the human body. Let's examine a few cases.

Professional boxers study how to anticipate the combination of punches that an opponent may perform by looking at subtle changes in the opponent's facial expressions. Apparently, there is some correlation between facial gestures and body movement. When a fighter lowers the chin to the side and closes the lips tightly there are high probabilities that a "hook punch" will be released from that side of the body (i.e. chin moving down to the left could mean that a punch is coming from the left). This may not be entirely surprising to someone with karate experience, since we know that, for example, a slight lifting or lowering of a shoulder implies that a front kick (*mae-geri*) may be coming from that side of the body. Some "readable" body traits that usually occur before, during, and after fighting include: increased breathing rate, flushed face (adrenaline rush), tense-rigid body, shaking (imminent attack), expanded pectorals, small pupils in wide-open-non-blinking eyes, twitching, and clenched fists.

Predicting aggressive behavior might be intuitive for most human beings. Life experiences provide us with basic skills to anticipate and avoid some potentially violent scenarios. However, anticipating how a trained fighter will use his mind during kumite requires a more elegant method than simple intuition. Kumite is a ritualized type of behavior which is performed in bouts (repetitive sequences of fighting techniques). It can be measured (i.e. time spent in sparring, number of strikes per minute, or total number of fighting bouts) and, consequently, its patterns can be predicted with some degree of accuracy. It is possible to record sparring sequences (the continuous and connected series of attacks) with a video camera, calculate their frequency of occurrence, and examine whether there are predictable combinations of strikes. The methods discussed here are relatively simple and any reader who has overcome the struggles of learning a karate routine (*kata*) should be able to understand them.

Kumite occurs in stereotyped sequences, which may be the result of a common casual factor (i.e. same block against a particular attack), or of one fighting technique stimulating or priming the next. The following examples illustrate the relative frequency with which certain karate techniques could appear in a fighter's repertoire. I will also discuss how to determine if some techniques occur in a predictable sequence or if certain strategies have a high probability of occurring together. The more frequent two techniques (or combinations of techniques) occur, the higher the probability that they will occur together. However, note that it is unusual for one technique to follow another 100% of the time. Instead, two related techniques may follow one another at some probability level that is less than 100% but higher than random chance.

Example 1: Kinematic Diagrams and Transition Frequencies

Kinematic diagrams (Greek, *kinesis* = motion) can be used to illustrate kumite sequences. In a kinematic graph (flow graph), arrows indicate transitions between techniques. An example is:

Straight Punch → Reverse Punch → Front Kick

This indicates that a front kick follows a reverse punch, which follows a straight punch (Sequence 1). (This notation is also known as Markov chains.) Transition frequencies are percentages that indicate how frequently one technique follows another. For example, a transition frequency of 60% between a reverse punch and a front kick would indicate that when a reverse punch occurs, in 60% of the cases it will be immediately followed by a front kick. Note that each technique may be followed by more than one other technique.

Sequence 1 — Frequent attacks used during kumite:
- A) straight punch,
- B) reverse punch,
- C) front kick,
- D) back-fist strike,
- E) side/back thrust kick,
- F) lower level side kick.

A reverse punch could be followed 60% of the time by a front kick and 40% of the time by a different technique (i.e. back-fist strike). In such cases, two arrows should be drawn from a reverse punch to the other two techniques.

Back-fist Strike → Reverse Punch → Front Kick
(40% of the time)　　　　　　　　　(60% of the time)

If this is the case, a karate practitioner receiving a reverse punch from this hypothetical opponent should also expect (based on probabilities) to receive either a front kick or a back-fist strike as follow-up attacks. Note that it is also possible that two techniques could follow one another and, in this case, arrows should be drawn in both directions: reverse punch ↔ front kick. When the same technique occurs twice, i.e. a front kick followed by another front kick, a "U" shaped arrow should be drawn indicating that the action repeats itself.

The majority of karatekas practice numerous techniques in a single training session. However, most participants in kumite tournaments are experts on no more than a handful of strategies, which are—of course—used intelligently. Therefore, anticipating how a future opponent will fight is by no means impossible. First, begin by compiling a list of all the individual techniques used by a karateka during kumite training (or tournament participation), as well as their frequencies of occurrence (number of techniques used per unit of time). A videotape camera will be essential in this case. Table 1 offers an example including five techniques.

Table 1

Techniques known or used by a karateka during different kumite sessions. Data corresponds to a total of ten minutes of continuous sparring sessions videotaped during various bouts of kumite. Data rounded to next highest values.

Techniques known or used by a karate practitioner	Number times the Technique was used	F = Frequency of occurrence Number of attacks per minute
Straight/lunge Punch	12 (8%)	1.2 (12÷10)
Reverse Punch	62 (40%)	6.2 (62÷10)
Front Kick	38 (25%)	3.8 (38÷10)
Back-fist Strike	10 (6%)	1.0 (10÷10)
Side Kick	32 (21%)	3.2 (32÷10)
TOTAL (%)	154 (100%)	15.4 (154÷10)

Second, record all the techniques in sequence of occurrence (i.e. straight punch → reverse punch → front kick) per attack and elaborate a Table similar to Table 2 shown below on this page. Note that most karatekas perform brief and explosive attacks with combinations of two (or three, see Example 2) techniques, which reduces the complexity of the analysis.

Third, a kinematic diagram should be elaborated with the transition-frequency values (percentages) summarized in Table 2. Figure 1 shows a graph of this kind.

Table 2

Number of times a technique in the left column was followed by other technique. Transition frequencies from one technique to another are expressed as percentages. Data rounded to next highest values.

	Straight Punch	Reverse Strike	Front Kick	Back-fist Strike	Side Kick
Straight Punch	2 (1%)	24 (15%)	14 (9%)	0 (0%)	9 (6%)
Reverse Strike	3 (2%)	0 (0%)	9 (6%)	0 (0%)	6 (4%)
Front Kick	6 (4%)	15 (10%)	7 (5%)	4 (2%)	4 (2%)
Back-fist Strike	0 (0%)	17 (11%)	3 (2%)	0 (0%)	12 (8%)
Side Kick	1 (1%)	6 (4%)	5 (3%)	6 (4%)	1 (1%)
TOTAL (%)	12 (8%)	62 (40%)	38 (25%)	10 (6%)	32 (21%)

Figure 1

Kinematic diagram showing transitions (arrows) and transition frequencies (percentages) among five different karate techniques. Data from Table 2.

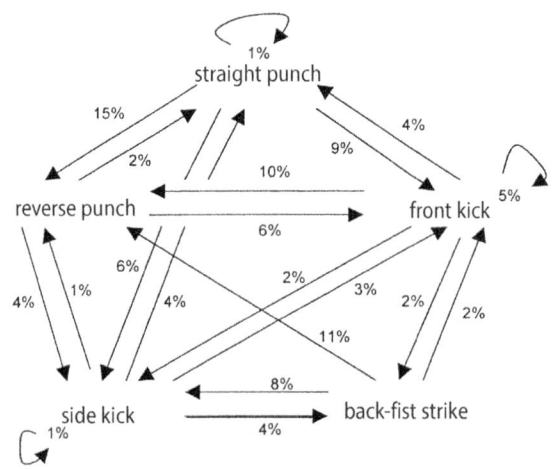

Fourth, determine the techniques that occurred with the highest frequency (most common ones). In this case, it is possible to group the data in three different ways:

❶ as a percentage of the total number of techniques recorded (i.e. the opponent uses a reverse punch in 40% of his attacks, Tables 1 and 2),
❷ as a frequency per unit of time (i.e. 6.2 reverse punch attacks per minute, Table 1), or
❸ as a percentage of the total samples (bouts) in which a given technique occurs (i.e. 8 out of 10 different combinations of techniques included at least 1 reverse punch = 80%, data not shown).

These three approaches provide different but complementary information on how to assess fighting strategies. Data presented in Tables 1 and 2 should be carefully studied, as well as the kinematic diagram. Based on this information, we can portray the fighting profile (distinctive signature) of this karateka: He uses a reverse punch, a front kick, and a side kick as his favorite techniques (40, 25, and 21% of the attacks, respectively). During a minute of sparring, we should expect him to throw a reverse punch twice as much times as either kick. And we should expect at least one reverse punch in any of his combinations of attacks.

The kinematic diagram shows how often this fighter connects with a straight punch, a back-fist strike, or a front kick with his most favorite technique, a reverse punch (15, 11, and 10% of the transition frequencies, respectively). It also shows how a front kick and a side kick follow one another in a few cases (2 and 3%, respectively). A straight punch is the technique that initiates most of the attacks, while a back-fist strike is preferably used for connection between attacks. Absence of arrows between techniques (i.e. between a straight punch and a back-fist strike) and unidirectional connections (i.e. between a back-fist strike and a reverse punch) are also possible. Can you hypothesize why?

Finally, the most relevant values summarized in Table 2 (i.e. data for a reverse punch, a front kick, and a side kick) should be analyzed statistically with a simple Chi-square test. This test is designed to assess the degree of correspondence between the real data (observed values reported in Table 2) and the values we should expect if the sequences were the result of random chance (expected values):

$$\text{Expected value} = \frac{\text{Row total} \times \text{Column total}}{\text{Grand TOTAL}}$$

Table 3

Observed and expected values (in parenthesis) in respect to the number of times a technique in the left column was followed by other technique.

	Reverse Punch	Front Kick	Side Kick	Column Total
Straight Punch	24 (22.1)	14 (13.5)	9 (11.4)	47
Reverse Punch	0 (7.0)	9 (4.3)	6 (3.6)	15
Front Kick	15 (12.2)	7 (7.5)	4 (6.3)	26
Back-fist Strike	17 (15.0)	3 (9.2)	12 (7.8)	32
Side Kick	6 (5.6)	5 (3.5)	1 (2.9)	12
Row Total	62	38	32	Grand TOTAL 132

The Chi-square value can be calculated using the equation:

$$X^2 = \sum_{i=1}^{k} \frac{(\text{Observed value} - \text{Expected value})^2}{\text{Expected value}}$$

$$X^2 = \frac{(24 - 22.1)^2}{22.1} + \frac{(0 - 7.0)^2}{7.0} + \ldots = 24.08$$

A high Chi-square value $X^2 = 24.08$ (df = 2, p ≤ 0.05) suggests that our transition frequencies (Table 2) and kinematic diagram (Figure 1) represent a valid prediction about the fighting profile of this karateka. The observed values are significantly different from the expected ones. The reader may realize that the analysis presented in this section could become even more sophisticated if it is applied to triplets of techniques, as shown below.

Example 2: Triplets of Techniques

This example includes additional calculations with the purpose to demonstrate that complex kumite strategies which include three continuous attacks can also be predicted. Relax, do not be afraid of more numbers. If you are able to perform the classical triplet of techniques practiced at any dojo— a straight punch, a reverse punch, and a front kick—you should find this case easy to comprehend.

Any average karate practitioner is capable of designing six different strategies based on these three techniques:

1) Straight Punch → Reverse Punch → Front Kick
2) Straight Punch → Front Kick → Reverse Punch
3) Reverse Punch → Front Kick → Straight Punch
4) Reverse Punch → Straight Punch → Front Kick
5) Front Kick → Straight Punch → Reverse Punch, and
6) Front Kick → Reverse Punch → Straight Punch

If the karateka in question is limited to use only these six alternatives during a sparring session, it should be expected that he will execute some triplets more frequently than others. The easiest and most comfortable combinations will be performed more often than the most difficult and awkward ones (Sequences 2 and 3). Again, a video tape could help quantify the occurrence of the various triplets. Since every individual is unique and his performance of techniques will follow, in general, a normal distribution (based on the individual's "universe" of knowledge or preference = six techniques), his karate mind will always process information in a distinctive way.

Sequence 2
A classical triplet of attacks designed to surprise the opponent by combining two punches and a sweep/kick to the leg. A) upper straight punch to the face, B) short-range punch to the stomach, C) a vigorous circular sweep to the leg. D) This last technique is intended to break the opponent's balance.

Sequence 3

Counter-attack against a direct straight punch to the face. In this case, the defender on the left, performs a very effective triplet consisting of: A) change in the trajectory of the attack by blocking with the edge of the hand, B) wrist grab, and C) back-fist strike to the face. This triplet can be executed in a fraction of a second.

Interestingly, the number of sparring strategies based on triplet combinations will increase significantly if more than three techniques are incorporated into the karateka's repertoire. How many triplets can a karateka design with ten different techniques in mind? We can calculate this value by applying a simple formula:

$$Nk = Nt \times 2 \left\{ (Nt - 2) + \sum_{a = (Nt - 2) - 1}^{n} \right\}$$

- Where, Nk = Number of kumite strategies based on a combination of three different techniques (number of triplets)
- Nt = Number of techniques known or used by a karate practitioner (in this case 10)
- $Nk = 10 \times 2 \{(10 - 2) + \Sigma [(10 - 2) - 1] + ... \}$
- $Nk = 20 \{ (8) + [7 + 6 + 5 + 4 + 3 + 2 + 1] \}$
- $Nk = 20 \{ (8) + [28] \}$
- $Nk = 720$

To illustrate the impressive amount of triplet combinations that can be created by any karateka, please refer to Table 4. As the reader may realize, knowing very few techniques is enough to create numerous combinations (something that karate students should keep in mind!).

Table 4

Number of triplet combinations that can be created by a karateka based on the number of techniques known or used by the karate practitioner.

N_t = Number of techniques known or used by a karateka	N_k = Number of triplet combinations that can be created by a karateka
3	6
4	24
8	336
10	720

It is evident that very few fighters will apply 720 different triplets of kumite techniques in their entire karate careers. Memorizing a dozen might be challenging enough for most of us. Therefore, we should expect the vast majority of karate practitioners to focus their training on few effective triplets. Table 5 summarizes frequencies and transition frequencies from one triplet to another. In this case, only five different triplets are shown. The corresponding kinematic diagram for this data is shown in Figure 2.

Table 5

Number of times a triplet in the left column was followed by another triplet. Transition frequencies from one triplet to another are expressed as percentages. Data rounded to next highest values.

Table 5	Straight Punch→ Reverse Punch→ Front Kick	Front Kick→ Straight Punch→ Reverse Punch	Straight Punch→ Side Kick→ Back Kick	Round House Kick→ Back-fist Strike→ Reverse Punch	Reverse Punch→ Front Kick→ Back Kick
Straight Punch→ Reverse Punch→ Front Kick	3 (2%)	9 (6%)	4 (3%)	16 (10%)	10 (6%)
Front Kick→ Straight Punch→ Reverse Punch	10 (6%)	3 (2%)	8 (5%)	4 (3%)	4 (3%)
Straight Punch→ Side Kick→ Back Kick	4 (3%)	5 (3%)	2 (1%)	8 (5%)	2 (1%)
Round House Kick→ Back-fist strike→ Reverse Punch	5 (3%)	12 (7%)	4 (3%)	3 (2%)	4 (3%)
Reverse Punch→ Front Kick→ Back Kick	8 (5%)	8 (5%)	2 (1%)	16 (10%)	3 (2%)
TOTAL (%)	30 (19%)	37 (23%)	20 (13%)	47 (30%)	23 (15%)

This karateka's favorite triplets are:

- Round House Kick → Back-fist Strike → Reverse Punch (30% of the attacks),
- Front Kick → Straight Punch → Reverse Punch (23% of the attacks), and
- Straight Punch → Reverse Punch → Front Kick (19% of the attacks).

The kinematic diagram suggests that whenever this fighter throws the combination "straight punch → reverse punch → front kick", he immediately follows up with the triplet "round house kick → back-fist strike → reverse punch" (10% of the follow up attacks). Similarly, when he uses the attack "reverse punch → front kick → back kick", the follow-up triplet is "round house kick → back-fist strike → reverse punch" (10%). This attacker tends to finish most of his explosive triplets with a reverse punch or a front kick (Table 5). Do you see why?

Figure 2

Kinematic diagram showing transitions (arrows) and transition frequencies (percentages) among five different triplets of karate techniques. Data from Table 5.

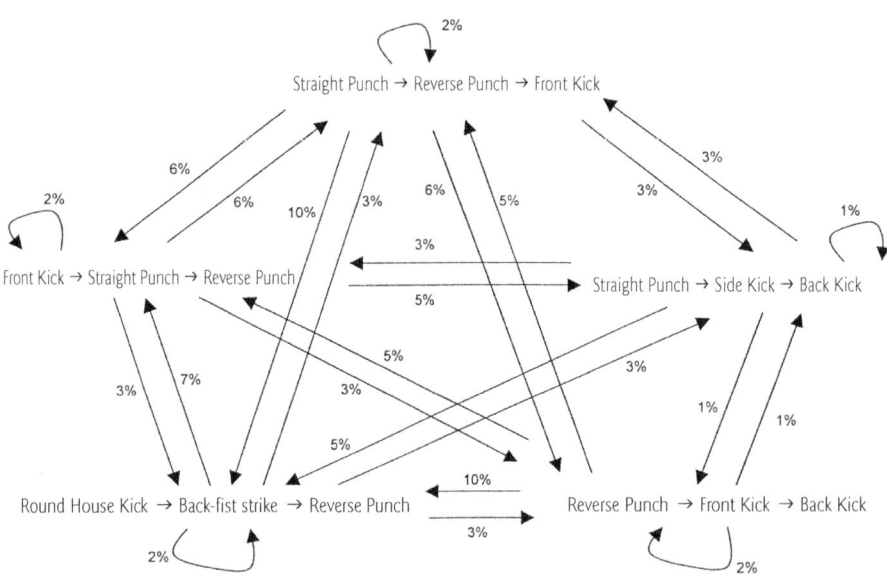

Finally, the most relevant values summarized in Table 5 (i.e. data for round house kick → back-fist strike → reverse punch; front kick → straight punch → reverse punch; and straight punch → reverse punch → front kick) can now be analyzed statistically with a Chi-square test (same as above). Here are the results: $X^2 = 23.3$ (df = 2, $p \leq 0.05$). Therefore, the transition frequencies (Table 5) and kinematic diagram (Figure 2) represent a valid prediction about the fighting profile of this karateka. The observed values are significantly different from the expected ones (analysis not shown).

Concluding Remarks

The reader may notice that kinematic diagrams can be drawn for fighting strategies that include single techniques, as well as combinations of any number of techniques (Examples 1 and 2 together). When listing the strategies on a table, what is important is to separate the attacks into distinguishable units (bouts of fighting behavior). Sometimes, the strategy may be a single front kick (the bout will be equal to one technique and that will be all!). In other cases, the bout may consist of a pair, a triplet, or a quartet of techniques in a sequence. Even blocks and shifting movements of the entire body can be included in the analysis (Sequence 4).

Sequence 4

Some single techniques are very effective during kumite, particularly when performed with confidence and explosive motion.

A) A "hybrid" technique against a direct punch. In this case, a rising-block is simultaneously combined with a back fist to the face; timing is perfect.
B) Prompt block of a front kick with a scooping block (*suki-uke*); the attacker is ready to be thrown.

C) Beautiful block of a punch and immediate counter-attack in close range with a reverse punch to the chin.
D) Similar counter-attack, but in this case with a "hook" punch.
E) Double combination at close range. Hooking block (*kake-uke*) is executed at the same time that a back-fist strike reaches the face.

Sequence 5

Application of karate series for demonstration and teaching purposes only.

A) Strong rising block aimed to stop the attacker while the defender enters into the attacker's individual space.
B) Inertia puts the attacker in a vulnerable position, ready for a
C-D) throw, or a back break.

In the examples discussed above, it has been assumed that a karateka's own fighting behavior is his primary source of stimulation for sequences of attacks or combinations of attacks (intra-individual sequences). That is, the fighting behavior of the opponent has been disregarded as an important variable. That decision is usually a subjective one left to the experience and discretion of who conducts the observations and analyses. It is evident that important stimuli may be originated from the opponent (inter-individual sequences), a situation that loosely could be described as "kumite communication" (which some readers may well argue about). Under those conditions, it is possible to cast the data into a table known as a sociometric matrix. As with the intra-individual analysis discussed earlier, associations found between an attacker's behavior and a receiver's behavior are only that, associations.

No casual relationship is explicitly demonstrated, although it is implied when the terms *nage* (transmitter) and *uke* (receiver) are used. This, however, will be the subject of a future article.

The value of kinematic graphs and transition frequencies is that they not only provide us with experimental methods to measure karate (or any fighting art) and develop testable hypotheses about it, but also that they give us alternatives for training and teaching (Sequence 5). Anyone could be the target of this kind of analysis based on the association of variables (different techniques subject to numerous interactions). And any instructor could explore multiple kumite and solo practice scenarios based on just a few techniques. The intellectual challenge for a karate practitioner should be to develop creative strategies for kumite and solo practice and, at the same time, make these strategies not too evident for others. A difficult task, indeed!

The readable and detectable body language that helps us predict some of the "attacker's intentions" should continue to be studied in our every day dojo training. Developing "good instincts" is always essential for karate improvement. However, mental strategies—usually undetectable by our common senses—can only be revealed with a probabilistic and mathematical assessment. It is obvious that a karate practitioner confronted with different fighters may perform different strategies, adapting himself to the challenges imposed by diverse stimuli (above). Nonetheless, his distinct individuality will remain detectable, measurable, and therefore predictable.

If karate is to become an Olympic sport, kumite will be fought not only on the mat, but also in the laboratory where sport science will take over the strategic planning of sparring. A collection of videotapes could help us document and scientifically measure the chronological drifting in kumite strategies of particular athletes, and even of karate schools that have unique ways of preparing their students for combat. Kinematic diagrams and transition frequencies may well be just a couple of methods, among many others, to quantify kumite. Consequently, our sophisticated analysis of kumite in particular—and of martial arts in general—may be only limited by the martial artist's imagination.

Acknowledgment

A special thanks to Sensei Robert Miller and Tabitha Miller, from the Institute for Traditional Karate Research-St. Louis, for their demonstrations of techniques and kumite sequences.

Glossary

Gyaku-zuki: reverse punch.

Kumite: sparring.

Mae-geri: front kick.

Mawashi-geri: round house kick.

Nage: person who transmits the technique.

Oi-zuki: straight/lunge punch.

Uke: blocking; person who receives the technique.

Uraken (Uraken-uchi): back-fist strike, also called *riken-zuki*.

Ushiro-geri: back kick.

Yoko-geri: side kick.

Suggested Readings

Evans, B. (1998). *Karate rules*. London, England: Ward Lock.

Lehner, P. (1996). *Handbook of ethological methods*. Cambridge: Cambridge University Press.

Martin, P., and Bateson, P. (1993). *Measuring behaviour*. Cambridge: Cambridge University Press.

Nakayama, M. (1978). *Best karate: Kumite I*. Tokyo: Kodansha International.

Nakayama, M. (1979). *Best karate: Kumite II*. Tokyo: Kodansha International.

Pieter, W., and Hejimans, J. (1997). *Scientific coaching for Olympic taekwondo*. Achen, Germany: Meyer & Meyer Verlag.

Sugiyama, S. (1992). *Kumite-gata*. Chicago: Harlem High Vocational Offset.

Siegel, S., and Castellan, N. (1988). *Nonparametric statistic for the behavioral sciences*. New York: McGraw-Hill.

Wagner, J. (2000). Reading hostile people. *Black Belt Magazine*, 38(1): 18-19.

chapter 11

Karate Pioneer Yabu Kentsu, 1866–1937

by Joseph Svinth, M.A.

Yabu Kentsu with his three oldest sons in 1906. The standing youth is 18-year old Kenden. On the left is Kenyu, who later shortened his name to Ken, and on the right is Kenshin. This photograph, or any negatives derived therefrom, may not be copyrighted. *Courtesy of the Yabe/Yasui Family Collection.*

Introduction

A couple years ago I was researching sumo and judo in Oregon before World War II, and during the research I started corresponding with Homer Yasui. One day Homer asked, "By the way, are you interested in karate, too? My wife's grandfather did karate."

"Sure," I replied. "So who was grandpa?"

"Kentsu Yabu," replied Homer. "Ever heard of him?"

Actually, I had. He was a well-known Shorin-ryu karate teacher of the early twentieth century, a peer of Funakoshi and others of that generation. He was supposed to have introduced karate to Hawai'i during the 1920's, but so far as I knew, there weren't too many pictures or reliable English-language stories about him.

"Oh," said Homer. "Would you like some?"

∙ ∙ ∙

The eldest son of Yabu Kenten[1] and Shun Morinaga, Yabu Kentsu was born at Shuri City, Yamakawa-cho, Ni-chome #8, in 1866. Known in childhood as Kamadu, he had three brothers, three sisters, and three half-sisters: second brother Kencho, a graduate of the Medicine and Biology Institute (Ishi Isei Kyoshujo), died at age 25; third brother, Kenkyu, was a well-known painter and calligrapher whose pen names included Kinto and Muka Sanjin (Yabu, 1986: 98-99).

The family was of mid-aristocracy (*pechin*), and had been ever since the Ryukyuan genealogical bureau was first established in 1689. As a group, the middle aristocracy worked in jobs such as civil administration and domestic law enforcement. So, besides often having acquired some proficiency in methods of physical restraint, male members of this class typically received training in calligraphy, politics, and Confucian pedagogy (McCarthy, 1994: 1). What this meant for the Yabu family was that Kentsu's paternal grandfather, Ken'yo, was the archery instructor for Lord Ikegusuku, while his father was a court calligrapher (Yabu, 1986: 98-99; Yasui, 1998 Sep. 6; Yasui, 1998 Dec. 12).

As a young man, Kentsu received training in what would become known as Shorin-ryu karate. Hokama Tetsuhiro says that Yabu's teacher was Matsumura Sokon (1998: 35). On the other hand, Dave Lowry says that Yabu's teacher was Itosu "Ankoh" Yasutsune (1985: 11). Since both Matsumura and Itosu were well-known Okinawan karate teachers, Yabu probably studied with each at different times.

When Yabu began this training is unclear. Dave Lowry says that as a child Yabu was bigger and stronger than his playmates, so was naturally attracted to karate (1985: 11). If this is correct, then he probably started circa 1880. On the other hand, in *Karate-Do Nyumon*, Funakoshi Gichin wrote:

> During the Sino-Japanese War [of 1894-1895] a young man trained earnestly with [Ankoh] Itosu for several months before joining the army. When he was assigned to the Kumamoto Division, the division medical examiner, noticing his well-balanced muscular development, said, "I hear you're from Okinawa. What martial art did you train in?" The recruit replied that farm labor was all he had ever done. But a friend who was with him blurted out, "He's been practicing karate." The doctor only murmured, "I see, I see," but he was deeply impressed. – 1988: 25-26

A group photo taken in 1908, in which Yabu Kentsu appears third from the right in the back row. The location is said to be the school where Yabu received his training as a teacher. If so, then the building was probably part of the Prefectural Teachers' Training College, where Itosu Ankoh taught karate from 1905. However, it could also be the Prefectural Number One School, where Yabu worked as a teacher. The original photograph belonged to a man named Nakahara Tetsushijo and is presently in the collection of Ryukyu University history professor Hiyane Teruo. Miyuki Yabe Yasui got her copy from her cousin Yohko Yabu Ikeda while visiting Shuri in 1993. This photograph, or any negatives derived therefrom, may not be copyrighted.

Detail from the above photo of Kentsu Yabu. He would have been about 42 years old when this photo was taken.
Courtesy of the Yabe/Yasui Family Collection.

So perhaps Yabu only began his training after deciding to go into the service in 1891.

Despite being exempt from Japanese military service—Okinawans were not yet subject to Japanese conscription—and although he had married Takahara Oto around 1887 and the couple had a son, Kenden, in 1888, Yabu was still among the first Okinawans to voluntarily serve in the Japanese Army. His goal was evidently to prove to the Japanese that Okinawans could be every bit as good of soldiers as any home island Japanese (Yabu, 1986: 98-99; Yasui, 1998 Sep. 6).

The Japanese Army sent Yabu to a school for noncommissioned officers. Upon graduation, he was promoted to sergeant. He was then sent to China, where he saw service during the Sino-Japanese War (Kim, 1974: 64-65; Noble, n.d.: 32; Yasui, 1998 Sep. 6).

There is a story told on Okinawa that Yabu was promoted to lieutenant before his discharge, and that his uniform and sword were subsequently kept in Shuri Castle (Kim, 1974: 64-65; Noble, n.d.: 32; Yasui, 1998 Sep. 6). However, family documents do not verify this, and Yabu's students often called him "sergeant." Research into Japanese military archives is probably required to resolve the question.

I am unaware of any further information concerning Yabu's military career. However, at the speculative levels, Richard Kim has written that Yabu perfected his karate on the battlefield against the Chinese (Kim, 1974: 64-65). George Alexander wrote that "Yabu [reportedly] fought over sixty lethal karate duels and was never defeated" (1991: 64). But, men who knew Yabu recalled that he was someone who despised hyperbole: "When Kentsu Yabu came into the room, all the brag, all the talk, all the opinions, they stopped," Dave Lowry has quoted an unnamed source as saying. Such stories are probably heroic rather than factual (1985: 13).

On a more plausible level, Graham Noble has cited hearsay evidence that one of Yabu's military subordinates died after Yabu struck him. During the subsequent inquiry, Yabu told investigators that he had struck the other man with his open palm, which was legal under Japanese military law, rather than with his fist, which was not.[2] The court accepted his statement after seeing him break some boards with his fist, and as a result dropped the manslaughter charge (Noble, n.d.: 32). Again, this story is hearsay and needs corroboration.

Upon separation from the service, Yabu returned to Okinawa. After settling in, he began studying at Shuri's Prefectural Teachers' Training College. While there, he frequently helped Itosu Ankoh, who was then leading a campaign to have karate made part of the Okinawan public schools' physical education curriculum, by giving public demonstrations of karate *katas*, or practice forms. His favorite kata was reportedly Gojushiho, an old Chinese form distinguished by its use of open-handed palm-heel and finger strikes (Noble, n.d.: 32-33). As for the way he did this kata, Dave Lowry cites an unnamed witness as saying that Yabu's version was unusual because "it was nothing at all like a dance, more like the motion of the surf, soft, soft, soft, as it comes in, then smash—hard like a rock" (1985: 12).

In 1902, Yabu became a karate instructor at Shuri's Prefectural Number One School (Hokama, 1998: 88). Former students recalled that his instruction stressed constant repetitions of Naihanchi kata. Toward that end, he liked to say that students should do 10,000 kata a year (Noble, n.d.: 33). Probably the latter statement was hyperbolic; in Japanese when one says "ten thousand," one is not necessarily being literal, but it still gives an idea of the level of technical proficiency Yabu expected from his karate students.

Since Yabu was one of Okinawa's earliest public school karate teachers, the modern Shotokai karate teacher Harada Mitsusuke, who met various Okinawan teachers while living in Brazil, has speculated that modern karate's tendency toward doing things "by the numbers" may be attributable to Yabu (Noble, n.d.: 33). But as Japanese scholars have since shown that all Japanese athletic training was heavily militarized during the 1930's and 1940's, that is probably exaggerating things a bit (Abe, Kiyohara, and Nakajima, 1990: 27-43).

During his life, Yabu's peers frequently honored him. For example, during the mid-1910's, he received the gift of a sword from Higa Toki, who had himself received the weapon from the Chinese leader Sun Yat-sen in appreciation for his service to China during the Chinese Revolution (*History of the Okinawans*, 1988: 12-14).[3] In 1924, Yabu was asked to become a charter member of the Okinawa Tode Research Club, an organization dedicated to protecting and preserving *tode*, as Ryukyuans then called *karate* (Bishop, 1989: 153). And in 1936, he was asked to join the council of distinguished karate teachers that ultimately agreed to change the name of karate from its old characters (*kanji*) meaning "Chinese hands" into its modern characters meaning "empty hands" (Funakoshi, 1973: 3-4; Funakoshi, 1988: 24-25; Hokama, 1998: 36, 93).[4]

George Alexander and Richard Kim have written that Yabu once defeated the famous karate fighter Motobu Choki during a private contest held at Motobu's Okinawan estate (Alexander, 1991: 64; Kim, 1974: 64-65). Kim said that during their battle, "The air cracked with the sound of loud *kiai*,[5] feet shuffling, punches and kicks landing on human flesh, and the excited gasps of the few privileged viewers" (1974: 64-65). However, less breathless researchers have been unable to find evidence proving that the two men ever fought, let alone such vivid descriptions of their contest (Noble, 2000; Silvan, 1998: 93).

Dave Lowry has speculated that the contest between Motobu and Yabu was not in karate, but in *tegumi,* or Ryukyuan sumo (1985: 13). That sounds plausible, especially since Yabu went out of his way to organize tegumi matches during the Okinawan celebrations held near Fresno in July 1921 and August 1922.[6] The *History of Okinawans* (1988: 339) reports that:

> Sergeant Kentsu Yabe[7] was a great fan of sumo. In Okinawa, he had been so enthusiastic that he got involved in every match that came up. His talking of sumo fired up all the younger men, and they decided to hold a big match. Considering the absence of entertainment in the life of the issei immigrant, those who participated in the sumo returned home pleased and happy.

Yabu Kentsu with his son Kenden and daughter-in-law Mitsuye. The photo was probably taken in 1921-1922, when Mitsuye was pregnant with eldest daughter Emi. This photograph, or any negatives derived therefrom, may not be copyrighted.
Courtesy of the Yabe/Yasui Family Collection.

Yabu was in Fresno visiting his eldest son, Kenden, who was then living in California. Although this visit is sometimes said to be the first visit of an Okinawan karate teacher to the US, this is not quite correct. According to the *History of the Okinawans in North America*, Nakaza Seijo, who moved to San Francisco around 1902, used karate during various physical confrontations with *hakujin* (European Americans) who enjoyed harassing Japanese. Neither did Yabu teach karate while in California. Instead, he was simply visiting his son, who had specifically asked his father to not "wear his sword" while visiting the United States (*History of the Okinawans*, 1988: 341).

Yabu Kenden emigrated to Hawai'i around 1908. After four years, he moved to California. His "Certificate of Fact of Issue of a Passport" signed by the Japanese consul in Los Angeles in 1912 says that his purpose for coming to America was to study Western theology. However, in Hawai'i, he was an agricultural worker and, in California, he worked for many years as a gardener. He eventually became more interested in socialism than Christianity (Yabu, 1986: 99; Yasui, 1998 Sep. 6; Yasui, 1998 Dec. 12).

In 1919, Kenden married a Japanese woman, Mitsuye Jyoko, and, by 1921, she was pregnant with the couple's first child. The family therefore believes that Kentsu's two visits to the United States were made in hopes that his eldest son would give him a grandson. Writes Kenden's son-in-law Homer Yasui (1998 Sep. 6):

> Since Kenden was Kentsu's firstborn and a son at that—the *chonan* —it was very important that a male child be produced. It didn't happen that way, because their fourth child was also a girl. That child is my wife, Miyuki Yabe Yasui, who was born on September 18, 1926.
>
> The story goes that it was Kentsu's intention—if the child was a boy —to take him back to Shuri to raise in a proper Okinawan fashion. Japanese fathers in those days were very powerful, so it wouldn't have been a bit surprising if Kenden and Mitsuye would have allowed that. Even in my generation, our fathers were powerful, and the chonans quite a bit less so, but still powerful nevertheless. Anyway, since Miki turned out to be yet another girl, Grandpa Kentsu returned home, probably disgusted, and certainly empty-handed.

The Yabes' oldest daughter, Emi, was born during Grandpa Kentsu's first visit and was about seven years old during his second visit. All she remembers of the second visit was that her grandfather dearly loved sweets and that her mother complained that Grandpa always wore shirts that were about an inch too big around the collar. Their other children (two of whom were still alive in 1998) were too young to remember anything of this visit (Yasui, 1998 November 7).

Eight of Okinawa's leading karate men. Back row, left to right: Shiroma Shinpan, Maeshiro Choryo, Chibana Chosin, Nakasone Genwa. Front row, left to right: Kyan Chotoku, Yabu Kentsu, Hanashiro Chomo, Miyagi Chojun. A frequently reproduced photo—it commemorates a major meeting hosted by an Okinawan newspaper in October 1936— its first known publication was in *Karatedo Taikan* in 1938.
Photo courtesy of Graham Noble.

On his way back to Okinawa, Yabu Kentsu visited the Territory of Hawai'i. There, a local Japanese association had Yabu give Hawai'i's first public karate demonstration.

The demonstration took place at the Nuuanu YMCA, then located at Fourth and Vineyard in Honolulu, on Friday, July 8, 1927. Special guests included American Army and Navy officers and a visiting Waseda University baseball team (Nippu Jiji, 1927 July 6). Afterwards, a *Honolulu Advertiser* reporter wrote (1927 July 9):

Compared with jiujitsu, karate is more destructive. Jiujitsu is the art of throwing and holding and is slow compared to karate. No weapons of any kind are used and blows are struck with the clenched fist and aimed at vital spots such as the solar plexus, point of jaw, and other nerve centers. It enables a little man to successfully defend himself in hand-to-hand conflict with a larger adversary.

Lieutenant Yabe stated that boxing was being introduced into Japan but he doubted if it would ever be as popular or used as universally as karate. Legs as well as arms are brought into play.

The various holds and poses of karate were shown and described as follows: Kusanku, Gojushiho, Naihanchi, Sanchin, preparatory drill, Pinan... Passai, etc. The talk and drill were highly pleasing and instructive. The big crowd appeared to be duly impressed with the possibilities of this sport.

The latter statement was not simply hype. Yabu's demonstrations encouraged *nisei* (people of Japanese descent, born and educated in the US), such as Thomas Miyashiro, to subsequently establish karate dojo that offered instruction to anyone, not just people of Okinawan descent (Haines, 1968: 119-121).

Yabu Kentsu circa 1927.
This photograph, or any negatives derived therefrom, may not be copyrighted.
Courtesy of the Yabe/Yasui Family Collection.

During this visit, Yabu also traveled to Kauai (Lowry, 1985: 12). "Although we digress a bit," notes the *History of the Okinawans in North America*, "Yabe learned a great deal about *samisen* (the stringed musical instrument) and the performing arts in Hawai'i from one of his students there, Ryokin Nakama" (1988: 341). Which is not surprising: apparently Yabu financed part of his trip by taking orders for Ryukyuan artifacts such as musical instruments and then mailing them to Hawai'i upon his return to Okinawa (Goodin, 1999 Apr. 9).

In 1936, Yabu visited Tokyo. Since he had terminal tuberculosis, it wouldn't be too surprising to learn that he was visiting physicians. Speculation aside, while in Japan, Yabu watched the young Nagamine Shoshin practicing karate. According to Mark Bishop, Yabu then warned Nagamine that karate's katas were undergoing rapid change in Japan and that it was up to Nagamine and other young men of his generation to preserve the Okinawan katas in their traditional forms (1989: 86).

Less than a year later, Yabu was dead. While the ancestral home was destroyed during the fighting in 1945, second son Yabu Ken later rebuilt the house and Ken's widow, Emi, lives there to this day.

Notes

1. "From early times until fairly recently," wrote Sakamaki Shunzo, "every [Ryukyuan] child was given a *domyo* (or *warabe-na*)—literally, his 'childhood name'. For a long time, it was generally his only name throughout his lifetime, since most members of the upper classes did not have surnames and formal names (*nanori*) until after 1689, and commoners did not have surnames until the 1870s" (1964: 13). In general, the oldest son took the same *domyo* as the paternal grandfather while younger sons took the names of relatives or friends. Although there were only about fifty individual *domyo*, suffixes ("Big," "Little," etc.) differentiated between grandfather and grandson while differences in pronunciation distinguished between aristocrats and commoners.

2. The Japanese Army used to encourage its commissioned and noncommissioned officers to use corporal discipline as a form of what would today be called "tough love." Indeed, the usual euphemism for the practice was *bentatsu*, or "act of love." For an introduction to the topic, see Chang, 1997: 217.

3. Arriving in San Francisco in 1896, Higa is also known as the first Okinawan

to have lived in the United States.
4   Although the Okinawan karate teacher Hanashiro Chomo proposed the new name as early as 1905, it was not formally adopted until October 1936. The fact that Japan was at war with Russia in 1905 and China in 1936 undoubtedly had something to do with the timing of the name change.
5   Literally, "a blending of vital energy," the word *kiai* properly refers to a manifestation of inner harmonics and discords transmitted directly from the psychic and physical center of the body. In a classic short story, "The Shout," English writer Robert Graves once wrote of an audible expression of such energy: "My shout is not a matter of tone or vibration but something not to be explained. It is a shout of pure [energy], and there is no fixed place for it on the scale." However, in North American and Japanese karate classes, the word is usually more narrowly defined as the noise that the athlete makes while executing a punch or kick.
6   In *tegumi*, officials restarted bouts whenever one of the players was thrown to his stomach or knees. Also, judges only counted falls to the back. A typical outdoor tournament started about 10:30 a.m. and continued until dark. To give everyone a better chance of winning, American competitors were sometimes divided by age and weight. If so, then divisions were usually 150 pounds and over, 130-149 pounds, and 129 pounds and under. Hawaiian blue laws, by the way, required players to wear a pair of shorts under their wrestling belts (for further details, see Adaniya, et al., 1988: 37-38).
7   "Yabe" is the Japanese pronunciation of the two Chinese characters pronounced "Yabu" in the Shuri dialect of the Ryukyuan language. The change in pronunciation was made unilaterally by some individuals (including Yabu's son Kenden) during the 1910's and officially by the Education Society of Okinawa in 1937. However, the changes "in the reading of surnames were more effective in overseas areas than in Japan proper," noted Higa Shuncho. "The reason for this was that in Japan proper, although a person announced a change in the reading of his name, the written characters were not altered, and other people did not readily accept the changed reading. On the other hand, in overseas areas, names were spelled out in Roman writing and there was immediate acceptance of the pronunciation indicated by the Romanized version" (Sakamaki, 1964: 38).

References

Abe, I., Kiyohara, Y., and Nakajima, K. (1990). Sport and physical education under fascistization in Japan. *Bulletin of Health & Sport Sciences*, University of Tsukuba, (13): 25-46; reprinted at http://ejmas.com/jalt/jaltart_abe_

0600.htm. Downloaded September 26, 2000.

Adaniya, R., Njus, A., and Yamate, M. (Eds.). (1988). *Of andagi and sanshin: Okinawan culture in Hawai'i*. Honolulu: Hui O Laulima.

Alexander, G. (1991). *Okinawa: Island of karate*. Lake Worth, FL: Yamazato Publications.

Bishop, M. (1989). *Okinawan karate: Teachers, styles and secret techniques*. London: A&C Black.

Chang, I. (1997). *The rape of Nanking: The forgotten holocaust of World War II*. New York: Basic Books.

Funakoshi, G. (1973). *Karate-do kyohan: The master text*. Tokyo: Kodansha International.

Funakoshi, G. (1988). *Karate-do nyumon: The master introductory text*. Tokyo: Kodansha International.

Goodin, C. (1999, April 9). Personal communication.

Haines, B. (1968). *Karate's history and traditions*. Rutland, VT: Charles E. Tuttle.

Kobashigawa, B. (Trans.). (1988). *History of the Okinawans in North America*. Translation of *Hokubei Okinawajin shi*. Los Angeles: University of California and the Okinawan Club of America.

Hokama, T. (1998). *History and traditions of Okinawan karate*. (C. Borkowski, Trans.). Hamilton, Ontario: Masters Publication.

Kim, R. (n.d.). The sergeant. *Karate Illustrated*, page unknown. (Xerographic copy courtesy Graham Noble).

Kim, R. (1974). *The weaponless warriors*. Burbank, CA: Ohara Publications.

Lowry, D. (1985). Yabu Kentsu, An Okinawan karateman. *Karate Illustrated*, (7): 10-13.

Lum, S. (1999, April 2). Wanted: Hawaii karate 'pioneers', *Hawaii Herald*, A-13.

McCarthy, P. (1995). *Bubishi: The bible of karate*. Rutland, VT: Charles E. Tuttle.

McCarthy, P. (1987). *Classical kata of Okinawan karate*. Burbank, CA: Ohara Publications.

McCarthy, P. (1994). The sapposhi, pechin, and samurai. *The Ryukyuanist 24*, 1-3.

Noble, G. (1998, November). Letter to the author.

Noble, G., McLaren, I., and Karasawa, N. (n.d.). Masters of the Shorin-ryu, Part II. *Fighting Arts International*, 32-33.

Noble, G. (2000). Master Choki Motobu. http://ejmas.com/jcs/jcsart_noble1_0200.htm. Downloaded September 26, 2000.

Sakamaki, S. (Ed.) (1964). *Ryukyuan names: Monographs on and lists of personal and place names in the Ryukyus*. Honolulu: East-West Center Press.

Silvan, J. (1998). Oral traditions of Okinawan karate. *Journal of Asian Martial Arts, 7*(3): 72-95.

Yabu, K. (1986, May 31). *Genealogy of the surname So family (from Kengi the founder): The Okushima family line, An annotated text.* Translated with supplementary notes by Ben Kobashigawa and Yoko Fukumura. Both the Japanese original and the English translation are privately published. The Japanese original is in the Yabu Family Collection while the English translation is in the Yabe/Yasui Family Collection.

Yasui, H. (1998, September 6). Letter to the author.

Yasui, H. (1998, Ocober 6). Letter to the author.

Yasui, H. (1998, November 7). Letter to the author.

Yasui, H. (1998, December 12). Letter to the author.

Acknowledgments

The following people provided assistance in completing this chapter: Michel Brousse, Charles Goodin, Richard Hayes, Eric Madis, Graham Noble, Robert W. Smith, Curtis Stanley, Homer Yasui, and Miyuki Yabe Yasui. The financial support of the Japanese American National Museum and the King County Landmarks and Heritage Commission is also gratefully acknowledged.

chapter 12

Koshin-ryu:
The Rebirth of Okinawa's Kojo Family Martial Arts

by Richard B. Florence, M.A.

Koshin-ryu fifth degree Joyce Stech in the Dragon Posture.
All photographs courtesy of Chuck Chandler.

Introduction

The need for self-defense goes back to the beginning of time. As time progressed, these early archaic and unstructured techniques gained structure as human society gained structure. Self-defense or offense systems developed under two primary influences: the military and individual families. These trends can be seen throughout the world, no matter the continent or country. On the military side, such styles as taijiquan in China and numerous weapons styles were developed. More often than not, an individual, or individuals working together who were soldiers, developed these styles. Oftentimes, civilian families further refined them. In China and Japan, numerous styles were given the name of the family that developed them.

Of course, this doesn't mean that all family styles were named after the family. Other familial-inherited lines were passed on without direct reference to the family, for instance, Ueshiba Morihei founded the art of aikido, who passed it on to his son, Kisshomaru, who passed it on to his son, Moriteru. In fact, the history of any one art would show how convoluted these arts are. Eventually the students of all arts and styles affect the development and naming of the mother art.

The martial traditions on Okinawa are no different.[1] This chapter will introduce, or re-introduce, one of the family styles once thought to have died out, the karate and weapon arts of the Kojo family. The development of the Kojo style is obviously directly linked to Okinawa's history.

A Short History of Okinawan Karate

Although most histories discuss the development of an indigenous mother art called *torite*, *tuidi*, or just *te/ti/di* (hand),[2] there is little actual information on its beginnings. However, *te* eventually took on primarily empty-handed elements of Chinese civilian martial systems. The Okinawa Board of Education places the major impetus on Okinawan development of a civilian martial art on the need for sailors to defend themselves against pirates (1995: 2). The flourishing trade with China and Japan brought about a large population of sailors to the Naha area. Of course, this influx of foreigners, as temporary as it may have been, did not preclude the need for self-defense throughout the island from local trouble makers.

Most karate styles can also trace their lineage to China[3] and the art called "Tang Hand." This term comes from the Tang Dynasty (618 CE-907), which came to mean China itself due to its cultural and political dominance, thus "China Hand" (Japanese: "karate"; Okinawan: "todi," also "toudi") originally.[4] However, Funakoshi Gichin, considered by some to be the father of modern karate, is uncertain if Okinawa ever actually adopted the "Tang" ideogram for karate (1988: 24-25).

Okinawa's relationship with China goes back a long way. It is possible that Okinawa came into at least indirect contact with China as early as the later half of the 3rd century B.C.E. (Kerr, 1958/1980: 29). Direct contact with China may have first occurred in 608 C.E., when a Chinese Sui Dynasty expedition looking for the fabled Land of the Immortals reached some Okinawan islands. In 1369, Chuzan[5] King Satto (r. 1422-39) accepted Chinese supremacy and sent representatives to the court of Chinese Emperor Hong Wu, founder of the Ming Dynasty (1369-1644). One result of this political relationship was that Okinawan "foreign students" (*ryugakusei*) were sent to Beijing and Nanjing to study Chinese culture and language. To further their education, young Okinawan scholars often traveled to Fuzhou, which was the closest large Chinese metropolis. Upon their return to Kume Village, these young men often became successful businessmen and pro-Chinese members of society.

In 1392, a group of Chinese businessmen, artisans, and officials arrived in Okinawa, which Okinawan history refers to as the "Thirty-Six Families."[6] The group lived in Kume Village, which became the nexus of Chinese culture in Okinawa. These Chinese taught Okinawan scholars their language and helped cement trade relations between Okinawa and China. Among families sent to Okinawa at this time was a branch of the Cai, who, by the 17th century, had become Okinawanized and adopted the family name of Kojo.

Left: Sign outside the Kojo Headquarters Dojo which reads "Kojo-ryu Koshinkan Karatedo". Right: Yabiku Takaya outside the dojo, which was opened in 1974.

Along with the growth and evolution of Okinawan society, new laws were made to keep the society stable. It has long been believed, especially by the martial arts community, that Okinawa King Sho Shin-O (r. 1477-1526) outlawed the private ownership and stockpiling of weapons, the first of two such prohibitions. Part of this is based on George Kerr's seminal history on Okinawa. In the first edition (1958/2000: 107), Kerr states this act came into effect when King Sho Shin-O ratified a decree in 1507 called "Eleven Distinctions of the Age." However, newer research refutes this. Sakihara Mitsugu says that the statement in question was found on a monument or stele erected in 1479 and called the Eleven Great Achievements of the Age. Sakihara explains that "(i)n 1926 Iha Fuyu misread the passage therein to mean 'this country used the armor for utensils,' and assumed that the king had confiscated all arms which were then made into practical tools such as farm implements. Thus originated the fallacy of a disarmed, peace-loving Ryukyu..." (1987: 199). Tuttle Publishing chose Sakihara to revise Kerr's work. In the afterword, Sakihara retells the above story, although changes some of the facts. He notes that "the Momourasoe Balustrade monument of 1509 ... eulogizes King Sho Shin ... listing his achievements." He states that in 1955, Zenchu Nakahara pointed out the error in Iha's translation (2000: 543-544).

Regarding the second widely believed myth that the Satsuma clan also imposed a weapons ban, Sakihara also provides an update. He notes that the clan conquered Okinawa in 1609; banned the importing of arms into the Ryukyus in 1639; and issued the "Prohibition of Those Who Travel to Ryukyu Carrying Arms," which allowed Okinawans to bring their arms to Satsuma for repair, but continued the 1639 ban on importing new weapons (2000: 544).

As time progressed, the Okinawan martial arts developed along some roughly constructed stylistic lines; however, these were not as diverse as many have assumed. According to Tokashiki Iken, a noted karate historian and Tomari-te and Goju-ryu instructor, "There were no clear distinctions between *te* styles, each master had his own specialty" (Tokashiki, 18 February 1997). Until the 18th century, Okinawan martial arts had no set curriculum and no organizations, either domestic or international. There were no ranks, either by belt or licensing. A teacher taught what he knew without reporting to anyone else, except for maybe his own teacher. A teacher gained students through his reputation, since he was known as either a good teacher and/or fighter or not.

At one time, *te*/karate was described in a relatively generic form based on perceived stylistic differences centering in the urban districts of Okinawa's modern-day capital of Naha: Shuri-te, Naha-te, and Tomari-te (*te*, "hand").[7]

Despite the long practice of martial arts in these areas, these geo-based names were not official designations. In fact, such a means of identifying the *te* arts did not exist until the winter of 1926-1927. In January 1927, judo founder Kano Jigoro made his third visit to Okinawa,[8] and was also the first time he saw *tode* on its native soil (McCarthy, 1994: 3, 8). The Okinawan planning committee for Kano's visit decided it would be best if they called the Okinawan martial art, then known as "China Hand," something besides a name that reflected links to Japan's enemy, China. The group decided to give the arts style names based on the geographic areas where they were most commonly found: Shuri, Naha, and Tomari (McCarthy, 1994: 3).

The next major stage in Okinawan karate was its development primarily along the so-called Naha-te, Shuri-te, Tomari-te models: Goju-ryu from the Naha-te lineage and Shorin-ryu from the Shuri-te[9] and Tomari-te lineages.[10] Two Okinawan styles that did not fall neatly within this model are Uechi-ryu, which was originally called Pangainoon-ryu (based on the Fujian dialect of spoken Chinese), but is sometimes considered a Naha-te style; and Kojo-ryu.

The Kojo Family

Like many other Okinawan families, the Kojo[11] family records only date back to the 1600's. Of those records, many were destroyed over time, including a large portion during the Japanese occupation and the Battle for Okinawa during World War II. The current family, non-practicing, head of the Kojo karate system, Kojo Yoshiaka, made many of these records available to Irimaji Seiji. These records link Kojo-ryu karate to Fuzhou through the Thirty-Six Families in Kume Village. Like much of the martial arts across Asia throughout the period of its development, Kojo-ryu remained pretty much a family style, handed down from father to son wherever possible. Occasionally, outsiders would get a glimpse of the style. This made sense since one's success in self-defense often depended on knowing something your opponent didn't, on the off chance that he was also a martial artist. Obviously, there is not strict secrecy in martial arts training, otherwise it would be nearly impossible to develop a viable system. The Kojo family system was therefore influenced by outside sources as well as the genius within the family.

Kojo Shinpo Uekata[12] appears to have been the first of a long line of Kojos to study Chinese martial arts. He was also known by the Sinified name of Sai (Mandarin: Cai) Ko. He was born in Kume Village in the late 1600's (family records are not specific as to the date). In the middle 1700's,[13] the records show that Kojo Shinpo studied gongfu (including weaponry and grappling) in Fuzhou, as a number of his family members and other Okinawans would do in later times. Kojo Shinpo may well have been one of the first martial artists to bring Chinese fighting arts to Okinawa. The art he taught to family members was simply called "fighting art" (*kumiaijutsu* or *kumiuchi*). As was the Kojo custom, he passed on what he knew to his eldest son, Shinunjo.

Kojo Shinunjo Peichin[14] (c. 1780-?) started martial arts training at a young age under Kojo Shinpo. In addition to his Kojo family training, he also apparently studied under Teruya Kanga, better known as Tode ("China Hand") Sakugawa, founder of Shuri-te.[15] He was sent to Fuzhou to further his studies. He added many new techniques to his father's system. In Kume Village, he was considered one of the finest Okinawan martial artists of his day. He seems also to have also used the name Matsu Higa, and was a senior Imperial guard at Shuri Castle (Sells, 1995: 33). He was nicknamed "Born Warrior." Most karate historians credit him with the founding of the Kojo-ryu karate system. He passed down his system to his son, Saisho, in the late 19th century.

Kojo Saisho (1816-1906) is also referred to by the Sinified name, Sai Sho, Sai Shoi, and Sai Shoei. He studied in Fuzhou, bringing back a four-foot staff art (*jojutsu*) to Kume Village. Palace guards favored the staff because the ceilings were low and the standard six-foot staff (*rokushaku bo*) was too long to maneuver inside. Saisho was a famous Okinawan weapons art (*kobujutsu*) practitioner and maintained a very strong interest in weapons, especially the long and short staffs, to the neglect of his empty-hand skills. However, later in life, he perfected his empty-hand skills and passed them down to his son, Isei (also Isho). He was given the sobriquet "Wise Old Man" (Bishop, 1989: 48). According to Bishop, he was stripped of his monetary privileges because he beat up two samurai who were attempting to rape an Okinawan woman. After such mistreatment from the Japanese authorities, he reportedly returned to Fuzhou, where he died (Bishop, 1989: 48).

In 1848, Saisho took his son, Isei, and nephew, Taitei, to Fuzhou and introduced them to Iwah,[16] a noted Shaolin crane, tiger, and dragon gongfu teacher. As well as teaching Kojo Saisho, Isei, Taitei, and Koho, Iwah also taught Matsumura Sokon (founder of Shorin-ryu) and Maezato (Miyazato) Ranho (founder of Koho-ryu).[17] Upon his death, Saisho left his art to Isei.

Little is known about Kojo Taitei (1837-1917), Saisho's nephew, and his relationship to the Kojo family karate style is only minimal. Taitei also studied under Wai Xinxian. Like his cousin, Isei, he was known for his skill with the bow and arrow and the small spear (Bishop, 1996: 115). He was given the sobriquet "Hard-Fisted Old Man." Taitei may have brought back a secret text that may be a version of the *Bubishi* (McCarthy, 1995a: 42). Among his students were Kojo Saikyo; and Higashionna (Higaonna) Kanryo, who may have trained under Taitei for two years and then at the Kojo school in Fuzhou under Wai Xinxian and possibly even Iwah (McCarthy, 1995a: 37).

In 1848, Kojo Isei (1832-1891)[18] went to Fuzhou with his father, Saisho, to study with Iwah. Reportedly, Isei quickly became Iwah's favorite student. A story passed down in the Kojo family notes that three of Iwah's students slipped into the dojo where Isei was practicing alone and attacked Isei. After Isei had quickly disarmed two of his attackers, the third one fled. These three Chinese may have been jealous of Isei's swift appointment as Iwah's assistant. Back in Okinawa, the story spread and became part of Kojo folklore as the saying, "One Kojo equals three others" (Bishop, 1989: 47; Yabiku, 2000: 40).

In 1862, at his teacher's request, Isei took over Iwah's dojo. This may have been the first time that a non-Chinese solely ran a martial arts school in Fuzhou.

During this period, Iwah was an imperial bodyguard. In 1868, he was apparently assassinated in the Chinese palace. In fear for his life, Isei returned to Okinawa believing that jealous imperial functionaries had killed his teacher.

When Isei returned to Okinawa in 1868, he taught his art to several family members. He brought with him three secret- or advanced-level katas: White Crane Fist, White Tiger Fist, and White Dragon Fist. Isei is also credited with preserving and bringing to Kumemura one of the several versions of the *Bubishi*. This textbook was carefully edited to fit the Kojo family's specific style of karate. Upon close examination, one can find the pressure point strikes and their correlation to the Kojo-ryu stances in this book.

Isei died suddenly of a blood clot in the brain, which left the art in the hands of his son, Koho.

Kojo Koho (also Kojo Kaho; 1849-1925) was born in Fuzhou, China. In addition to being the fourth headmaster of the family martial arts system, he was also a skilled calligrapher and government translator. In 1855, he began studying gongfu under Iwah and his father, Isei, in Fuzhou. On his family's return to Okinawa in 1868, he continued to train and perfect his father's art.

In 1880, he returned to China and located his father's old dojo. Two Chinese teachers, Wai Xinxian[19] and Ko Ryuru, were now running it. Because he was a Kojo, Koho was allowed to rejoin the school. Wai Xinxian taught Koho two more Crane katas, Nepai and Hofa, which Koho did not teach to anyone else. In 1889, Koho took over the dojo. This made him the second non-Chinese to operate a dojo in China, who just happened to be a Kojo as well. He called his martial art, "Kogusuku." His assistants are listed as Udon Makabe and Matsuda Tokusaburu, Okinawan friends of the Kojo family in Kume. In 1900, Koho returned to Okinawa.

Koho completed the format of the Kojo family system. He created Kojo-ryu's three staff, two sai, and three empty-hand katas from the upper-level katas of the White Tiger Fist, White Crane Fist, and White Dragon Fist. The three Koho-created empty-hand katas are Tenkan, Kukan, and Chikan. Each of these forms contain four different stances, which are to be used to fight an opponent at different times of the day, much in line with the meridian theory discussed in the *Bubishi:* Tenkan stances are theoretically used to strike vital areas of the body from 6 to 10 am; Kukan stances are used between 10 am and 2 pm; and Chikan between 2 and 6 pm.

In Okinawa, Koho's system became known as Kojo-ryu Jutsu. In addition to teaching his grandson, Yoshitomi, to whom he left the system, Koho also taught his son Saikyo; his brother, Koshiro Shuren (1883-1945),[20] one of the first Meiji Era (1868-1912) native Okinawan police inspectors in the prefecture; and Matsuda Tokusaburo (Nakaya, 1986: 51).

Kojo Saikyo (1873-1941) was known as the "King of Kume" because of his wealth. He studied the Kojo system under his grandfather, Kojo Isei; his father, Kojo Koho; and Kojo Taitei. Saikyo's business concerns may have precluded him from learning the entire system and thus taking over the family system from his father, Koho. Saikyo taught his son, Yoshitomi.[21]

The fifth generation headmaster, Kojo Yoshitomi, (also Kojo Kafu; 1909-1995) began training in his family's karate and weapons system in 1921 under his grandfather, Koho. There is very little written about Yoshitomi. The only extensive information available is an oral history from his eldest living son, Yoshiaka, and one of his senior martial arts students, Irimaji Seiji. Yoshitomi began training under his father, Saikyo, and uncle, Shuren, soon after his grandfather's death in 1925. In the late 1930's, Yoshitomi was drafted into the Japanese Army and became a highly decorated soldier while fighting in the Philippines.

In 1958, Yoshitomi and his eldest son from his first marriage, Shigeru, opened a dojo in Naha and began teaching Kojo-ryu karate and weaponry. Among their first students were two sons from his second marriage, Kaoru and Tatsumi, and Shigeru's brother, Yoshiaka. Yoshitomi's first non-family student was Irimaji Seiji. Two non-family, mainland Japanese members, Hayashi Shingo, a dentist in Totori, Totori Prefecture, Japan, and Sokomoto (first name unknown) would begin study under Yoshitomi later on.

In the later 1960's, Yoshitomi was a nominal member of Higa Seitoku's (b. 1921) All-Okinawa Karate and Kobudo United Association (Bishop,

1996: 140). In 1974, Yoshitomi closed the Naha dojo because Shigeru was diagnosed with cancer. He decided not to reopen it because he liked the quiet living and few students were willing to undergo the harsh training (Silvan, 1993: 78; Bishop, 1996: 116; Yabiku, 2000: 42). Sometime before 1980, Yoshitomi and his two sons, Shigeru and Tatsumi, self-published ten textbooks on Kojo karate and weaponry. And with the help of senior students of Go Kenki, Yoshitomi reconstructed and brought back into the Kojo-ryu system the katas Nepai and Hofa, the two Crane katas that were lost when his grandfather died. He also created the sparring versions of katas Hakukoken, Hakutsuruken, and Hakuryuken (Yabiku, 2000: 42).

Yoshitomi built a very large family home in Naha that resembles an American ranch-style house. This house has several wings that housed his sons and guests. His son, Yoshiaka, now lives in and owns the house.

Yoshitomi often practiced alongside his students in his rigorous training regime. Classes were three to five hours long. Although known as a strict teacher, he was apparently well liked (Irimaji, 2000 August).

In November 1991, Yoshitomi promoted Yabiku Takaya to 8th-degree. In 1995, he promoted Irimaji Seiji to 9th-degree and gave him a full instructor's license, which authorized him to teach the Kojo family system. Since Shigeru died before Yoshitomi, the Kojo system was left to Kojo Yoshiaka as headmaster and Irimaji as chief instructor. Also in 1995, Yoshitomi awarded Yabiku his instructor's license.

Kojo Shigeru (1934-1993) began training under his father, Yoshitomi, in 1948. In 1958, they opened the first commercial Kojo-ryu dojo in Okinawa and began teaching family members and a select few non-family members, although Shigeru depended primarily on his job as a taxi driver for living expenses.

His right hand and arm were severely injured in a teen-age accident. Because of this, Shigeru become an expert in the use of his legs. Irimaji Seiji and Yabiku Takaya note that Shigeru performed over three hundred kicks with each leg during a training session (Chandler, 2000). Among Kojo Shigeru's few students was Yabiku Takaya, who trained under Shigeru from 1973 until his first retirement in 1975.

When Shigeru was diagnosed with cancer in 1975, the Kojos closed the dojo and turned the building into a chicken coop to make money. In 1980, with his health seemingly restored, he taught a few private students on a part-time basis. However, the cancer eventually killed Shigeru.

As the eldest surviving son of Kojo Yoshitomi, Yoshiaka remains the headmaster of Kojo-ryu karate and kobudo, although he does not practice or teach the art himself.

The Next Generation: Kojo-ryu Reaches Outside the Family

Irimaji Seiji (b. 1941) was born to an Okinawan couple in Iceland. After World War II, his family moved back to Okinawa and bought a home in Naha. In 1958, he enrolled in Kojo Yoshitomi's dojo, becoming the first non-Kojo family member to be fully instructed in the art.

From 1965 to 1968, as a 3rd-degree, Irimaji was the all-Okinawa full-contact champion. He stopped competing because he kept winning, thus proving, at least within the confines of the punch-kick arts in Okinawa, his claim that the style was able "to overcome any and all other types of martial arts" (Yabiku, 2000: v).

Before 1974, Irimaji taught at the Kojo-ryu headquarters dojo in the morning. At night, Irimaji, Yabiku, and Shigeru would train together in their free time at the taxi company where all three worked.

In 1974, Kojo Yoshitomi made Irimaji the first non-family member to be awarded the senior teacher's certification (*kyoshi*) in the style and also named Irimaji the Kojo-ryu chief instructor. Because he had nowhere to train after Kojo Yoshitomi closed the Naha headquarters dojo in 1974, Irimaji asked Yoshitomi for permission to open another dojo in Naha, making him the second person, and first non-Kojo family member, to open a Kojo-ryu dojo in Okinawa. Called the Kojo-ryu Koshinkan, Irimaji's school served as the official Kojo-ryu headquarters until he retired from teaching in 1990. In 1990, Irimaji closed this school and became a nighttime manager for a taxi company. Irimaji has taught only one private student, Yabiku Takaya, who became his student in 1976.

Irimaji is well known for cutting chopsticks in two with a playing card, which has been filmed a number of times. To perform this feat, someone holds a pair of chopsticks between the thumb and index fingers of each hand at chest level. Irimaji takes a standard playing card and cleanly slices the chopsticks in two. He is the only one known who can perform this feat and says that Yoshitomi taught it to him (Yabiku, 2000: 44).

In 1995, Kojo Yoshitomi promoted Irimaji to Kojo-ryu 9th-degree, and, as the style's chief instructor (Yabiku, 2000: 53). He is the seniormost Kojo-ryu instructor in the world and is recognized as such by the current headmaster, Kojo Yoshiaka.

After the death of his teacher in 1995, Irimaji founded the Koshin-ryu Kohokan Karate and Kobudo Organization in honor of Yoshitomi; therefore, Irimaji is the headmaster, 10th-degree grandmaster for Koshin-ryu. As is often the case with a family-named style, when the family-member headmaster dies and the style is left to someone outside the genetic line, the new chief instructor will give the style a new name, using elements of the old name. In this case, Koshin uses "Ko," the first character of the Kojo family name and the character "shin," for "original methods." Kohokan means "yellow mountain peak house/hall" or "Koho's Hall," and was named in honor of Kojo Koho.

Irimaji Seiji (L.) and Yabiku Takaya,
Directors of the Koshin-ryu Kohokan.

Irimaji lives with his current wife, Mieko, in rural Naha and continues to teach Kojo-ryu karate to his senior student, Yabiku Takaya. In October 1999, he appointed Yabiku Koshin-ryu Kohokan chief instructor, chief examiner, and vice chairman. In August 2000, he promoted Chuck Chandler, a senior student of Yabiku, to 7th-degree. Chandler is the first non-Oriental to train in Kojo-ryu and the first to be awarded a 7th-degree in the style—apparently Kojo Yoshitomi did not like Americans. Chandler is the international director, an international examiner, and chief instructor in the U.S. for the Koshin-ryu Kohokan (as well as for Yabiku's Okinawa Konan-ryu Kohokan Karate and Kobudo Kyokai).

On 5 August 2000, during the Obon Festival, Messrs. Yabiku and Chandler participated in a historical event. During the Thirty-Fifth Karate and Kobudo Festival in Honor of Kinjo Takashi, they and Mr. Irimaji were presented to the public as the next generation of Kojo-ryu. It was also announced that Yabiku was opening up the Koshin-ryu system to the public (as Irimaji has retired from public teaching). Messrs. Yabiku and Chandler also presented to the public the Kojo-ryu kata Hakukuken and Tenkan, respectively (Yabiku, 2000: iv).

Yabiku Takaya demonstrating a technique from the Nepai kata
with Koshin-ryu Kohokan U.S. Director Chuck Chandler.

Yabiku Takaya (b. 1945) was born in Kumamoto City, Kumamoto Prefecture, Japan. He is a descendent of Gosamaru, the Okinawan noble who built Nakgusuku Castle in the 15th century. Like many Okinawan karate and weapons masters of his generation, Yabiku studied a number of styles under a number of instructors before deciding to concentrate on the Kojo family system. He started his journey in the martial arts in 1951, under Sakihama Seijiro (1903-1997), a cousin of his grandfather and founder of Goju Shizen-ryu karatedo (in 1945); and his father, a Shorin-ryu practitioner. From 1960 to 1978, he was a private student of Soken Hohan, third grandmaster of Matsumura Seito Shorin-ryu karate and weaponry. From 1960 to 1990, he studied Yamane-ryu weaponry under Kochinda Saburo (1904-1998), a student of Chinen Masami. He studied Kojo-ryu under Kojo Shigeru from 1973 to 1975 and then under Irimaji Seiji from 1976 to the present. Yabiku is a taxi driver for the same company where Irimaji is a supervisor and Kojo Shigeru worked. Yabiku has also made an extensive study of Uechi-ryu and China's White Crane.

In August 2000, Irimaji said: "I trained and taught as teacher Yoshitomi taught me. I've had many students come and go. I believe my training methods were too hard and severe for those who wished to train there. Maybe six months and they were gone. Only one [Yabiku Takaya] stayed for the duration of my 15-years teaching at this dojo" (Yabiku, 2000: 44).

Kojo-ryu is seeing a rebirth through the Koshin-ryu. Its founder, Irimaji Seiji, was the chief instructor of Kojo-ryu after the death of Kojo Yoshitomi and Shigeru. He created the Koshin-ryu because a Kojo family member, Yoshiaka, is still alive, although he doesn't train or teach.

Two mainland Japanese, Hayashi and Sokomoto (first name unknown) trained on Okinawa for two to three years in the early 1970's. Hayashi returned to Totori City, Totori Prefecture, to work as a dentist and to teach what he had learned of the Kojo-ryu. He apparently has not been back to Okinawa since then, although Irimaji Seiji has maintained contact with him. Further information regarding Hayashi and the enigmatic Sokomoto would be a great boon to the history of Okinawan karate.

THE SYSTEM

Fighting Postures

One of Kojo-ryu's, and thus Koshin-ryu's, hallmarks is its emphasis on twelve somewhat stylized fighting postures, much like the postures or stances familiar to practitioners of swordsmanship and those who watch Japanese sword movies. Each posture is related to one of the Chinese zodiac signs.

Sparring is often initiated from these postures. The intent is that the practitioner sets up his opponent who will "run into" the practitioner's technique, much like a spider trap. Below are the characteristics of these stances (Yabiku, 2000: 57-80):

- **Front or Forward Stance** (*Seishin*): The primary sparring stance. The practitioner stands in a cat stance (heels on a line, one foot in front of the other, one stride in length, front heel up). The arms are held straight out in a relaxed manner. The hands are held palms down, wrists straight, and fingers slightly curled. It is linked to the Rat Zodiac sign and is emphasized in kata Tenkan.
- **Immovable Stance** (*Fudo*): Done with the feet about two fists apart, one foot in front of the other, and both heels planted (rooted or grounded); the arms are held hanging down, hands open, and fingers straight like sword hands. It is used for resting, quick changes of body postures, awareness of the environment and the opponent, and facilitates counter techniques. It is linked to the Ox Zodiac and is emphasized in the kata Tenkan.
- **Wind Hands Stance** (*Jinpu*): Done much like a cat stance, only the front heel rests lightly on the ground; both hands are open, palms out, the back hand is held above brow level (looking much like a military salute), and the front arm hangs down so that the lower arm and open hand protect the thigh. It is an

aggressive posture used primarily against quick opponents. It is linked to the Tiger sign and is emphasized in kata Tenkan.

- **Cross Stance** (*Jumonji*): Done from a cat stance. One arm is held straight resting atop the wrist of the other arm, the hand in the spear-hand position. The other arm is bent and held parallel to the ground, the hand is in the spear-hand position, perpendicular to the other hand. It is linked to the Rabbit and is emphasized in kata Tenkan.

- **Cloud Dragon Stance** (*Unryu*): Done from a cat stance. One arm is held forward, palm open and facing the opponent, as though feeling for movement. The other hand is held above the ear, palm open in a 45-degree position to the front. It is linked to the Dragon and is emphasized in kata Kukan.

- **Blending Stance** (*Aiki*): Done from the cat stance. The arm above the front leg is bent, parallel to the ground, palm open and facing the ground, covering the body's centerline. The other arm is held forward, slightly bent, parallel to the ground, palm facing down. It is considered an aggressive stance, making body transitions and quick hand attacks easier. It is linked to the Snake sign and is emphasized in kata Kukan.

- **Sword in the Eyes Stance** (*Seigan*): Done from the cat stance. The arm above the front leg is held straight, parallel to the ground, with the palm facing down. The other hand is held in a fist above the fist in the classic ready-to-punch position. It is considered a good stance to use when facing an opponent with a weapon. It is linked to the Horse sign and is emphasized in kata Kukan.

- **Moving Rock Stance** (*Dogan*): Done from a one-leg kneeling position. The hands are held as in the Front Stance position: arms held straight out in a relaxed manner; hands held palms down, wrists straight, and fingers slightly curled. It is considered a good stance against kicks. It is linked to the Sheep sign and is emphasized in kata Kukan.

- **Heaven and Earth Stance** (*Tenchi*): Done from is done with the feet about two fists apart, one foot in front of the other, and both heels planted, as in the Fudo Stance. The arm over the front leg is held forward, elbow bent at a 45-degree angle, palm open and facing the opponent, also at a 45-degree angle. The other hand is held above the ear, but not above the head, palm open in a 45-degree position to the front. It is considered a good stance for quick attacks. It is linked to the Monkey sign and is emphasized in kata Chikan.

- **Blowing Down Stance** (*Fukiroshi*): Also called the Crane Method (*Tsuru Ho*). It is done with the feet about two fists apart, one foot in front of the other, and both heels planted, as in the Fudo Stance. The hands are held somewhat similar to the Jinpu stance. However, in the Blowing Down Stance, the back arm is bent at approximately 90-degrees, the forearm pointing to the heavens, the palm open and facing forward. It is linked to the Rooster sign and is emphasized in kata Chikan.

- **Pointing at the Ground Stance** (*Chi Seigan*): Done with the feet about two fists apart, one foot in front of the other, and both heels planted, as in the Immovable Stance. The front arm hangs down so that the lower arm and open hand protect the thigh. The back arm is bent, parallel to the ground, crossing the body's center line; the palm is open and facing down. It is considered a good stance from which to defend against kicks. It is linked to the Dog sign and is emphasized in kata Chikan.
- **Number One Stance** (*Ichimonji*): Done from the cat stance. The front arm is bent, the fist resting a little bit above the solar plexus area. The back fist is held above the waist in the ready-to-punch position. It is linked to the Boar sign and is emphasized in kata Chikan.

KATA	STANCE	CHINESE ZODIAC ANIMAL
Chikan	Ground (Chiseigan)	Dog
	Number One (Ichimonji)	Boar
	Blowing Down (Fukioroshi)	Rooster
	Heaven & Earth (Tenchi)	Monkey
Kukan	Blending (Aiki)	Snake
	Forward (Seigan)	Horse
	Moving Rock (Dogan)	Sheep
	Cloud Dragon (Unryu)	Dragon
Tenkan	Immovable (Fudo)	Bull
	Wind Hands (Jinpu)	Tiger
	Cross (Jumonji)	Rabbit
	Front (Seishin)	Rat

Use of Open-Hands

In addition to the emphasis on fighting postures, another unique feature of the Kojo system is its preference for open-handed techniques rather than the classic karate punch (*seiken*).

In hand-to-hand combat, a Kojo-ryu fighter likes to slide in close to his opponent, lock the opponent's leg with his own leading leg, and strike, generally with an open hand. As he is striking, the Kojo-ryu fighter will often use the locking leg to sweep his opponent to the ground.

The importance of grappling and open-hand strikes is best symbolized by the three higher-level, animal katas created by the Kojo family: White Crane, White Tiger, and White Dragon. The Crane arts emphasize grabbing and open-hand strikes, usually with the finger tips. The Tiger arts emphasize striking with harder parts of the still open hand, such as the thumb, and dividing and ripping muscles and ligaments. The Dragon arts are predominately grappling oriented.

Kojo-ryu and Uechi-ryu are the two Okinawan karate styles that most emphasize open-hand strikes over close-fisted punching. Both styles' techniques reflect the same three animals: crane, tiger, and dragon, emphasizing of the shared Fuzhou training hall. In Kojo-ryu, there are eleven primary open-handed strikes:

- **Tiger Claw**: The hand looks somewhat like a tiger's claw and is used for grabbing, tearing, and ripping.
- **Tiger Thumb**: The protruding thumb joint in the Tiger Claw position is used to strike soft tissue areas.
- **Tiger Paw Strike**: Also called the four-knuckle punch. The thumb is laid across the palm and the four fingers are bent at the second knuckle.
- **Tiger Palm Heel**: The palm heel of the Tiger Claw position used as a strike against harder targets, such as the chin.

In the photographs shown here and on following pages, Chuck Chandler demonstrates various techniques with his student, Richard Florence.

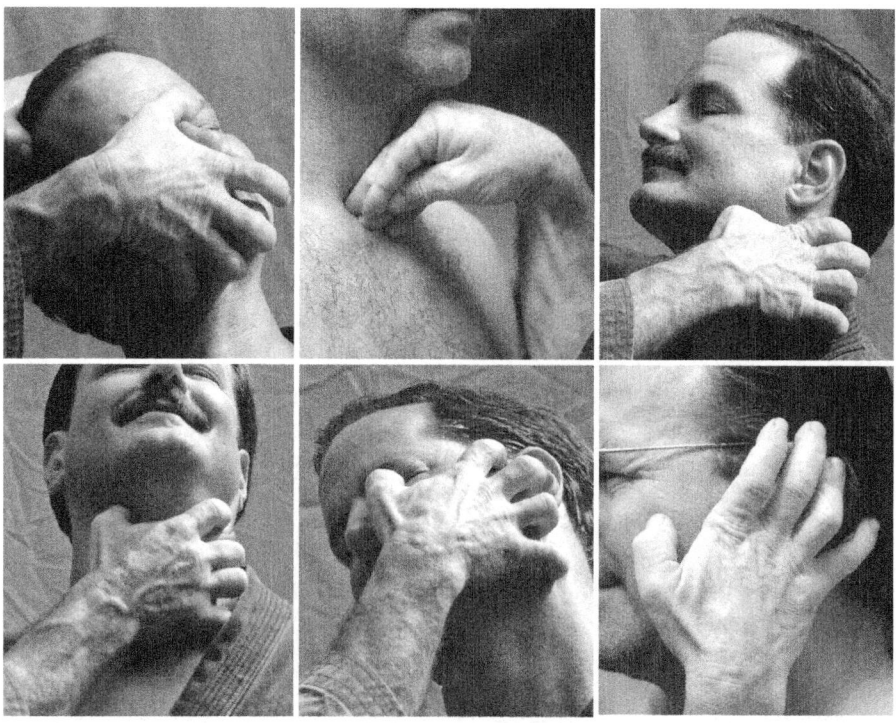

- **Crane Beak**: The fingertips are held folded together and used in pinpoint strikes.
- **Crane Wing**: The fingertips are held together but flat, as opposed to the Crane Beak, and generally held with the palm facing the ground, striking soft tissue areas.
- **Dragon Claw**: A position similar to the Tiger Claw, and also used for grabbing, tearing, and ripping.
- **Cobra Strike**: The middle finger crosses over the ring finger, with the pointer finger lying atop of the ring finger and next to the middle finger, used for supported, pinpoint striking to penetrate soft tissue areas, such as the spot behind the collar bone. It was also taught in the Tiger, Crane, Dragon school of Shushiwa, the Chinese teacher of Uechi Kanbun, the founder of Uechi-ryu, who took the strike out of his style because he considered it too dangerous and replaced it with the Crane Beak strike (Dollar, 1996: 66).[21]
- **Iron Palm**: The hand is open and the fingers tensed backward. The striking area is the set of small bones at the top of the palm, right below the last segment of the fingers. In such a position, the Iron Palm is much like an Iron Bar.
- **Sword Hand**: Also called the Spear Hand. The wrist and fingers are held straight, with the fingertips doing the striking. The classic "karate chop" position.

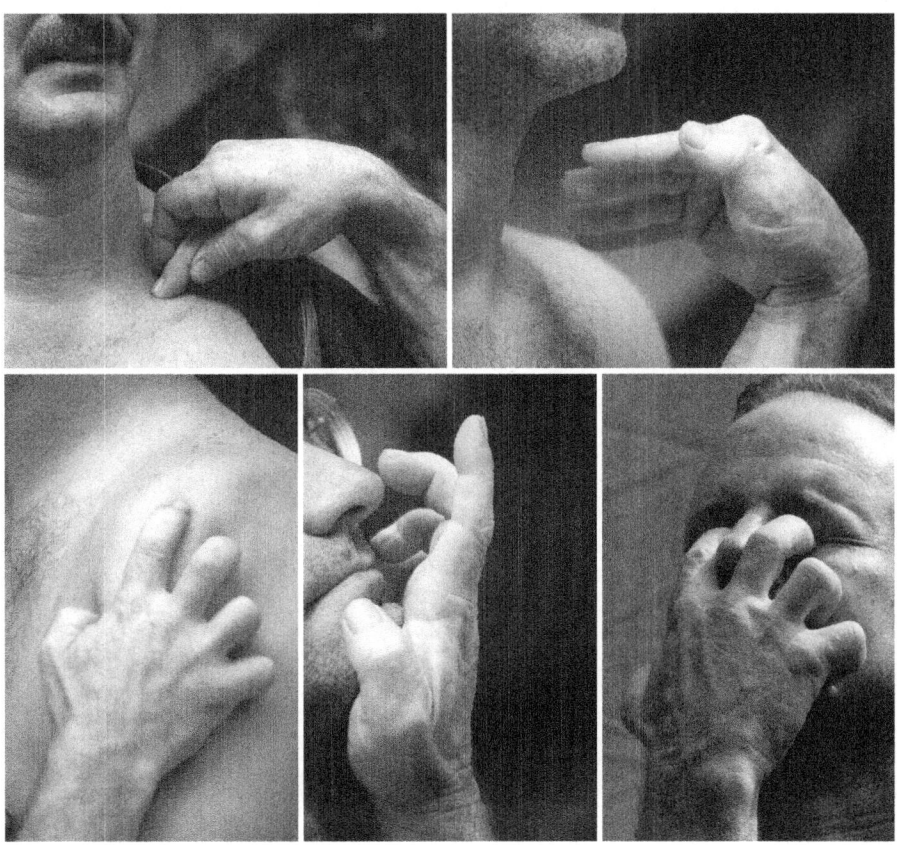

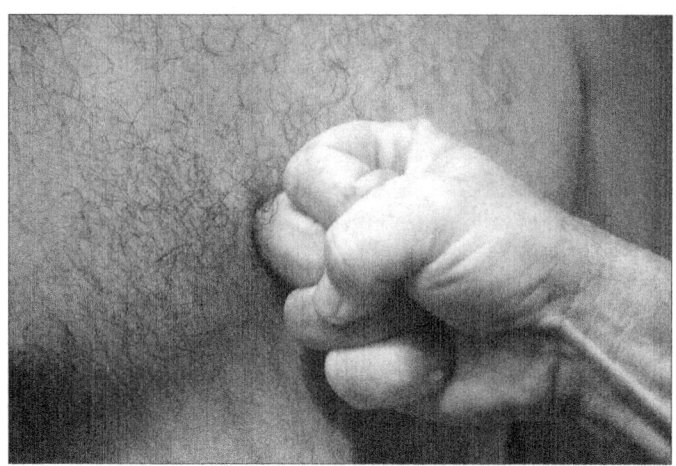

Katas

The Kojo-ryu katas reflect the history of Okinawan karate. They include Chinese forms learned in southern China, family-created forms based on the Chinese forms, traditional Okinawan (Shorin-ryu) katas adopted in the 20th century to serve as a bridge for outsiders, and modified family katas to help introduce the system to the next generation. These katas are:[23]

Empty-Hand Katas

- **Pinan Shodan**: A kata from the Shuri-te/Shorin-ryu lineage. Kojo Yoshitomi learned this kata while in elementary school and brought it into the Kojo-ryu.
- **Pinan Nidan**: A kata from the Shuri-te/ Shorin-ryu lineage. Kojo Yoshitomi learned this kata while in elementary school and brought it into the Kojo-ryu.
- **Naihanchi Shodan**: A kata from the Shuri-te/Shorin-ryu lineage. Kojo Yoshitomi learned this kata while in elementary school and brought it into the Kojo-ryu.
- **Passai**: A kata from the Shuri-te/Shorin-ryu lineage. Kojo Yoshitomi learned this kata while in elementary school and brought it into the Kojo-ryu.
- **Chinto**: A kata that originally came from the Tomari-te tradition. Kojo Yoshitomi learned this kata while in elementary school and brought it into the Kojo-ryu.
- **Tenkan** (Heaven): One of three Kojo-ryu katas created by Kojo Koho based on the teachings of Iwah and principles found in the *Bubishi*. The other two are Chikan and Kukan. "Tinkan" in Okinawan.
- **Kukan** (Sky): One of three Kojo-ryu katas created by Kojo Koho based on the teachings of Iwah and principles found in the *Bubishi*. The other two are Chikan and Tenkan.
- **Chikan** (Earth): One of three Kojo-ryu katas created by Kojo Koho based on the teachings of Iwah and principles found in the *Bubishi*. The other two are Kukan and Tenkan.

- **Hakutsuruken Kumite** (White Tiger Fist Sparring): A Kojo-ryu kata that extracts non-lethal sparring principles from kata Hakukuken. Kojo Yoshitomi created this kata for his son, Shigeru, to teach the public the basic concepts without danger of hurting the student. It can also be called "Hakukuken Kumite."
- **Hakutsuruken** (White Crane Fist): Also called Hakukuken. A Kojo-ryu kata created by Kojo Shigeru. It was created as the international version of Hakukuken for competition. Shigeru taught it to Irimaji Seiji, who taught it to Yabiku Takaya.
- **Hakukuken** (White Crane Fist): One of the three Kojo-ryu higher-level katas. It is also called "Hakutsuruken." The others are Hakuryuken and Hakokoken.
- **Hakukoken Kumite** (White Tiger Fist Sparring): A Kojo-ryu kata that extracts non-lethal (ie., sans pressure point applications) sparring principles from kata Hakukoken. Kojo Yoshitomi created this kata for his son, Shigeru, to teach to the public the basic concepts without danger of hurting the student.
- **Hakuryuken Kumite** (White Dragon Fist Sparring): A Kojo-ryu kata that extracts non-lethal sparring principles from kata Hakuryuken. Kojo Yoshitomi created this kata for his son, Shigeru, to teach the public the basic concepts without danger of hurting the student.
- **Hakuryuken** (White Dragon Fist): One of six primary Kojo-ryu katas. The others are Hakakuken, Hakutsuruken, Chikan, Kukan, and Tenkan.
- **Nepai**: One of the thirteen forms taught at the Wai Xinxian gongfu school in Fuzhou. It is based on Hofa.
- **Hofa or Houfua**: One of the thirteen forms taught at the Wai Xinxian gongfu school in Fuzhou. It is also called Nipaipo. It is the base from which the kata Nepai is taken.
- **Nunfa**: One of the thirteen forms taught at the Wai Xinxian gongfu school in Fuzhou.
- **Paichu**: One of the thirteen forms taught at the Wai Xinxian gongfu school in Fuzhou.
- **Paishi**: One of the thirteen forms taught at the Wai Xinxian gongfu school in Fuzhou.
- **Pachin**: One of the thirteen forms taught at the Wai Xinxian gongfu school in Fuzhou.
- **Tanchin**: One of the thirteen forms taught at the Wai Xinxian gongfu school in Fuzhou.
- **Nijikken**: "Twenty Fists." One of the thirteen forms taught at the Wai Xinxian gongfu school in Fuzhou.
- **Sodenkan**: One of the thirteen forms taught at the Wai Xinxian gongfu school in Fuzhou.
- **Gogiho**: "Five Skills Way." One of the thirteen forms taught at the Wai Xinxian gongfu school in Fuzhou.

- **Shitenkan**: "Four Points Fist." One of the thirteen forms taught at the Wai Xinxian gongfu school in Fuzhou.
- **Suiken**: One of the thirteen forms taught at the Wai Xinxian gongfu school in Fuzhou.
- **Shimonken**: "Four Gates Fist." One of the thirteen forms taught at the Wai Xinxian gongfu school in Fuzhou.
- **Kokukakuken**: "Royal Crane Fist." Kojo Koho may have created this kata.

In the 20th century, Kojo Yoshitomi reconstructed the two crane-based kata, Nepai and Hofa, that were lost when his grandfather, Koho, died in 1925. In the kata names, Hakutsuruken/Hakukuken, Hakukoken, and Hakuryuken, "haku" (white) is added to the animal names to indicate that they are the pure, original methods of the crane, tiger, and dragon.

Because the three elemental katas (Tenkan, Kukan, and Chikan) are so difficult for beginner-level students to understand, in 2000, at the request of Chuck Chandler, Irimaji Seiji and Yabiku Takaya put their mark on Kojo-ryu by adding two katas:

- **Tenkan Kihon Ichi**: "Heaven Basics One." A Koshin-ryu kata created by Irimaji Seiji and Yabiku Takaya.
- **Tenkan Kihon Ni**: "Heaven Basics Two." The second of two Koshin-ryu katas created by Irimaji Seiji and Yabiku Takaya.

In 2001, Irimaji and Yabiku developed three basic-level katas for the Kukan series. Eventually, they will develop a series of basic katas to help learn kata Chikan as well.

Weaponry

There are three weapons taught, with a total of five weapons katas in Kojo-ryu:

- **Bo Shodan**: The first staff kata created by Kojo Koho.
- **Bo Nidan**: The second staff kata created by Kojo Koho.
- **Sai Shodan**: The first sai kata created by Kojo Koho.
- **Sai Nidan**: The second sai kata created by Kojo Koho.
- **Jo**: Kojo Saisho brought this 4' staff form back from Fuzhou.

Conclusion

In this day and age when many seem to be searching for the origins of the martial arts, and Okinawa karate in particular, the Kojo family system may be an answer. It is one of the oldest of the Okinawan systems still practiced today. As noted above, the system is a good paradigm of the evolution of Okinawan karate, reflecting the various stages and influences that describe those systems: it has strong ties to the Chinese martial arts, both historically and stylistically; it provides its own unique touch in the six family-created katas; a touch of traditional Okinawan karate, adopting some Shorin-ryu katas to provide a more familiar transition to outsiders; and has changed with the times with the contributions of Irimaji and Yabiku. The Kojo family is intimately linked with many of the better known names of Okinawan karate: among others, Kojos trained under Iwah, Ko Ryuru, Wai Xinxian, Tode Sakugawa, Matsumura Sokon; Kojos trained alongside Maezato Ranho and Go Kenki; and Kojos trained Higashionna Kanryo.

Koshin-ryu is the continuation of the relatively unknown but often spoken about Kojo family karate. There is a direct historical link to the Kojo family arts through Koshin-ryu's founder, Irimaji Seiji, who is the most senior ranking Kojo-ryu practitioner and was personally selected by the last practicing family member to be the style's chief instructor.

There is no question that Irimaji Seiji and his Koshin-ryu are the legitimate heirs of Kojo-ryu. However, like all things historical, there is much yet to uncover about Okinawa karate in general, and Kojo-ryu in particular. For instance, since the Kojos trained in China with Chinese instructors who taught other Okinawans who became well-known and because the Okinawan martial arts world was relatively small and its members knew each other and often shared techniques with each other, how did Kojo-ryu remain out of the public for so long? When Mark Bishop came around to research his book, *Okinawan Karate: Teachers, Styles and Secret Techniques* (1989), why didn't Kojo Yoshitomi note that Irimaji was his senior student?

In any case, the Koshin-ryu Koshinkan is a good place to start this search.

Notes

1. Okinawa is the main island in the chain of islands called the Ryukyus. Today, the entire chain is a Japanese prefecture using the main island's name.
2. In Japanese and Okinawan, words are Romanized differently when appearing alone and when in combination with other words/sounds. For instance, the Okinawan term "ti" and the Japanese term "te" use the initial "t" sound when appearing alone; however, when appearing as the second or later syllable of a word, they sound more like "di" and "de," respectively. I have tried to reflect this dichotomy throughout the chapter. I have also adopted the Japanese pronunciation over the Okinawan because it is the more readily recognized.
3. Nagaboshi Tomio (adopted name of Englishman Terence Dukes; 1994: 456) believes that the major influence on any indigenous Okinawan martial arts was Chinese Buddhist monks and traders.
4. In Korea, Hwang Kee chose to name his Shotokan-based art "Tang Soo Do," which also means "China Hand Way."
5. Okinawan legend says that the Tenson ("Heaven") Dynasty ruled over a unified Okinawa for 1500 years until 1314, when Tamagusuku succeeded his father, Eiji. Because of Tamagusuku's weak character and abilities, Okinawa broke up into three "kingdoms": Nanzan ("southern mountain"), Chuzan ("central mountain," ruled by Tamagusuku), and Hokuzan ("northern mountain"). Chuzan King Sho Hashi conquered Hokuzan in 1416. With Sho Hashi's conquest of Nanzan in 1422 (or 1429), Okinawa was again unified. And much as the Tang Dynasty came to signify all of China, Chuzan then became synonymous with all of Okinawa (Sakihara,

1987: 9, 82; Kerr, 1958/2000: 60, 86).

6. The number thirty-six does not mean literally only thirty-six families went to Okinawa at this time. It was a symbolic term meaning a large number of Chinese, with their families, moved to Okinawa, at least temporarily.
7. Today, *Shuri* ("first village" or "head village"; *Sui* in the Okinawan dialect) and *Tomari* ("port"; *Tumai* in Okinawan) are districts of Naha, the Okinawan capital. Before Okinawa became a Japanese prefecture in 1879, Shuri was the royal district housing the king's castle; Tomari was the port district; and Naha (Nafa in Okinawan) was the business and residential district. There were, and are, other, lesser-known districts of Naha.
8. Kano lectured on judo at the Okinawa Teacher's College in 1922 and in the summer of 1926. See McCarthy, 1994: 8-9.
9. Tomari-te is said to have been much like Naha-te, which would explain their marriage in Tokashiki Iken's Gohakukai, a combination of Goju-ryu and Tomari-te. However, Tomari-te kata are quite frequently found in the Shorin-ryu styles as well. For more information, see my "Where Goju-ryu and Tomari-te Meet: Tokashiki Iken and the Gohakukai," *Bugeisha*, Summer 1998.
10. In Okinawa karate systems, it is actually more common for a senior student to give his interpretation of the original style a new name without reference to the founder's name, often the name is based on the name of the new founder's school, such as Shorin-ryu Kenshinkan, Shorin-ryu Shorinkan, Goju-ryu Meibukan, and Goju-ryu Jundokan. Then there are cases in which a founder has studied several arts and gives the art a name that in some way reflects those arts, such as Higa Seitoku's *Bugeikan Te* ("Martial Arts Place/Hall Hand," based on Shorin-ryu, Motobu-ryu Udun-di, and Yamane-ryu kobujutsu), and Kyoda Juhatsu's *To'on-ryu* (a variant reading of the "Kanryo" in Higaonna Kanryo, founder of Naha-te/Nafa-di).
11. In Okinawa, "Kojo" can also be pronounced "Koshiro," "Kogusuku," "Kugushiku," and "Kogushiku." In Chinese Mandarin, the characters for the name are pronounced "Hucheng" and mean "lake wall" or "lake city."
12. The *oyakata* (or *uekata*) were the third highest class in Okinawa, coming beneath the royal family and the *aji* (or *anji*), feudal-type lords, often the sons of the king's brothers and uncles (McCarthy, 1995: 48, citing Douglas Haring, *Okinawan Customs: Yesterday and Today*, 1969, Rutland; VT: Charles E. Tuttle).
13. Sells says Shinpo went to China in 1665 (1995: 23).
14. *Peichin* were the fourth class in Okinawa, under the royal family, aji, and oyakata.
15. Sakugawa was a student of Wai Xinxian and/or Ko Ryuru (Nagamine,

2000: 61).

16 Iwah taught other Okinawans, including Matsumura Sokon.
17 Upon his return to Okinawa, Ranho settled in Kume Village, where the Kojo family also lived.
18 These dates are based on family records available to Irimaji Seiji and provided to Chuck Chandler. Bishop (1996: 115) gives the dates as 1839-1891.
19 Like most history of this period, little is known about Wai Xinxian. He may have been senior to Ko Ryuru, or a practitioner of equal skill in another style. He may have taught Higaonna Kanryo and did teach Aragaki Seisho, who did teach Higaonna; and Uechi Kanbun for a short time (McCarthy, 1996: 34-35, 60).
20 Shuren also studied under Maezato Ranho, who was another student of Iwah in Fuzhou.
21 There are unsubstantiated rumors that Kojo Saikyo taught Maezato Ranho's grandson, Miyazato Eiko. However, the current Kojo-ryu headmaster, Irimaji Seiji says that Kojo Yoshitomi was Saikyo's son and inherited the system from his grandfather, becoming the fifth-generation headmaster.
22 This book is poorly produced, with no editing, a poor index, and no footnotes. However, I use it here because its main source, the opus *Uechi-ryu karatedo* (1975) by Uechi Kanbun and Takamiyagi Shigeru, is a font of information regarding Okinawa history, culture, and karate. It has also been replicated in other self-promoting books such as *The 100 Year History of Shorin-ryu Karate* (1986) by Frank Hargrove.
23 The series Shoshingata, Fudogata, Chinpugata, Jumonjigata, Unryugata, Aikigata, Segangata, Domyogata, Techigata, Suikagata, Ichimonjigata, listed in Nakaya (1986: 86), Silvan (1993: 78), and copied onto the Internet at Paranto (1996) are not Kojo-ryu katas. They are actually the twelve stances taught in the katas.

Bibliography

Bishop, M. (1989). *Okinawan karate: Teachers, styles and secret techniques*. London: A&C Black.

Bishop, M. (1996). *Zen kobudo: Mysteries of Okinawan weaponry and te*. Rutland, VT: Charles E. Tuttle Co.

Chandler, C. (2000, September). Personal conversation with the author.

Dollar, A. (1996). *Secrets of Uechi ryu karate and the mysteries of Okinawa*. Antioch, CA: Cherokee Publishing.

Florence, R. (1998, Summer). "Where Goju-ryu and Tomari-te meet:

Tokashiki Iken and the Gohakukai." *Bugeisha* 6: 46-54.

Funakoshi, G. (1973). *Karate-do kyohan: The master text*. Tokyo: Kodansha.

Funakoshi, G. (1975). *Karatedo: My way of life*. Tokyo: Kodansha.

Funakoshi, G. (1988). *Karate-do nyumon: The master introductory text*. Tokyo: Kodansha.

Haines, B. (1995). *Karate's history and traditions: Revised edition*. Rutland, VT: Charles E. Tuttle Co.

Irimaji, S. (2000, August). Personal interview conducted by Chuck Chandler in Naha, Okinawa.

Jones, C. M. (2001, August 31). Personal correspondence with the author.

Kerr, G. H. (1958/1980). *Okinawa: The history of an island people*. Tokyo: Charles E. Tuttle Co.

Kojo, Y. (nd). Kojo family records.

McCarthy, P. (1995a). *The bible of karate: Bubishi*. Rutland, VT: Charles E. Tuttle Co.

McCarthy, P. (1995b). When masters meet: The 1936 meeting of Okinawan karate masters. *Furyu*, 1(4): 10-17.

Nagamine, S. (2000). *Tales of Okinawa's great masters*. Rutland, VT: Charles E. Tuttle Co.

Nakaya, T. (1986). *Karate-do: History and philosophy*. Carrollton, TX: JSS Publishing Co.

Okinawa Prefecture Board of Education. (1995). *Okinawa karate "kobudo" graph*. Naha: Okinawa Prefecture Board of Education.

Paranto, N. (1996). http://www.kojosho.com/kata.html; International Kojosho Karate Federation (IKKF) home page; downloaded: 8 Oct. 2000.

Sakihara, M. (1987). *A brief history of early Okinawa based on the Omoro soshi*. Tokyo: Honpo Shoseki Press.

Sells, J. (1995). *Unante: The secrets of karate*. Hollywood, CA: W.M. Hawley.

Silvan, J. (1993). *Okinawan karate: Its teachers and their styles*. New York: Vantage Press, Inc.

Tokashiki, I. (1997, 18 February). Personal interview; oral. Bank of Japan; Naha, Okinawa, Japan.

Yabiku, T. (2000, September). *Ryukyu hiden karate-do: The pathway to Okinawa's secret karate—My 50 years as a karateka*. Summerville, SC: Resources Unlimited.

Acknowledgment

I would like to express my appreciation to Chuck Chandler who provided me with the results of his own research and Kojo family information from his instructors, Irimaji Seiji and Yabiku Takaya.

chapter 13

Kobudo:
Okinawan Weapons are Not All Flash

by Mary Bolz, B.S.

All photographs courtesy of Mary Bolz.

Introduction

People who practice martial arts do so for a variety of reasons. An often touted reason is to obtain self-defense skills. Another reason often given for studying a martial art is for cultivating self-discipline and building self-confidence. Yet, anyone experienced in the fighting arts will declare that these arts are more flash than useful self-defense. In actuality, what is usually seen is some sort of aerobic workout based on "punching and kicking," sometimes with music played in the background. If we wish to study a martial art for true self-defense and character development, we should utilize some guidelines to help us distinguish which practice methods realistically offer these benefits.

Hopefully, this chapter will offer some practical information in this respect by looking at the "ancient martial art methods" associated with the Okinawan weapons (*kobudo*).*

* Notice: Anyone who wishes to practice with weapons, such as the nunchaku, should be aware of any local laws governing their use. Please check with local authorities.

Weapons: "Flash" v.s. Realistic Self-Defense

What is involved in turning choreographed movements into practical self-defense? And, what manner of practice can guarantee character-building that is commonly associated with Asian martial traditions? Additionally, how does weapons practice fit in to these goals?

To answer the first question, the techniques taught must be of practical use—they must work when used against a real attack by a physically and mentally powerful opponent. Much of today's weapons practice is awe-inspiring with its associated acrobatics, speed, and beauty. However, such practice is usually of little use against a serious attacker.

An argument regarding weapons practice is that, in modern society, nobody carries weapons with them: defensive training with weapons is useless when facing any assault on the street. However, the practicality of weapons practice goes beyond this apparent limitation. The physical and mental skills obtained through weapons practice can be applied in the street by adapting and utilizing common everyday objects in place of the traditional weapons. For example, staff (*bo*) techniques can be easily be applied with a broom or mop. A frying pan can be used as a shield and a spoon used as a *tinaka* or *shuchu*.

If fighting techniques are practiced without realism and without active visualization of an attacker, either a false sense of self-confidence will develop, or certain physical and mental skills necessary for self-defense will not develop at all. Practice geared for health, for aerobic fitness, or performing routines to music is simply not enough. Although Okinawan kobudo may seem ancient and outdated, it can be very useful for developing real fighting skills and the mental toughness required in our modern world.

The following section presents a few Okinawan kobudo techniques and looks at a few training methods that bring out the proper physical skills and mind-set necessary for realistic self-defense. The drive to practice solely for flash, fun, and ego is a great obstacle to overcome. We can make our practice more realistic if we wish. The key is in *how* the practice is done.

TECHNICAL SECTION

TWO-PERSON DRILLS

Distancing: Two opponents square off. The distance between two people (*maai*) is an extremely important aspect in all fighting arts, especially with weaponry. Here, in preparation for an actual attack, the distance between the two opponents should be such that neither of the two can reach the other with their weapon without having to step closer. This is a relatively safe distance at which to square off. The positions shown below are typical postures taken prior to practicing any technique.

Staff vs. Staff

1a The aggressor advances.

1b He attempts a strike to the neck. The defender counters while slide-stepping to the outside.

1c The defender raises the right end of her staff, sliding it along the opponent's staff and then flipping her staff over his into a pressing maneuver. Note that it is the lower body, the hip and the legs, that lead this movement. Her body has turned to an even greater side-position by the movement of her hips and the sliding of the rear leg.

1d The defender slide-steps even more to the right, leading with the hip and forcefully pressing down on her opponent's staff with a twisting action of the wrist. Notice the direction of the defender's navel, compared to the previous photos.

1e The defender counter-attacks to her opponent's face with the staff's tail-end. The hips lead all of these movements and is the leading force in propelling the staff at maximum force.

Staff vs. Staff

2a   The opponents square off.
2b   The attacker moves in with a thrust to the throat.
2c   Leading with her hips, the defender steps forward and slightly to the right to simultaneously execute a full-force block with the side of her staff.
2d   The defender sharply turns her hips and simultaneously twists her wrist upwards, causing a powerful counter-attack to the attacker's head at the temple.
2e   Detail of the grip used in the beginning block (2B).
2f   Detail of an incorrect grip to use while pressing.
2g   Grip used for a properly executed press.

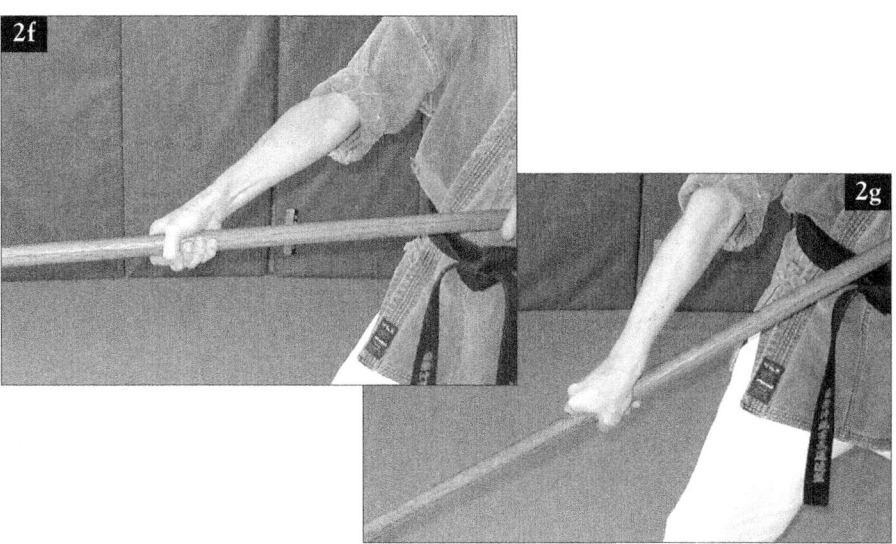

Nunchaku

3a A would-be attacker facing a defender with a nunchaku hidden behind her back that is tucked through her belt.

3b As he reaches to grab her, she reaches for the nunchaku.

3c As he grabs her collar, she starts to swing the nunchaku over his arm.

3d She prepares to "choke" his wrist.

3e Detail of the nunchaku being swung over the arm.
3f She catches the other end of the nunchaku and begins the choke.
3g The nunchaku is slid down the arm to the wrist. The defender twists forcefully, causing the nunchaku to choke the attacker's wrist. This brings pain and immobilizes the attacker.
3h The defender is now in control and can bring the attacker to the ground where she can follow-up with another technique if she wishes.

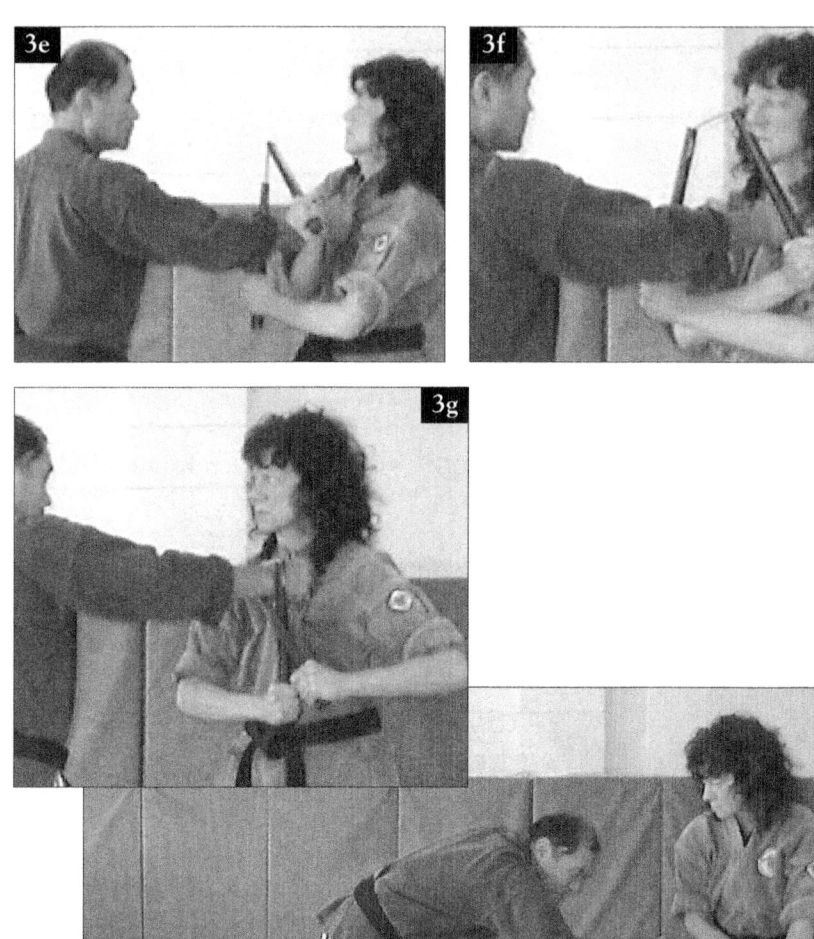

Nunchaku

4a A would-be attacker approaches.

4b He comes in closer to punch toward the face. To avoid the punch, the defender quickly drops and prepares to counter.

4c-d The defender drops further and prepares to wrap the nunchaku around the attacker's ankle.

4e She snares his ankle and tightens the grip, causing the attacker excruciating pain and leaving him immobile. He can not attack and she can follow with another technique if she wishes.

Nunchaku

5a   A would-be attacker approaches.

5b   He moves in closer, reaching out with both hands to grab.

5c   The defender has the nunchaku in her right hand and, as the attacker grabs, she lifts both her arms to the outside and above his arms. In one fluid motion, she releases one handle and immediately catches it in her left hand.

5d   She then pulls the nunchaku down over his wrists.

5e   The defender entraps both of the attacker's wrists to immobilize him. She can follow-up with another technique if she wishes.

Staff vs. Nunchaku

6a Attacker/defender square off.
6b The attacker strikes toward the face. Side-stepping, the defender executes a powerful block and presses the nunchaku down forcefully by using the hips to turn the whole body.
6c She begins to flip the nunchaku underneath his right wrist.
6d The flipping action brings the free handle underneath the staff and into her left hand.
6e She executes a wrist choke.

6f After stunning the opponent with the painful wrist choke, the defender quickly initiates a throat choke.

6g-h Tightening the hold. Additional pressure is given on the neck.

6i Finishing the technique by securing the nunchaku under the jaw and pressing firmly upward.

Single-Person Training Drill: Strike

7a Ready posture.
7b Starting to throw the butt-end of the nunchaku to its target.
7c Strike to the eye.
7d Alternate strike to the throat area.

Single-Person Training Drill: Throat Choke

8a   Incorrect position of nunchaku for a throat choke.

8b   Correct position.

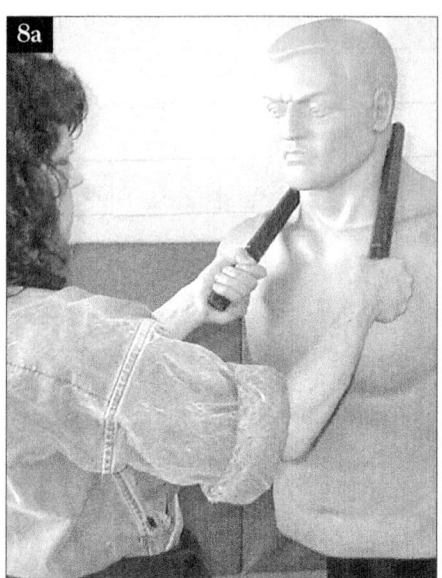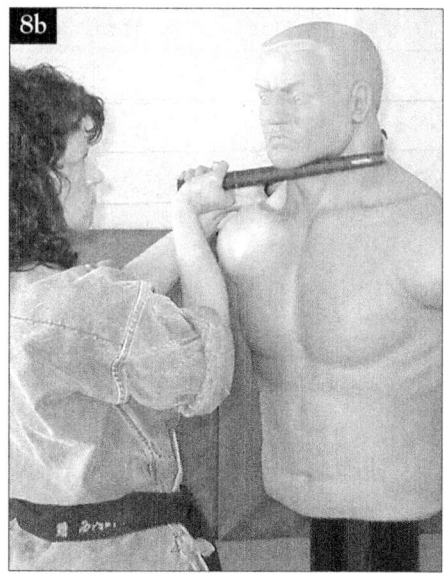

Guidelines for Realistic Practice*

In order for self-defense techniques to be truly practical and effective, the mode of practice must be closely scrutinized. Constant practice develops habits—habits which can be valuable or totally useless, depending on whether practice drills are effective or not. Important guidelines are provided below which should be helpful when practicing with a partner.

* Editor's Note: The theories presented in this chapter are not universal, but are expressed as the main themes of this particular school.

1) At advanced levels, real weapons must be used. Practicing only with weapons of rubber or wood do not provide the true "feel" of a real weapon, or the mental alertness required wielding a lethal weapon as a sharp bladed sword.

2) Do not look at the opponent's limbs or his or her weapon. Gaze at the opponent neutrally and objectively. Serious practice required serious focus.

3) Do not start a technique over again if a mistake is made by either party. Keep on going! There are no second chances in the real world.

4) In defending, use side-stepping and parry. Never remain head-on with the

opponent. Try to move forward, to the side, or circle, but not back. Side-stepping or circling is ideal, but going forward in response to an attack is highly discouraging to an attacker. Moving forward must be regulated by the reach of the technique you intend to try with your weapon. Don't let aggression interfere with proper distancing!

5) The best form of self-defense is to attack. In our particular style, we try never to step back from an attack. A block is only the first part of an attack. The best form of self-defense is often in attacking. In our particular style, we rarely step back from an attack. A block is only the first part of an attack.

6) Keep the mouth closed by keeping the lips and teeth together and the tongue touching firmly to the roof of the mouth. This produces focus, spirit and concentration of mind. It also lessens any probability of damage to the face and head if a blow of less than full-force is received. It also presents a stronger image. When the lips are apart and the mouth open, a weak countenance is shown. But you can breathe. Fighting is an aerobic activity, or should be!

7) While practicing with a partner, do not converse. Too much socializing and casual practice can be seen in many martial art classes. This type of practice will not produce true defensive fighting ability. Remember that a partner is an opponent and enemies do not casually talk or smile while fighting each other.

8) Always move from the hips. The hips lead the rest of the movement. Many martial art practitioners move their hands first. This is limiting in power and effectiveness. For beginners, make a habit of moving the hips and feet first, then the hands. The movements will become unified as training progresses. If the habit of moving one's hands first is not corrected, one's technical ability will never improve.

9) "Upper empty and lower full." Relax the shoulders and keep them down. Make the feet, legs, and hips bear the responsibility of stability, power, and speed of movement, i.e., the hips should be low and more contracted and does more muscular work than the upper body in a ratio of 70/30. Keeping the hips low and square in training is conducive to this.

10) Realistic distance (*maai*) in prearranged sparring is very important. If the attack does not reach the opponent, he or she should not block. Conversely, if a proper attack is made and it is not blocked, the defender should be hit! ...within the limits of what is safe, of course.

Self-Defense as a Unified Effort

For many, the study of a martial art is a quest for spiritual and mental development and is not separated from the physical aspects of the art. The previously mentioned points will go far to develop the mental side. For the sake of clarity, we can treat these aspects separately.

How can one apply martial training to one's personal life and somehow "better" one's mental and spiritual side? And, why should anyone even try? Can't spiritual/mental training best be developed by practices solely designed for that purpose, such as *zazen* and other forms of meditation? There are many methods for forging the spirit. However, in the martial traditions, a fundamental thought is of duality, in Japanese called *in-yo* (Chinese, *yin-yang*). These represent the complimentary and seemingly contradictory aspects found throughout all of nature. Since they are inseparable, can each be trained in isolation by themselves? It seems logical that both in and yo be trained simultaneously in a united effort. One way to do this is through martial arts practice, such as those with Okinawan weapons (*kobudo*). Here are some specific reasons why kobudo practice can develop the spiritual and mental aspects:

1) Fighting is very demanding physically, more so than non-fighting activities because of the fundamental associations it has with survival. The risk of injury is high. The intensity of the practice forces the "whole person" to participate in the practice. Thus, for spiritual development and mental discipline, one must practice kobudo as a fighting art, not merely as exercise or for fun.

2) Physical practice (*yo*) has an effect on the spiritual and mental (*in*), so the elements listed above should not be ignored.

3) To develop spiritually as well as physically, a person must train regularly, at least three times a week, several hours during each session. Otherwise, *in* and *yo* become lazy!

4) To go beyond the basics of practicing useful techniques, a growing awareness of the mental aspects involved in martial arts training is required. This can be achieved through serious practice, especially weapons practice with a partner which brings you closer to reality.

chapter 14

Basic Foundations in Okinawan Karate: Interview with Canadian Tsuruoka Masami

by Olga Toth and Robert Toth

Left: Karate demonstration by a young Tsuruoka Masami.
Right: Tsuruoka Masami discusses fine points
of karate practice during a recent seminar.
Photos courtesy of Tsuruoka Masami.

Introduction

The first man to set foot on the moon was Neil Armstrong. The first person to break the four-minute mile was Sir Robert Bannister. Sir Edmund Hillary and Tenzing Norgay were the first to reach the summit of Mount Everest. Firsts have always been important to us: the breaking of new ground, standing above everyone else, and going where no one has gone before. Not following the pack, but leading it! Seventy-three-year-old Tsuruoka Masami is such a man in the karate world.

Born in Canada of Japanese parents in 1929, Tsuruoka's early life reads like an adventure story. Like many other people of Japanese ancestry living in North America, he was placed in an internment camp during World War II. Just after the war, Tsuruoka moved to Japan and trained with Dr. Chitose Tsuyoshi, a leading figure in modern karate. In 1958, Tsuruoka returned to Canada and opened the first karate school in the country, where he taught traditional karate at a time when most people had never even heard of it.

Today there seems to be martial arts schools on many corners of every major city in North America. But it was different forty-five years ago when Tsuruoka Masami was the first to introduce the Japanese art of karate to the Canadian public.

INTERVIEW — A CANADIAN BEGINNING[1]

▶ MR. TSURUOKA, COULD YOU START BY TELLING US A BIT ABOUT YOURSELF?

I was born in Cumberland, British Columbia, in 1929. My dad immigrated to Canada in the early 1900's and brought my mum a little later. There was an influx of immigrants from Japan at that time. They were the young buckaroos. They wanted to make a fortune and then go back to Japan.

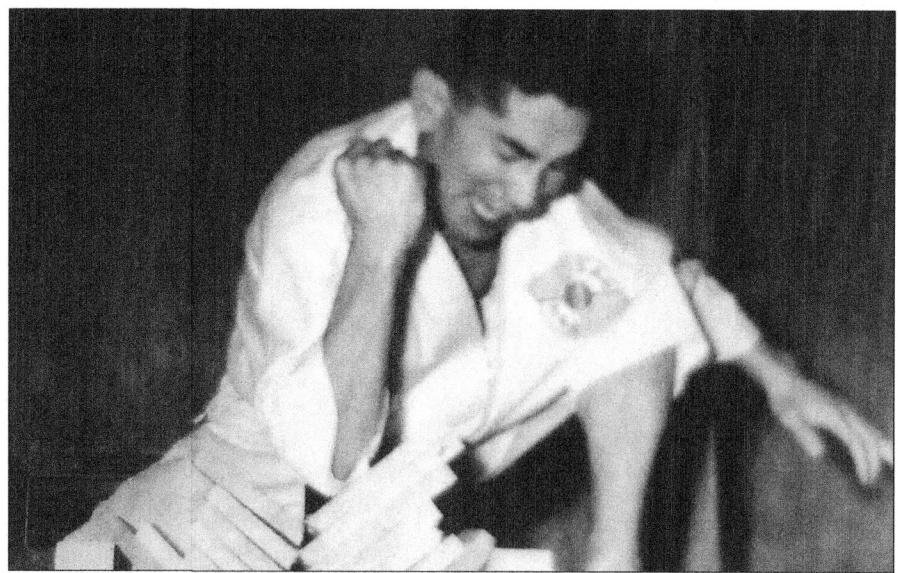

Karate demonstration by
a young Tsuruoka Masami.
Photo courtesy of Tsuruoka Masami.

▶ I'VE HEARD THAT YOUR FAMILY WAS PUT IN AN INTERNMENT CAMP DURING THE SECOND WORLD WAR. COULD YOU TELL US A LITTLE ABOUT THAT?

About a week or two weeks after the war began, they rounded us up and put us in the internment camp.² That was at Hastings Park, where they also kept the pigs and horses at the Pacific National Exhibition. We didn't know what we were getting into. It was very difficult. I'm sure that my parents and my brothers were devastated because they figured they were Canadians and would never be treated like that. They only gave us around twenty-four hours to prepare. So, we left everything behind . . . everything. The army people came with a big truck and just loaded us and we didn't know where we were going.

A lot of people went from the camp into the army. They volunteered for the Canadian Army and they were shipped to the Far East because they spoke Japanese.

IN JAPAN

▶ I'VE READ THAT AFTER THE WAR YOU MOVED TO JAPAN. WHEN EXACTLY?

Yes. About eight months after the war. The Canadian government asked who wanted to go to Japan and who wanted to stay. And my dad wanted to see his mother before she died, so we moved to Kumomoto, Kyushu Prefecture.

You've never been to a country that lost a war. It's quite a sad thing, because there's no food. The only reason that we were okay was because we went to the country side, so we had enough to eat. A lot of people that went to the city had a hard time.

▶ THAT WAS YOUR FIRST TIME IN JAPAN. HOW DID YOU FEEL ABOUT THAT?

Whenever you go to a foreign country that you've never seen before, you notice the atmosphere, attitudes, etc., are very different. Although I looked Japanese, they looked at me in a funny way, as if thinking to themselves: You look Japanese, but you're not Japanese.

▶ DO YOU CONSIDER YOURSELF CANADIAN?

I never really thought about that. Both my parents were Japanese, I spoke Japanese, I went to Japanese school so I had no problem in Japan. I was very fortunate because my dad sent me. I mean, he didn't send me, he forced me to go to Japanese school. When you're a kid, you were forced. I was very grateful for that.

MARTIAL ARTS TRAINING

▶ When did you first start training in the martial arts?

In Canada, I first studied a little bit of judo. When I went to Japan, I was studying judo and a little kendo. Then I got mugged one time. I was mistaken for somebody else out on the street. I got left lying on the street because nobody wanted to help. Nobody intervened. I vowed to myself that nobody's going to do that to me again. When I was in Tokyo, I saw a demonstration of karate at a park. So, when I came back to my city, I started looking for a karate school and found my teacher.

Actually, I had a hard time finding him. There was a person that I knew who said that there is a karate master in the town. So, I went looking for him and found Dr. Chitose.[3] He had a small place on the outskirts of Kumomoto and about four or five students. At that time, right after the war, MacArthur said, "No martial arts."[4] So, they weren't allowed to teach openly. Chitose's *dojo* [training hall] wasn't even a dojo. He didn't have a dojo like the dojos here. It was his backyard. So when it rained, we were in the mud.

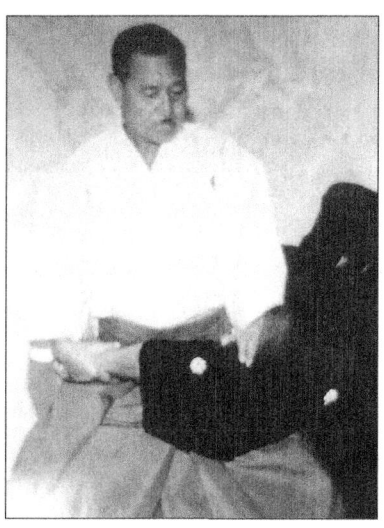 

Dr. Chitose Tsuyoshi.
Photos courtesy of Tsuruoka Masami.

▶ What was the training like under Dr. Chitose?

Well, I watched the other students and imitated them. It's not like over here. Here they take you by the hand and teach you. Over there you're on your own. Just don't open your mouth. You watch and imitate. That's all. We did basics, basics, basics, basics.

We didn't do *kumite* [free sparring] for awhile. Because if you did kumite and happened to get lucky and hit a black belt, you were going to get beat up. So you didn't do kumite.

Dr. Chitose always emphasized attitude in the training. And as a teacher he was a very kind man. During the war, Dr. Chitose was stationed in Tokyo. He was a doctor. His name was Chinen. But the name Chinen was very Okinawan and, at that time, many with Okinawan names wanted their names to be pronounced in standard Japanese. So, he changed it to a Japanese name.

▶ DID HE EVER TALK WITH YOU ABOUT HIS TEACHERS?

Not very much. He'd always say, I learned from him or I learned from him. You know, Naha-te and Shuri-te, and then the combination of both.[5] He learned both styles. Chito-ryu was a 50/50 combination of both.

▶ DID YOUR TEACHER GIVE YOU A BLACK BELT TO WEAR?

Oh, yes. And he gave a certificate, too. We had only white, brown, and black belt then.[6] I never even put a brown belt on. I just waited until I got a black belt. At the time, you had to register your name with the police in Japan. The master would register it for you. You wouldn't go to register yourself. Now it's all different. Black belts are a dime a dozen now. Don't forget in the old days karate had a very bad name in Japan. Kendo, judo, these were the Japanese arts that they cherished. So, when karate came, it was considered a foreign art.

KARATE IN CANADA

▶ WHY DID YOU MOVE BACK TO CANADA?

Well, I was born here. I always wanted to come back here. My brother was in Toronto. He didn't go back to Japan. I had to have a sponsor, so he sponsored me.

▶ DID YOU START TEACHING KARATE AS SOON AS YOU MOVED BACK TO CANADA?

No. I had no intention of teaching. I was happy. I was training in judo with a very good friend of mine. I used to go and help him teach judo. In Japan, judo is okay, but here there are many 6' 5", 250-pound guys. For a 129-pounder to move them, it is difficult to do. It's hard to throw them.

But somebody must have heard from Japan that there was karate here. Somebody came to me and said, "I heard that you know a little karate." I said, "I don't know karate enough to teach, but I did a little." And then they kept on bugging me. There was a body building place in Toronto and the owner found out I studied karate. At the time they used to have a body building contest and one year he invited me to go up there and put on a demonstration. The only demonstration we could do was to break bricks and boards because we had to show the difference between judo and karate.

When we came back after the demonstration, he had a big sign at his place advertising "Karate Training." I never even consented to it. However, I taught there for about two months. It didn't work out. But the people that were taking karate wanted me to continue teaching. So, they got the club going. The first dojo in Canada was on top of a bowling alley [laughs].

Things were quite difficult because people didn't know what karate was. All they wanted to know was how to break boards and bricks. A boxer would come in and I'd have to pull my punch, but the boxers train to hit, so they would hit you! Then I'd use my feet and they'd say: That's dirty fighting.

▸ WHAT WERE YOUR CLASSES LIKE BACK THEN?

Well, the students were in great shape. So, we did a lot of physical exercise. At that time, everyone used to work out hard. That's why the exercise part of a karate class that we still see today is for twenty-five or thirty minutes. You know, that's not necessary. For karate, you should do about ten to fifteen minutes of stretching exercises so you don't pull a muscle. But the trend at that time was to exercise for thirty minutes. Even if you were fit, you still had to do thirty minutes.

▸ DID YOUR CANADIAN STUDENTS WANT TO LEARN THE SAME WAY THAT YOU WERE TAUGHT IN JAPAN?

Oh, they did because my place was the only place. If they wanted to leave, I'd say leave. I didn't care. And I kept that trend up. That's why we had a lot of good champions coming out of our school.

Today, I try to keep the same way as much as possible. I still teach nothing but the basics. But now there's a lot of ladies and kids. I never used to teach kids. So, you have to kind of adapt your way of teaching. Right now, it's more sports orientated. There's more people practicing karate but they're getting away from the basics. That's why I have a very small class. My class is maybe, fifteen or twenty at the most. A lot of teachers have hundreds of students. But I just have my small group.

KARATE ORGANIZATIONS

▸ WHAT DO YOU THINK IS THE MOST IMPORTANT THING IN KARATE TRAINING?

If it's training, I say basics. Basic stance, basic block, basic punch, basic kick. Because once you can do your basics, the rest you can improvise yourself.

▶ YOU WERE INVOLVED WITH ORGANIZING THE NATIONAL KARATE ORGANIZATION. HOW DID THAT COME TO BE? WHY DID YOU START THAT?

It was in 1964. At that time, there were so many associations coming into Canada, especially from the United States. So, I figured we must have one governing body. We were very fortunate, the government accepted us as the National Association of Canada. Now, whoever came had to join us. After we had the national association, we started forming provincial organizations. At that time we only had Quebec, Manitoba, Ontario, and New Brunswick. Only four provinces had karate at that time. Then it started spreading.

Tsuruoka Masami with Dr. Chitose Tsuyoshi.
Photos courtesy of Tsuruoka Masami.

▶ COULD YOU TELL US ABOUT YOUR LEAVING DR. CHITOSE AND THE CHITO-RYU FEDERATION?

It was all politics and I don't like politics. Like any master, Dr. Chitose got information from many people. So, he got all muddled up. I told him, I was the one that got karate out of Japan and made Chito-ryu known across the world. Then, the people from the United States, they started squabbling … and I said: OK, that's enough! Now, let me alone. Just let me teach my karate. I've got no time to spend on politics. I told Dr. Chitose that he'd be my only teacher. The last time I saw him was the year before he died. He and I had the opportunity to talk then.

After I left, Yamaguchi Gogen and Ohtsuka Hironri came to me and said: Why don't you come to our organizations?[7] But I said: No, I have my teacher. I'll come and practice with you, but I have one master and I'll live with my master.

▶ COULD YOU TELL US ABOUT TSURUOKA KARATE?

It's a karate organization. That's it. We practice any style. I still practice Chito-ryu. I practice Shotokan. I practice Goju-ryu. Any opportunity to have a master come, I'll practice with him. I'll invite him to my club and let him teach, because my students must have some knowledge of different styles. I don't like that idea that "this is the only one good style." My master used to be very upset because I used to practice other styles. I said, I have to learn the other styles to be able to compete against that style.

People ask: Why don't you belong to Shotokan, because you claim to be Shotokan? I claim nothing. I say, I practice Shotokan. I practice Goju-ryu. I practice Chito-ryu. There's a difference between being part of an organization and practicing a style.

I think that the openness between different karate styles is important. Judo, at one time, had many styles. Now it's judo, which is one. So, karate ... as long as the masters are alive, there will be styles. But after all the masters die, who's going to claim they're a master? Then there's no master and there's no organization. So, eventually, I think it will be like judo or swimming or basketball.

There will always be a traditional and a sports aspect. There should always be the traditional. I hope that will never die. Because once it's sport, rules dominate, and rules keep on changing every year. You should see the World Karate Federation rules. I can't keep up with them. In 1970, we were at the First World Championship [Tokyo] and we stuck to the rules printed then until 1978. Now it's completely changed. I mean, they have points after points. To me they do that [Tsuruoka demonstrates a back fist], it's a half a point. What? In those days we never even considered something like that because it was "one punch, one kill." And if you make a mistake, you're out [laughs]! Ten seconds. You traveled all the way to Japan to participate in a tournament for ten seconds?

TODAY AND TOMORROW

▶ WHAT'S THE BIGGEST CHANGE THAT YOU'VE SEEN IN THE KARATE WORLD?

Flashy people seem to get all the glory, and the people that are very dedicated get left behind. So, people that can go out in public and talk about how they are big heroes and are well-known, but the people that are at the grassroots, the ones that do all the work, they are not thought of like they should be.

▶ IF YOU COULD CHANGE ONE THING IN THE KARATE COMMUNITY WHAT WOULD YOU CHANGE?

I don't think that I'd change anything. When I go around the world or across the country I see little children. They are our future. They make me very, very happy. First of all, they learn discipline. They learn to respect. Their attitude is good and they're honest. I think that karate has given a lot to the country. If nothing else, it pleases me to see that. It doesn't matter what dojo it is. They are all trying their best. The black belt who teaches is teaching sincerely, and that's what I like about it.

You know, nobody has to belong to any big organization. Your student might open a club next door to you, but at least he picked up all the good points that you taught him and can pass it on to the little ones. At least he tries to emulate you and teach the children respect and discipline. When I see that, everybody's the same. There's no such thing as bad karate. Technically maybe you can say it is bad or good. But that doesn't matter, because your club is always the best anyway. If you see somebody else's technique, you think that they're no good [laughs]! …That's the way it is.

▶ WHAT ADVICE WOULD YOU OFFER TO A YOUNG BLACK BELT WHO WANTS TO OPEN HIS OWN SCHOOL?

Keep the basics up. If you don't practice the basics, you won't be able to go forward. If you learn the basics, then you can create your own thing. Karate is about creation. It's not about copying one person. You must produce your own.

"All Your Spirit in One Punch"
Calligraphy by Dr. Chitose presented to Tsuruoka Masami and the
Tsuruoka Karate School. *Photo courtesy of Tsuruoka Masami.*

▶ DURING SUCH A LONG CAREER, IS THERE ANY ONE THING THAT STANDS OUT IN YOUR MEMORY?

Not really, because I think that I've got a long ways to go yet [laughs], because everyday I learn something. I learn from the beginners. I learn more from my beginners than the black belts. Black belts have to go find their own way. If they don't want to work hard, that's not up to me.

▶ IS THERE ANYTHING THAT YOU'D LIKE TO PASS ON TO THE NEXT GENERATION OF KARATE PRACTITIONERS?

As I said before, let the teacher teach the student discipline, respect and honesty. Try your best and teach with passion.

TECHNICAL SECTION

> To search for the old is to understand the new.
> The old, the new — This is a matter of time.
> In all things, man must have a clear mind.
> The Way: Who will pass it on straight and well?
> – Funakoshi Gichin, 1973

Tsuruoka Masami's advice to young karate instructors on what to teach students is to focus on perfecting basics. "If you learn the basics, then you can create your own personal style. Karate is about creation. It's not about copying. You must produce your own" (personal communication, 2 November 2002). The foundation for reaching this creative stage has always been strong basic techniques. Basic techniques are made up of balance and centering, stance and posture, the use of the hips to create power, and the use of the hands and feet as weapons (Nakayama, 1966: 9). These traditional movements should remain as they were originally created by past generations. Many years were put into their development and each karate student should be sure that these techniques remain in their purist form to be passed on to the next generation (Bowerbank, 1997: 75).

Scientific training of the basic techniques is essential. Faulty training methods can result in acquiring bad habits or even injury. But karate training can be considered scientific only if correct physiological principles are used. An examination of the techniques that past generations created reveals that the ideas agree with modern scientific principles (Nakayama, 1966: 11, 15).

These basic techniques provide the foundation for all of the concepts that follow in karate training. For example, these same basic techniques are used to make up the forms that are a large part of traditional karate. As well, it is the basic techniques that are the most likely to score in free-sparring. This shows how the basic techniques play an important role in all parts of karate practice (Bowerbank, 1997: 72).

To create a strong, balanced natural stance, one must stand up straight, straighten and tighten the legs, push out the stomach, and push the buttocks up, being careful not to concave the chest (Tsuruoka, personal communication, 2 November 2002). Stability depends on good balance. Without correct balance, it is impossible to deliver powerful techniques (Figures 1 and 2).

When standing erect, the body's center of gravity is located in the area slightly below and behind the navel (*tanden*). In Japan, the importance of the tanden has been taught from early times. This region of the body was emphasized because it was felt that it is where the human spirit is centered. This area also provides the basis of power and balance. A correct stance will enable the student to maintain the balance of both the upper and lower parts of the body.

If the power concentrated in the tanden is used in executing karate techniques, the interlocking support produced by the pelvic and hip bones supported by the thighs and the trunk by the spine will produce strong basic techniques (Nakayama, 1966: 18). It is necessary to recognize the importance of the lower body as this is what provides balance and support and generates initial power through contact with the ground.

For a front leaning stance, maintaining posture is necessary to create stability. The front knee must be over the foot, but must not extend past the middle of the arch. The heel of the front foot, the knee, and the hip all line up (Bowerbank, 1997: 51).

A front leaning stance is taught with a 60/40 weight distribution. But weight distribution is not what to look for. The pressure ratio is more important. It is the back leg that is going to hold the stance and that's where the pressure must be. Straighten the back leg to brace the stance, square the hips, shift the hip up, and tighten the buttocks (Tsuruoka, personal communication, 2 November 2002) (Figure 3).

The hip bone is where lower-body strength connects to upper-body movement. This is the largest bone in the body. If one learns to use the hip properly by contracting the muscles around it, one will be able to control movement of the entire body. All basic punches and blocks employ the use of the hip by rotating the pelvic bone (Bowerbank, 1997: 64).

If the hips are correctly pushed forward, power travels through the thrusting leg to the hips. From the hips it continues to the backbone, the shoulder, and through the arm to finally end in the fist. To transmit this power effectively from the hips to the arm, a proper connection must exist between the hips and the upper body. To achieve this connection, tense the muscles around the abdomen and the lower back. If the muscles are loose, only a part of the potential power will be created (Nakayama, 1966: 63) (Figures 4 thru 9).

The punch is the very essence of karate (Tsuruoka, personal communication, 2 November 2002). The fore-fist is the most frequently used striking point in karate. It consists of the first knuckle of the forefinger and middle finger. An imaginary straight line can be drawn from the center of the forearm to the point between the knuckles of the forefinger and middle finger. The forearm and the knuckles form a straight line (Nishayama, 1959: 47).

Left column, Tsuruoka Masami making corrections.
Right column, applying the principles in practice.
Photos courtesy of Robert Toth.

The starting point of a punch is the chamber position. It doesn't matter where the hand is held in chamber. Each of the different karate styles has its own way. The chamber hand creates the rotation and power necessary for a punch. By twisting the wrist, the shoulder will drop and, as the fist is an extension of the elbow, the elbow will scrape the body when the arm is extended for a punch. The punch, then, will have more power. The more the wrist is twisted, the more power there will be in the punch (Tsuruoka, personal communication, 2 November 2002) (Figures 10 and 11).

Mr. Tsuruoka points out how back muscles are effected when the arm is chambered and afterward when a punch is delivered.

Practicing a basic punch, and letting the hips and shoulders rotate.

The punch must penetrate. If the punch is jerked out and the fist hits and then stops, it is possible to get tennis elbow (Tsuruoka, personal communication, 2 November 2002). When most people execute a punch, their intent is directed at the surface of the target. The punch is actually meant to extend behind the surface of the target (Bowerbank, 1997: 68).

The arm must extend. Lock the elbow and lock the hip. The shoulders should be square and flat. The shoulder blade disappears as the latissimus dorsi tightens. When punching with penetration, the fist can be felt to go through the opponent's stomach. That is where the injuries should happen. That is why most teachers say to punch though the body (Tsuruoka, personal communication, 2 November 2002) (Figures 12 to 14).

Kicking techniques have the most varied methods of application because of the anatomical makeup of the lower trunk and hip area of each person is different. Factors such as flexibility, muscle density, bone length, body fat, and age determine the ability to demonstrate good kicks. Because of these physical differences, karate practitioners subconsciously change the method of kicking rather than follow the ways that were created by past generations.

Contributing factors for maintaining good form for kicking are foot position, hip thrust, retraction, body angle, and balance (Bowerbank, 1997: 41, 44). To achieve maximum effect, it is necessary to kick with the whole body and not just the leg (Nakayama, 1959: 136).

One thing that will enhance kicking performance and give the karate student a better chance to attain technical proficiency is the knee. Too many karate students focus on the end result of a kick. But, the kicking foot only makes contact with the target in the last part of the technique. The knee leads the kick to the target. First, the knee must rise above the belt line before the foot releases. Then, the knee must thrust toward the target. Finally, the knee stays above the waist as the foot retracts after the impact. Finally, the foot is set back down on the floor (Bowerbank, 1997: 44, 45) (Figures 15 thru 19).

Lifting and bending the knee completely requires the use of the hip and thigh muscles. These muscles are connected to the hip bones. The hips must be stabilized to allow the muscles to operate properly; strong abdominal muscles help this to happen (Nakayama, 1959: 138).

• • •

Tsuruoka Masami recently provided instruction for a black belt class hosted by Robert Toth at the St. Catharines Martial Arts Center in Ontario.

Practice of the basic stances, blocks, punches, and kicks should be continuous. It is necessary for karate practitioners to develop a strong foundation of basic techniques because it is only through this method that it is possible to move on to the creative stage of the martial arts. Karate is about creation. It's not about copying. Without creativity, the martial arts will stagnate and die. At the same time, without a foundation of basic techniques, the martial arts will crumble. It is only by practicing and understanding the old techniques that it is possible to create something new.

Most of the old karate masters of the last generation have passed on. Mr. Tsuruoka and his contemporaries were students of the old masters. They learned the old ways. But it was their creativity that brought karate into the 21st century. Hopefully, Tsuruoka Masami's advice will help guide the practitioners of traditional karate far into the next generation.

Notes

1. This interview was conducted with Mr. Tsuruoka at his karate school in Toronto on 22 October 2002.
2. The Japanese attack on Pearl Harbor on 7 December 1941 brought the problem of resident Japanese in British Columbia into focus. Canada formally declared war with Japan even before the United States did, but it was obvious to Prime Minister Mackenzie King what the war would mean to the resident Japanese.

    The Pearl Harbor bombing provided anti-Japanese interests in British Columbia with a propaganda item. Mass evacuation of the resident Japanese was announced late in February 1942 (Adachi, 1991: 199, 201).
3. Chitose Tsuyoshi was born Chinen Gochoku in Okinawa in 1898. He was the grandson of Bushi Matsumura. His martial arts instructors included Kyan Chotoku, Motobu Choyu, Hanashiro Chomo, Higashionna Kanryo, and, most of all, Arakaki Seisho.

    Chitose changed his name for personal and political reasons, as was common for Okinawans to do at the time. He attended university in Tokyo studying medicine. While in Japan, he assisted Funakoshi Gichin with instructing karate at one of the first karate schools.

    Chito-ryu was not named after him. "Chi" means thousand and "to" refers to China or the Chinese Tang Dynasty. Chitose used the name Chito-ryu to commemorate the thousand years of history behind the art of karate (Sells, 2000: 77, 78, 79, 138, 140).
4. General Douglas MacArthur was the Allied commander of the Japanese occupation in 1945. He effectively, if autocratically, directed the demobilization of Japanese military forces, the expurgation of militarists, the restoration of the economy, and the drafting of a liberal constitution (*Encyclopedia Britannica*, 2003).
5. The systematized fighting arts were named after the areas from where they propagated. Shuri-te is found in Shuri and was rooted in Bushi Matsumura Soken's teachings. Naha-te was found in Naha and was the result of a tradition of training originating with Nakaima Kenri and Sakiyama Kitoku. Later tradition says that Naha-te was established by Higashionna Kanryo. Sakiyama and Nakaima brought back essentially the same type of martial art that Higashonna later taught: Southern Chinese gongfu from Fujian Province (Sells, 2000: 30, 31, 37).
6. *Kyu* are the lower grades of the martial arts below black belt; *ikkyu* is a first kyu brown belt, the rank right before first-degree black belt; *nikyu* is a second kyu brown belt (Frederic, 1994: 142).
7. Yamaguchi Gogen (1909-1989) was the head of the Japanese Goju-ryu

karate system. He began Goju-ryu karate in 1929 under Okinawan master Miyagi Chojun. In 1935, Yamaguchi organized the All-Japan Goju-Kai Karatedo Association and became its chief instructor.

Ohtsuka Hironori (1892-1982) began martial arts training at six years of age in Shindo Yoshin-ryu jujutsu. Eventually, he was awarded the *menkyo kaiden*, becoming the successor of this style. A year later, he commenced karate training under Funakoshi Gichin.

In 1939, Ohtsuka founded Wado-ryu karatedo, which became one of the four major styles of Japanese karate. In the same year, he organized the All Japan Karatedo Federation, Wado-Kai, which serves as the worldwide sanctioning body for the Wado-ryu system (Corcoran and Farkas, 1993: 363, 396).

Bibliography

Adachi, K. (1991). *The enemy that never was*. Toronto: McClelland and Stewart.

Bowerbank, A. (1997). *The spirit of karate-do: Teaching of Masami Tsuruoka*. Toronto: Morris Marketing.

Corcoran, J., and Farkas, E. (1993). *The original martial arts encyclopedia*. Los Angeles: Pro-Action Publishing.

Encyclopedia Britannica, 1994-2003 ultimate reference suite (2003). CD-ROM.

Frederic, L. (Paul Crompton, Trans. & Ed.) (1994). *A dictionary of the martial arts*. Rutland, VT: Charles E. Tuttle.

Funakoshi, G. (1973). *Karate-do kyohan*. Tokyo: Kodansha International.

Nakayama, M. (1966). *Dynamic karate*. Tokyo: Kodansha International.

Nishiyama, H., and Brown, R. (1959). *Karate: The art of empty hand fighting*. Tokyo: Charles E. Tuttle.

Acknowledgment

The author would like to thank Tsuruoka Masami, Betty Mochizuki, and Monty Guest for the photographs, Adam Kieswetter for proofreading the article, Mike DeMarco for his editorial suggestions, and all of the black belts for their help with the photographs in the technical section.

index

Ahagon, Naonobu, 10
aikido, 38, 40, 188
Akamine Eisuke, 56, 60-61, 94-95
All-Japan Karatedo Federation (Zen Nihon Karatedo Renmei), 136
All-Okinawa Karate and Kobudo United Association, 194
All-Okinawa Karatedo League, 18
Aragaki, Seisho, 143 note 1, 145, 212 note 19
Asayama Ichiden-ryu, 91-92, 98, 100
baguaquan, 91-92, 100, 106
basic techniques (kihon waza), 41-42, 65, 134, 140, 238-239, 245
breathing methods, 41, 73-74, 77, 79-80, 84-86, 89, 149-150
Bubishi, 96, 137-138, 150, 155, 156 note 7, 192-194, 204, 213
bull fighting, 15, 21, 25
Cauley, Thomas, 36-40, 42-45
Chandler, Chuck, 197-198, 206
Chatan Yara no Kusanku (kata), 22
Chen, Panling, 100
Chibana, Choshin, 14, 16-17, 20, 33, 91-93, 95-96, 98-99, 101-102, 111, 147-148, 181
chiishi (weights), 82-83, 140, 146
Chinen, Masami, 95, 198
Chinen Shichiyanaka no Kon, 105-106
Chinese kenpo, 31-34, 98, 101, 145
Chinto kata, 98, 204
Chito-ryu, 233, 235-236, 246 note 3
Chitose, Tsuyoshi, 230, 232-233, 235, 237, 246 note 3
Choun-no-Kon, 10
competition, 99, 133, 205
Dai Ni Seisan, 6
Daito-ryu, 98
forward stance (zenkutsu dachi), 6, 65, 68-71, 89, 199
free sparring (kumite), 14, 30, 34, 42-43, 158-172, 233
Fukuchi, Seiko, 23-25, 33
Fujian Province, 2, 32, 145, 150, 191, 246 note 5

Fujita, Seiko, 93-94, 99
Fukuda, Shoen, 37
Funakoshi, Gichin, 40, 138, 143 note 6, 174-175, 188, 238, 246 note 3, 247 note 7
Fuzhou city, 138, 143 notes 4 and 5, 145, 147, 149, 156 note 6, 189, 191-193, 202, 205-206, 208, 212 note 20
Geki-sai Dai Ichi/Dai Ni, 139
Go, Kenki (Wu Xianhui), 136-137, 143 note 5, 147, 195, 209
Goju-ryu Keishin Kai, 10
Goju Shizen-ryu, 198
Gojushiho kata, 98, 178, 182
grappling (tuite, torite, tuidi), 35, 125-127, 191, 201-202
Greater Japan Martial Virtues Association (Dai Nippon Butoku Kai), 148
gripping pots (nigirigame), 97, 140, 146, 148
Gushukuma, Shimpan, 26, 148, 181
Hakko-ryu, 38
Han Konan-ryu (see Pangainoon-ryu)
Hanashiro, Chomo, 33, 37, 147-148, 181, 184 note 4, 246 note 3
Harada, Mitsusuke, 178
Hatsumi, Yoshiaki (Hatsumi Masaaki), 100
Hawai'i, 34, 174, 180-181, 183, 184 note 6
Higa, Nobuyuki, 10
Higa, Seiko, 23-25, 33-34
Higa, Seitoku, 91-92, 95, 98, 111, 194, 211 note 10
Higaonna/Higashionna, Kanryo, 34, 92, 96, 98, 192, 211 note 10, 212 note 19
Higaonna, Morio, 74
Higashionna, Tanmei, 135, 143 note 3
Hokama, Tetsuhiro, 13, 23-24, 175
Inoue, Motokatsu, 37-38, 64, 91-95, 98, 103, 111
Inoue, Takekatsu, 37
International Okinawa Kobudo Association, 11
International Seibukan Karate Association, 20
Iraha, Choko, 155

248

Irei, Tadashiki, 10
Irimaji, Seiji, 191, 194-198, 205-206, 209-210, 212 notes 18 and 21
Isshin-ryu, 134
Itokazu, Seiki, 1-2
Itosu Anko Yasutsune, 16, 32-34, 37, 98, 145, 147-148, 175-177
Iwah, 192-193, 204, 209, 212 notes 16 and 20
Ji'in kata, 64
Jion kata, 64, 134, 138, 143 note 6, 147, 153-154
judo, 25, 29-30, 38, 92, 111, 174, 191, 211 note 8, 232-234, 236
Kamiunten, Fumiko, 29
Kanchin kata, 6
Kanegawa, Gibu, 64
Kanshiwa kata, 6
Kanzaki, Shigekazu, 130-143, 149-151, 153, 155
Kanzaki, Shigeru, 97,
Karate Research Society (Karatedo Kenkyu Kai), 137, 143 note 5
kendo, 38, 90, 111, 232-233
Kihon-gata I and II, 148
Kim, Richard, 61, 177-178
Kinjo, Kazufumi, 56
Kinjo, Masahiko, 11
Kinjo, Takashi, 1-11, 197
Ko, Ryuru, 27-28, 193, 209, 211 note 15, 212 note 19
Kobayashi-ryu, 33, 60, 91
Kobayashi Shorin-ryu, 14, 20, 92, 111
Kobayashikan Kyokai, 91, 111
Kobu no Ti Naka, 10
Kobukai Konan-ryu, 1, 6
Kobuken ("Kinjo's Martial Fist"), 6
Kobuzai (sai kata), 6
Kochinda Saburo, 198
Koga-ryu, 99
Kogusuku, 194, 211 note 11
Kojo, Isei, 193-194
Kojo, Koho, 193-194, 197, 204, 206, 208
Kojo, Saikyo, 192, 194, 212 note 21
Kojo, Saisho, 192, 208
Kojo, Shigeru, 195, 198, 205
Kojo, Shinpo, 191-192
Kojo, Shinunjo, 192
Kojo, Taite, 145, 192, 194
Kojo, Yoshiaka, 191, 194-196, 199
Kojo, Yoshitomi, 194-199, 204-206, 210, 212 note 21
Kojo-ryu, 189, 191-199, 201-202, 204-206, 208-210, 212 notes 21 and 23
Konan-ryu, 1-2, 6-7, 10, 197
Kongo no Ko (bo kata), 94, 105
Konishi, Yasuhiro (aka Konishi Koyu), 37-38, 40, 93, 99
Koshin-ryu, 187, 196-199, 206, 209-210
Koshin-ryu Kohokan Karate and Kobudo Organization, 196-198
Koshiro, Shuren, 194
Kume Village, 104, 145, 189, 191-192, 212 note 17
Kusanku kata, 17, 22,
Kyan, Chofu, 33
Kyan, Chotoku (nickname: Chan Migwa), 16-17, 19-22, 33, 148, 181, 246 note 3
Kyoda, Juhatsu, 19, 92-93, 96-98, 102-103, 111, 130-131, 136, 138-139, 144-146, 148-155, 211 note 10, 253
Kyoda, Juko, 97, 131-133, 140, 153-155
Mabuni, Kenwa, 23, 40, 98, 143 note 6, 147, 155
Maeshiro, Choryo, 181
Maeshiro, Shusei, 2
Maezato no Nunchaku Sho/Dai, 95, 105
Maezato no Tekko, 58, 64, 105
Makabe, Chan, 17, 21
makiwara, 26, 97, 139, 148
Matayoshi, Shinpo, 2, 6, 8, 10, 23, 156 note 6
Matayoshi Nicho Zai (two-sai kata), 6
Matsubayashi Shorin-ryu, 38
Matsuda, Tokusaburo, 194
Matsugawa no Tecchu, 61, 64
Matsumora, Kosaku, 32, 34
Matsumura, Sokon ("Bushi"), 15-16, 18, 21, 32-33, 37, 175, 192, 209, 212 note 16, 246 notes 3 and 5
Matsumura Sokon's wife, 15-16, 18
medicine, 17, 27, 43, 246 note 3
Mie Junshin, 60
Minowa, Katsuhiko, 55-72, 94
Minowa no Kon Sho/Dai, 60
Minowa no Sanbon Nunchaku, 60-61, 65

Minowa no Tecchu, 60
Miyagi, Chojun, 24, 26, 34, 40, 73, 87, 92, 96-97, 130, 134-136, 138-139, 143 note 4, 144, 146-152, 156 note 6, 181, 247
Miyahira, Katsuya, 14, 111
Miyashiro, Thomas, 182
Motobu, Anshi, 35
Motobu, Choki, 14, 28-30, 33-34, 40, 178-179, 211 note 10
Motobu, Choyu, 28, 30, 35, 147, 246 note 3
Motobu-ryu, 10, 38, 91-92
Motobu-ryu Udun-di, 28-29
Murakami, Katsumi, 91-111
Nagaishi, Fumio, 56
Nagamine, Shoshin, 183
Naihanchi/Naifanchi kata, 17, 99, 178, 182, 204
Nakaima, Kenri, 246 note 5
Nakama, Chozo, 20
Nakamoto, Aisho, 143 note 4
Nakamoto, Masahiro, 56, 60, 63-64, 94
Nakasone, Genwa, 143 note 7, 148, 181
Nakasone, Koshin, 56
Nakazato, Joen, 17-18
Nakazato, Shugoro, 15, 91-93, 95, 103, 111
Nanbansato-ryu, 93-94, 99
Nepai kata, 131, 134, 147, 154-155, 193, 195, 198, 205-206
Nishiuchi, Mikio, 11
"no mind" (mushin), 41, 101
Northern Japan Yuishinkai Kobudo, 37
nunchaku (flail), 41, 60-61, 65, 95, 103, 105, 139, 215, 219-226
oar (eku/ieku/kai), 8-9, 62, 103, 132
Ochiai, Hidy, 38
Ogasawara, Jiro, 37
Ogasawara, Tokushiro, 38-39
Ohtsuka, Hironori, 99, 236, 247 note 7
Okada, Jiro, 38-40, 44-45
Okinawa Budo International (OBI), 10
Okinawa Karatedo Federation, 33
Okinawa Karatejutsu Kenkyu Kai (Okinawa Karatejutsu Research Club/Association), 147
Okinawa Kokusai Budo Karatedo Renmei, 10
Okinawa Konan-ryu Karatedo Kyokai, 2
Okinawan Prefectural Karate Association, 14

Okinawa Prefectural Karatedo Promotion Society, 148
Oyadomari, Kokan, 33-34
Pangainoon-ryu, 1-2, 191
Passai kata, 17, 98, 182, 204
Pinan kata, 32, 54, 182, 204
prearranged attack (yakusoku kumite), 60-61, 68, 146
pressure points (kyusha), 35, 94, 193, 205
push-hands (kakie), 139, 146
reverse punch (gyaku-zuki), 5, 117, 160-165, 167-168, 170
Rokkishu kata, 96, 150
rokushaku bo (six-foot staff), 62, 65, 67-68, 103, 192
Ryukyu Kobudo Hozon Shinko Kai (Ryukyu Kobudo Preservation and Promotion Association), 55, 62, 64
sai (three pronged truncheon), 6-7, 36, 41, 61-62, 103, 105, 139-140, 194, 208
Sakihama, Seijiro, 198
Sakiyama, Kitoku, 246 note 5
Sakugawa, Kanga ("Tode"), 17, 31-32, 37, 192, 209, 211 note 15
Sakugawa Koshiki Shorinji-ryu, 36-39, 41-42, 45
Sakugawa no Kon Sho, 61, 95, 98, 105-106
sanbon nunchaku (three-section flail), 60-61, 65
Sanchin kata, 6, 30, 73-76, 78, 80-81, 83-87, 89-90, 96, 113, 115-118, 129, 132-134, 138, 141, 146, 149-150, 152, 156 note 1, 182
Sancho Zai (three-sai kata), 6
Sanseiryu kata, 6, 96, 152
Sato, Kinbei, 91, 98-100, 111
Seibukan Shorin-ryu, 20
Seichin kata, 6
Seiro, Iju, 25
Seiryu kata, 6
Seisan kata, 6, 96, 132, 134, 137-138, 146, 150-152, 156 note 1
Shimabukuro, Zenpo, 20
Shimabukuro, Zenryu, 20
Shindo Jinen-ryu, 37-38, 40, 93, 99
Shindo Yoshin-ryu, 247 note 7
Shindokan Shorin-ryu, 14
Shinshukai (Association for True Study), 57

Shinzato, Katsuhiko, 13
Shiroma, Shinpan
    (see Gushukuma Shimpan)
Shirotaru no Kon, 95, 105
Shito-ryu, 23, 40, 155
Sho Ko (king), 15, 21
Sho Shin-O (king), 103, 190
Sho Tai (king), 35
Shorei-ryu, 143 note 6
Shorin-ryu, 10, 14, 20, 31, 38, 64, 91-92, 96, 98, 100, 111, 143 note 6, 148, 156 note 2, 174-175, 191-192, 198, 204, 209, 211 notes 9 and 10
Shorin-ryu Shorinkan, 91
Shorinji-ryu, 17-18, 36-39, 41-45, 61
short spear (tinbe), 145, 192
Shudokan, 91
Shotokan, 38-40, 210 note 4, 236
Shuri Police Department, 33
shuriken, 93-94
Shushi no Kon ko-shiki, 95, 98
Shushi no Kon Sho/Dai (kata), 94, 105
sickles (kama, nichogama), 1, 27, 41, 59, 67
Sochin kata, 139, 154
Soeishi no Kon (bo kata), 95, 105
Soeishi-ryu, 95
Soken, Hohan, 11, 198
sport karate, 43, 99, 130, 172, 182, 234, 236
staff (bo), 15, 41, 51, 62, 103-104, 106, 139, 192, 194, 208, 215-219, 223
sumo, 92, 111, 174, 179
Sunsu kata, 134
suruchin (weighted chain), 41, 105
taijiquan, 91-92, 98-100, 106, 108, 111, 187
Taira, Shinken, 38, 55, 57-58, 62, 64, 93-95, 111
Takahara Peichin, 31
Takamatsu, Sumisuke, 100
tecchu/tetchu (palm size stick-like weapon), 2, 10, 60-65, 67-68, 72
Tensho kata, 96, 139, 150
Teruya, Rinko, 132
Tokashiki, Iken, 138, 190, 211 note 9
Tokuda, Anbun, 14
Tomari-te, 32-34, 190-191, 204, 211 note 9
Tomoyose, Ryuko, 26-27
tonfa/tuifa, 41, 52, 61-62, 103

To'on-ryu, 91-93, 96-98, 111, 130-155, 156 note 2
Toyama, Kanken, 91-92, 98, 102, 111
Tsuken Akachu no Ieku De, 8
Tsuken Bo Sho/Dai, 60, 105
Tsukensunakake no Kon Kata, 57, 105
Tsuruoka, Masami, 229-245
Uechi, Kanei, 2, 26, 56-58
Uechi, Kanbun, 1, 26, 28, 203, 212 notes 19 and 22
Uechi-ryu, 1-2, 6, 10, 26, 56-57, 64, 72, 191, 198, 202-203
Uehara, Seikichi, 28-30, 35
Ueki, Masayuki, 39
Ueno, Takashi, 100
Ueshiba, Morihei, 40, 188
Wado-ryu, 99, 247
Wai, Xinxian, 192-193, 205-206, 209, 211 note 15, 212 note 19
Wang, Shujin, 98, 100
Washin-ryu, 39
weapons ban, 62, 103-104, 190
White Crane boxing, 131, 143 note 5, 147, 155, 193-194, 198, 201, 205
White Dragon, 193-194, 201, 205
White Tiger, 193-194, 201, 205
Xie Zhongxiang, 145
Whooping Crane boxing, 138
World War II, 17, 33, 56, 58, 147-148, 174, 191, 196, 230
Wu, Xianhui (Go Kenki), 137, 143 note 5, 147, 195, 209
xingyiquan, 91-92, 98, 100, 106, 111
Yabiku, Takaya, 189, 195-198, 205-206
Yabiku, Moden, 38
Yabu, Kentsu, 33, 98, 134, 138, 147-148, 154, 174-184
Yamaguchi, Gogen, 236, 246 note 7
Yamane-ryu, 91-92, 95, 98, 111, 198, 211 note 10
Yamazaki, Masanao, 37-38
Yara, Choui, 92, 111
Yonegawa no Ko, 95, 105
Yoshimura, Hiroshi, 56-57, 68-71
Yuishinkai kobudo, 37-38, 91
Zen Okinawa Kobudo Renmei, 2
Zhang, Zhankui, 100

Printed in Great Britain
by Amazon